The
Psych
101
Series

James C. Kaufman, PhD, Series Editor

Department of Educational Psychology
University of Connecticut

James Michael Lampinen, PhD, is the youngest of six siblings (Sharon, Linda, John, Judi, Joe). He was born a bit north of Chicago. From a young age, he was interested in science. He received his bachelor's degree in psychology from Elmhurst College and his PhD in cognitive psychology from Northwestern University. He also did a stint as David G. Payne's post doc at Binghamton University. He is currently professor and associate chair in the Department of Psychological Science at the University of Arkansas in Fayetteville. His work focuses on memory errors and their applications to legal contexts. This includes eyewitness testimony, memory illusions, and searches for missing or wanted persons (prospective person memory). Jim lives in Fayetteville and is married to Jamie Lampinen. They are raising three children and a dog and are busy making lots of memories together, as evident from the ever-expanding magnet collection on their refrigerator.

Denise R. Beike, PhD, is a would-be novelist who discovered psychological science along the way and never looked back. She received her bachelor's degree in English and psychology from Indiana University and her PhD in social psychology from Indiana University. She is currently professor and chair of the Department of Psychological Science at the University of Arkansas. Her research interests include the effects of autobiographical remembering on emotions, the self-concept, relationships, and behavior (it affects all of them—see Chapter 6!). She also studies the emotional experiences of regret and missing someone, both of which involve memory. She is the author of various articles and book chapters on these topics, but her proudest accomplishment is her students' success.

Memory 101

James Michael Lampinen, PhD
Denise R. Beike, PhD

SPRINGER PUBLISHING COMPANY
NEW YORK

Springer Publishing Company, LLC
11 West 42nd Street
New York, NY 10036
www.springerpub.com

Acquisitions Editor: Nancy S. Hale
Composition: Amnet

ISBN: 978-0-8261-0924-8
e-book ISBN: 978-0-8261-0925-5

14 15 16 17 / 5 4 3 2 1

The author and the publisher of this Work have made every effort to use sources believed to be reliable to provide information that is accurate and compatible with the standards generally accepted at the time of publication. The author and publisher shall not be li-able for any special, consequential, or exemplary damages resulting, in whole or in part, from the readers' use of, or reliance on, the information contained in this book. The publisher has no responsibility for the persistence or accuracy of URLs for external or third-party Internet websites referred to in this publication and does not guarantee that any content on such websites is, or will remain, accurate or appropriate.

Library of Congress Cataloging-in-Publication Data

Lampinen, James M.
  Memory 101 / James Michael Lampinen, PhD, Denise R. Beike, PhD.
    pages cm
  Includes bibliographical references.
  ISBN 978-0-8261-0924-8 (print : alk. paper) — ISBN 978-0-8261-0925-5
(e-book) 1. Memory. I. Beike, Denise R. II. Title.
  BF371.L25 2015
  153.1'2—dc23

                                                                        2014029370

Special discounts on bulk quantities of our books are available to corporations, pro-fessional associations, pharmaceutical companies, health care organizations, and other qualifying groups. If you are interested in a custom book, including chapters from more than one of our titles, we can provide that service as well.

For details, please contact:
Special Sales Department, Springer Publishing Company, LLC
11 West 42nd Street, 15th Floor, New York, NY 10036-8002
Phone: 877-687-7476 or 212-431-4370; Fax: 212-941-7842
E-mail: sales@springerpub.com

Printed in the United States of America by Gasch Printing.

Contents

CONTENTS

Acknowledgments

We thank James Kaufman for inviting us to make a contribution to such a great and innovative book series. We also want to thank Nancy S. Hale for her tremendous patience in guiding us through this process. Several students, former students, and colleagues eagerly discussed the ideas in this book and offered us comments on earlier drafts of this manuscript. We thank them in no particular order: Lindsey Sweeney, Chris Peters, Jack Arnal, Blake Erickson, Kara Moore, Brittany Race, Nicole Wentling, and Holly Cole. More broadly, we want to thank our students and colleagues for all the interesting conversations we have had with them over the years, which have shaped our thinking and our lives. We'd also like to thank the many Facebook friends who cheered us on as we posted daily reports on our book progress—"likes" to you all. And of course, we thank our families and significant others for their love and support, even when we were grouchy as deadlines loomed. In particular, Jim wants to give a special shout-out to Jamie for being his inspiration. We could not have completed this project without the efforts of these remarkable people.

Creativity 101
James C. Kaufman, PhD

Genius 101
Dean Keith Simonton, PhD

IQ Testing 101
Alan S. Kaufman, PhD

Leadership 101
Michael D. Mumford, PhD

Anxiety 101
Moshe Zeidner, PhD
Gerald Matthews, PhD

Psycholinguistics 101
H. Wind Cowles, PhD

Humor 101
Mitch Earleywine, PhD

Obesity 101
Lauren M. Rossen, PhD, MS
Eric A. Rossen, PhD

Emotional Intelligence 101
Gerald Matthews, PhD
Moshe Zeidner, PhD
Richard D. Roberts, PhD

Personality 101
Gorkan Ahmetoglu, PhD
Tomas Chamorro-Premuzic, PhD

Giftedness 101
Linda Kreger Silverman, PhD

Evolutionary Psychology 101
Glenn Geher, PhD

Psychology of Love 101
Karin Sternberg, PhD

Intelligence 101
Jonathan Plucker, PhD
Amber Esping, PhD

Depression 101
C. Emily Durbin, PhD

History of Psychology 101
David C. Devonis, PhD

Psychology of Trauma 101
Lesia M. Ruglass, PhD
Kathleen Kendall-Tackett, PhD, IBCLC, FAPA

Memory 101
James Michael Lampinen, PhD
Denise R. Beike, PhD

Memory 101

Everything Is Memory

This book is about human memory: how it works, how it sometimes doesn't work, why it's important, and why it's interesting. The authors of this book are a cognitive psychologist (Jim) and a social psychologist (Denise). Cognitive psychologists study how people think, remember, categorize, and use language. Social psychologists study how people think about and interact with other people. One of us is primarily interested in how memories can sometimes become distorted and in the role that memory plays in the legal system. And one of us is primarily interested in the role memory plays in shaping one's personal autobiography, how memory is used in coping, and why it sometimes makes sense just to forget and move on with things. But we both agree that memory is central to all human endeavors. In fact, a major reason why we chose to focus our careers on memory is because we think that memory is the sine qua non of human psychology. We think you should be interested in memory, too. We think you should be interested in memory because how we process, store, retrieve, and use memory is intrinsically interesting. We also think you should be interested in memory because memory is important for a variety of different reasons, some obvious and some not so obvious. We think you should be interested in memory because memory is foundational. It is the bedrock on which thinking and reasoning depend. We think that once you read this book, you will agree that memory research is interesting, perplexing, and important.

MEMORY IS INTRINSICALLY INTERESTING

Memory is intrinsically interesting because it involves a re-experiencing of the past in the present. Look around the room that you are in right now. Presumably, you notice things like the wall, the floor, the ceiling, tables, chairs, wall décor, the book in your hands, other human beings, your pet iguana (or whatever), and so on. Those things all exist in the present, and although it is no simple feat for your brain to process this information in the present, doing so involves, at the very least, making sense of a set of things that are physically there. A digital camera can also process information about what is in the room in the present without too much difficulty, although this occurs in a much different manner from how your visual system processes the same scene.

But now think about the home where you grew up. Can you picture the walls? Can you picture the furniture? Can you remember walking into the house after a hard day at school? Can you mentally count how many windows there were in the house? Can you remember hugging your parents there? Can you remember arguing with your siblings there? Can you picture the bed you used to go to sleep in? Do any embarrassing stories come to mind about things that happened there? Most people can mentally reimagine those sorts of things, even though none of those things are present in the present, so to speak. Yet those memories, in many cases, can have a kind of perceptual vividness that makes them almost like reliving the original experience. Researchers have found that many of the same brain regions involved in perceiving an event become active again when one remembers the event (Slotnick, 2004). This led Payne and Blackwell (1998) to coin the phrase "re-perception" when describing how memory operates.

But how does this "re-perception" occur? One possible answer is that the brain somehow stores the pattern of activation from the original event in more or less pristine form and then just replays it, the way one would replay a musical concert on CD or a film on DVD. This idea has a great deal of intuitive appeal considering how vivid and detailed some memories seem, but—as we will learn in Chapter 3—it is almost certainly wrong. The reason it's wrong, partly, is because memory did not evolve for the purpose of answering questions on history tests or reciting lyric poetry, but instead evolved for the purpose of adapting to circumstances based upon experience.

When one of us (Jim) was in his early 20s, he was driving back to college after spending the weekend at home. He was in a hurry because his friends and he had a weekly gathering in which they watched reruns of a program called *Star Trek*, which involved human beings on a big spaceship with a "mission to explore strange new worlds, to seek out new life and new civilizations, to boldly go where no man has gone before" (opening narration of *Star Trek*). As he headed down the highway, exceeding the speed limit in a manner that would have pleased James T. Kirk but undoubtedly befuddled Mr. Spock, Jim noticed that his car seemed to be losing power. The car was running, but even as he pressed the accelerator, the power seemed less and less and less. You can probably imagine Jim freaking out, because he certainly didn't want to be stranded along the side of the road in the middle of nowhere. Remember that this was back when telephones were big, bulky things attached to walls by electrical wires. Telephones had not yet been conceived that fit in your pocket, let alone allowed you to text during class or play Candy

Crush Saga. Before the car was completely out of steam, he managed to get it to a rough-looking truck stop, too late at night on a Sunday for the repair shop to be open. He didn't have enough money for a hotel. He slept in his car at the truck stop, dreaming of creepy-looking dudes peering in through his car windows (if it were a dream).

The next day, his dad, an expert mechanic among other things, trekked out to see what was wrong with the car. The alternator belt had broken, allowing the battery to eventually run out of power. To this day, Jim can picture that entire event, and to this day, he also knows to check the alternator belt if a car starts to lose power. Did that event happen precisely how he remembers it happening? Probably not. But he has retained the gist of it: how bad and scary it was to have a car break down like that; what caused the car to break down; what to do if a car breaks down in that particular manner. Memory is our teacher, and it evolved to teach us, not to serve as a recorder of minutia and trivia.

Memory teaches us about other things as well. Memory teaches us about other human beings. We interact with someone and, after many experiences with the person, start to form an impression of that person. Is the person smart, or not so smart? Nice, or not so nice? Honest, or not so honest? Fun, or not so fun? We don't have to remember everything the person said or did in exquisite veridical detail. We just need to remember enough to form an impression and to assure ourselves that the impression is a solid one. We need enough information to approach or avoid. We use memory in the same way when forming impressions of ourselves. Indeed, as we will discuss in Chapter 6, the impression we have of ourselves revolves at least partly around the life story that we have concocted for ourselves in our own personal autobiography. Is that autobiography completely true and accurate? Almost certainly not. It's been said that one should never let the truth get in the way of a good story, and it seems that human memory obeys that maxim when telling stories about the self. But the story, unless one is pathologically self-deceptive, does get the broad strokes right. And this makes sense. Memory did not evolve to be your individual VCR player; it evolved to get the gist right.

As discussed in a ton of detail in Chapter 6, memory serves many other functions as well. Memories can serve to entertain. When people get together what do they do? They tell stories. The stories, of course, are based on memories, even if they end up being exaggerated for effect. You may even reminisce a bit when you are by yourself and feeling kind of bored. Memories can serve to define ourselves to others. When someone asks you to tell them something about yourself, you may well respond with a particular memory that you think aptly summarizes who you are. These have been called self-defining memories (Singer & Blagov, 2004) and may at times also be self-serving memories (Alston et al., 2013). And memory can also serve as a kind of control on our emotions. When we are sad, we can try to buck ourselves up with our memories. How exactly memory operates to serve these important functions is the tale told in the early part of this book. Chapter 2 describes some of the nuts and bolts of how memory operates. And Chapter 3 goes into a good deal of detail about how memory is basically a simulation of the past, not merely a tape replay.

MEMORY IS FOUNDATIONAL

Try this. Go to PsycINFO, the online searchable database of articles published in psychology journals. Type in the search term "memory" and see what you get. When we did this on April 30, 2014, we obtained 187,059 hits. When we add to the search terms related to the word "remember" or "mnemonic," the number jumps to 210,586. Those are very large numbers and should convince you that nobody could be familiar with everything that has been written about memory. Roughly 1 in 20 articles listed in PsycINFO includes some variant of one of those three words. But that's not the half of it. There are many topics in psychology for which memory is an implicit part of the conversation even if it's not mentioned directly.

Payne et al. (1999) once asked readers to imagine what it would be like if they had no memory, if their memories were completely shot—kaput. They pointed out that the first thing people imagine in these circumstances, no doubt from watching too many movies, is walking around muttering things like, "Who am I?" and "Where am I?"—not recognizing friends, family, or pets. As Payne et al. point out, those things would almost certainly not happen if one had literally no memory. The reason they would not happen is because if one had no memory, it would be impossible to walk around in the first place—the ability to walk depends crucially on memory for the sequence of muscle contractions necessary to ambulate. Nor would you be muttering anything, since the ability to mutter depends on memory for words and memory for how to speak. You wouldn't be asking "Who am I?" because you wouldn't have any self-concept in the first place. You might think you'd be stuck in the moment, thinking only about the present, but that's not true either, since the ability to think about the present requires you to make use of categories learned in the past. You couldn't think thoughts like "What a pretty birdie," because concepts such as *birdie* and *pretty* are all things that are stored in memory as well. Not only would your memory be destroyed, but your perceptual apparatus would also be greatly compromised, because perception depends crucially on memory (Kang et al., 2011). Without memory you'd just be lying there like a blob, which makes it especially hard to get a date on Friday nights.

Of course, actual memory deficits are not that extreme. Usually they involve impairment of one type of memory or another, not the whole kit and caboodle. In fact, as will be discussed in Chapter 8, even people with fairly dense amnesia have some ability to use their memories and some memory systems that are preserved. But the thought experiment illustrates an important reason to study memory—memory is foundational. Memory is important in pretty much everything human beings do. So if you are interested in human beings, then you should be interested in memory.

The Psych 101 Series, of which this book is a part, deals with just about every branch of specialization within psychology. And every book also deals with memory in one way or another. Interested in intelligence? Intelligence requires recalling information to reason about it and recalling reasoning strategies and heuristics that have worked in the past. Interested in depression? People with depression have memory biases that cause them to focus on negative life events. Interested in language? Language requires a memory for words and grammar, as well as tying together clauses with prior clauses stored in memory. Interested in social cognition? Social cognition requires accessing memory for information one has stored concerning other people. There is no aspect of human psychology that does not depend crucially on memory. If you are interested in psychology in any of its facets, you had better also know a lot about memory.

PRACTICAL APPLICATIONS

At a more practical level, memory research has a number of important applications. One obvious field is the field of education. In fact, a burgeoning field of cognition of instruction deals with applying research from experimental psychologists to help improve learning (Carver & Klahr, 2001). Obvious examples of this include helping children learn basic facts such as the meanings of words, historical facts or figures, mathematical equations, and parts of speech. However, memory is also important for helping children learn how to think and solve problems. In fact, most attempts to teach problem solving involve some variation on giving children examples and hoping that they will learn from these examples. So you show a child how to solve one type of mathematical equation and hope that over time he or she will be able to use those examples to solve new math problems on his or her own. For this approach to work, it requires the student to be able to remember the prior example and how it was solved, then transfer that solution to the new problem. No easy task! Such learning is sometimes called analogical learning or case-based learning (Gentner & Markman, 1997; Riesbeck & Schank, 1989).

Memory is important for schoolwork, but it doesn't stop being important after you've left school. There are many cases in which being able to accurately recall the details of events can be of crucial importance. Imagine you are sitting at home watching the latest episode of *Flip or Flop* when all of a sudden your cell phone rings. It's a number you don't recognize, but against your better judgment you answer the phone. It's a survey researcher from the local university, wanting to know about your eating habits. You guiltily think about the Cheetos you had earlier in the day. They ask you: In the past week, how many times have you eaten various foods (e.g., spinach, kale, powdered doughnuts)? How accurate do you think you would be in answering those questions? Research suggests not very accurate at all (Krosnick, 1999). And yet public health researchers rely on such surveys in helping them to understand topics such as America's obesity epidemic. Or how about this. You are subpoenaed to come into court as part of a lawsuit being filed against the company that you work for. You are asked about meetings in which you took part 1, 2, or even 3 years ago. You are asked to testify fully and truthfully. How accurate do you think your memory would be? In Chapter 3, we'll talk about research showing that when people try to remember events, they sometimes remember the events in a way that diverges from historical reality. These are called memory illusions or false memories and can be a big problem in legal proceedings (Lampinen, Neuschatz, & Payne, 1998).

A specific example of cases in which memory needs to be accurate is when witnesses make an identification of a potential criminal. Eyewitness identification is part of approximately 77,000 criminal cases per year, but evidence suggests that eyewitness identification is often subject to error (Lampinen, Neuschatz, & Cling, 2012). We know this partly because of the large number of DNA exonerations that have happened in recent years. In fact, not too long ago, Nathan Brown was released after spending 17 years in prison for an attempted rape in Metairie, Louisiana (Possley, 2014). The main source of evidence against Mr. Brown was an identification made by the victim. DNA testing proved by clear and convincing evidence that someone other than Mr. Brown was responsible for the attack. In Chapter 4 we discuss some of the factors that influence the accuracy of memory in eyewitness identifications.

Another example of how memory is important is in helping us to achieve our goals. The average person's day is filled with a large number of tasks and goals that he or she needs to accomplish. Sometimes people write to-do lists to remind themselves of these goals, but other times people rely entirely on their memory. Such memories are called prospective memories (McDaniel & Einstein, 2000). Prospective memory is not always successful and is a major source of consternation for the person who forgets to do the particular task, as well as for other people who were expecting the person to do the task. How prospective memory works, and how it can be improved, is discussed in Chapter 5.

But wait—there's more. Memory is part and parcel of how we define ourselves. For instance, the philosopher John Locke (1690/1995) argued that what makes us the same person now that we were in the past, what gives our life unity, is simply our memory of the past. When I remember myself delivering pizzas at age 19 and think of myself now teaching psychology classes at an age slightly older than 19, the thing that unifies my self-concept over time is my life story, which is stored in my autobiographical memory. Because autobiographical memory is so intimately tied to the self, it not only defines us, but is also tied to our goals and our emotions in an especially strong manner. Autobiographical memory is discussed in Chapter 6. Sometimes the events that happen in our lives are none too pleasant. They are things that

9

we'd just as soon forget. Yet, those memories sometimes are very hard to forget and can even become intrusive. The role of trauma in memory is something we'll get into in Chapter 7.

We also know that memory is of practical importance, because we know that when people suffer certain kinds of brain damage, they can experience severe memory problems. Because memory is involved in pretty much every aspect of life, such memory problems can be particularly debilitating and can affect work, social interactions, navigation, and daily living. Yet despite the problems caused by memory deficits, research has also shown that even people with dense amnesias retain some ability to form new memories. The complex set of loss of function and preserved function that occurs in amnesia is the topic of Chapter 8.

Finally, we conclude the book by talking about the role memory plays in our lives and the lives of people with superior memories. We talk about how superior memories differ from average, run-of-the-mill memories and how such abilities can be developed and maintained. We also talk about whether one really needs a superior memory in the first place. This all happens in Chapter 9, the concluding chapter of the book.

LET'S GET STARTED

We are all familiar with our own memories, but often we think of memory only in the context of memorizing. This isn't surprising since, as students, we spent an awful lot of time with highlighters and flashcards trying to cram information into our brains. Traditional presentation of memory research within general psychology and cognitive psychology textbooks reinforces this view. But human memory is a much richer, more nuanced, and more interesting topic than that. In fact, memory is an important part of just about every human activity. People certainly use memory when they study for exams. But they also use memory when they talk with their friends, plot against their enemies, celebrate their victories, solve problems, and try to remember what was on their shopping list. People so value memory that they will gladly pay more to obtain life experiences than material goods, because experiences can be savored indefinitely in memory. And many of the material goods we purchase, we purchase simply to serve as reminders to salient life events (e.g., consider souvenir shops).

Our guiding assumption in writing this book is that all psychological processes depend on memory and that memory is shaped by the functions that it serves. Memory is a foundational mental ability, important in its own right, but also important in the role it plays in other mental functions. To understand memory is to understand much of human psychology. We look forward to having you join in this journey with us. But as the old adage says, the longest journey starts with a single step. So let's get stepping!

REFERENCES

Alston, L. L., Kratchmer, C., Jeznach, A., Bartlett, N. T., Davidson, P. S., & Fujiwara E. (2013). Self-serving episodic memory biases: Findings in the repressive coping style. *Frontiers of Behavioral Neuroscience, 7*, 117. doi: 10.3389/fnbeh.2013.00117. eCollection 2013.

Carver, S. M., & Klahr, D. (2001). *Cognition and instruction: Twenty-five years of progress.* New York, NY: Psychology Press.

Gentner, D., & Markman, A. B. (1997). Structure mapping in similarity and analogy. *American Psychologist, 52*, 45–56.

Kang, M.-N., et al. (2011). Visual working memory contaminates perception. *Psychonomic Bulletin and Review, 18*(5), 860–869. doi: 10.3758/s13423-011-0126-5

Krosnick, J. A. (1999). Survey research. *Annual Reviews of Psychology, 50*, 537–567.

Lampinen, J. M., Neuschatz, J. S., & Cling, A. (2012). *The psychology of eyewitness identification.* New York, NY: Psychology Press.

Lampinen, J. M., Neuschatz, J. S., & Payne, D. G. (1998). Memory illusions and consciousness: Exploring the phenomenology of true and false memories. *Current Psychology, 16*, 181–224.

Locke, J. (1690/1995). *An essay concerning human understanding.* Amherst, NY: Prometheus Books.

McDaniel, M. A., & Einstein, G. O. (2000). Strategic and automatic processes in prospective memory retrieval: A multiprocess framework. *Applied Cognitive Psychology, 14,* S127–S144.

Payne, D. G., & Blackwell, J. M. (1998). Truth in memory from human memory: Caveat emptor. In S. J. Lynn & N. P. Spanos (Eds.), *Truth in memory.* New York, NY: Guilford Press.

Payne, D. G., Klin, C. M., Lampinen, J. M., Neuschatz, J. S., & Lindsay, D. S. (1999). Memory applied. In F. T. Durso, R. Nickerson, R. W. Schvaneveldt, S. T. Dumais, D. S. Lindsay, & M. T. H. Chi (Eds.), *The handbook of applied cognition* (pp. 83–113). New York, NY: John Wiley and Sons.

Possley, M. (2014). *Nathan Brown.* National Registry of Exonerations. University of Michigan School of Law and Northwestern University School of Law. Retrieved from https://www.law.umich.edu/special/exoneration/pages/casedetail.aspx?caseid=4457

Riesbeck, C., & Schank, R. (1989). *Inside case-based reasoning.* Northvale, NJ: Erlbaum.

Singer, J. A., & Blagov, P. (2004). The integrative function of narrative processing: Autobiographical memory, self-defining memories, and the life story of identity. In D. R. Beike, J. M. Lampinen, & D. A. Behrend (Eds.), *The self and memory* (pp. 117–138). New York, NY: Psychology Press.

Slotnick, S. D. (2004). Visual memory and visual perception recruit common neural substrates. *Behavioral and Cognitive Neuroscience Reviews, 3,* 207–221.

Nuts and Bolts: The Basics of Your Memory

magine you receive a phone call from the International Olympic Committee. They want to hire you as a consultant to come up with a test of athletic ability. They plan to offer you a six-figure salary. You think about it for a while and say, "Sure, why not?" You start coming up with potential tests for athletes. How about how much weight a person can lift in a box squat. Or how high one can jump from a stationary position. What about 40-yard dash time? Time in the 1,500 meters? Pushup count? Reaction time? Flexibility? You start listing ways you could evaluate potential athletes. You think of ways of combining the results from all the different tasks. But then it hits you like a ton of bricks: You can't give the Olympic Committee what it wants.

The problem, you realize, is that being an athlete isn't a single thing. There's a big difference between the set of skills and abilities that a world-class beach volleyball player has and those a major-league catcher has. There's a big difference between the set of skills and abilities that an NFL linebacker has and those an ultramarathoner has. And there's a big difference between a professional wrestler and a prima ballerina. They are all athletes, but the exact mix of skills they have differs. You call the Olympic Committee and tell them that—as much as it pains you—you can't take their money. There's no single set of skills that makes someone a great athlete. Rather, what being a great athlete amounts to depends a lot on the particular sport being played. Being an athlete isn't one thing. Rather, athletic ability is a set of partially overlapping skills that, when combined, produce outstanding performance.

When people wonder how memory works, they are making a similar kind of mistake. In this chapter, we hope to convince you that memory isn't a single thing. Rather, there are different types of memory that emerge in different contexts, that are measured in different ways, and that operate by slightly different rules. It's not that these different types of memory are completely unrelated—they aren't. But memory is a mixture of different skills and abilities that allows us to make use of information from the past. The precise mix of these skills and abilities varies for different types of memories. We begin by cataloging different ways that memory can be measured, and then we talk about different types of memory. After that, we outline some of the basic theories of how memory is organized and how it functions.

NOT ONE THING: MULTIPLE MEMORY MEASURES

Before we talk about different types of memory and different systems of memory, we must first make a distinction between different ways of measuring memory (Richardson-Klavehn &

Bjork, 1988). When doing so, it is important for us not to fall into a trap: It's tempting to think that different ways of measuring memory correspond in a fairly direct way to different underlying memory systems or different underlying memory processes. Wrong! This is a mistake because responses on particular types of memory measures can be influenced by multiple underlying memory processes. That is, memory measures are not "process pure" (Jacoby, 1991). We'll give examples of this later, but keep it in the back of your mind for now.

The first distinction among memory measures is between *direct measures* of memory and *indirect measures* of memory (Flory & Pring, 1995; Howard, Fry, & Brune, 1991; Light & LaVoie, 1993; Light, LaVoie, Valencia-Laver, Albertson-Owens, & Mead, 1992; Lorsbach & Morris, 1991; Merikle & Reingold, 1991). A direct measure of memory is one in which the person being tested is well aware that his or her memory, per se, is being tested. What town were you born in? Who is Vladimir Putin? What is the decimal expansion of π? What did you do last Friday? What's your most embarrassing moment? What did you dream last night? These questions all tap memory in fairly direct ways. In an indirect measure of memory, researchers are interested in measuring your memory, but they are kind of sneaky about it. They act like they are interested in measuring something else. For instance, I might show you a large set of abstract patterns and ask you to rate how aesthetically pleasing you find them. Imagine that every now and then, I repeat a pattern that you have already seen and have you rate it again. Some studies have found that prior exposure to a stimulus increases liking for that stimulus (Zajonc, 1968), so one might take increased liking of a pattern as evidence that someone has a memory for that pattern. So in this hypothetical experiment, I am measuring your memory, but it seems to you like I'm collecting judgments of your aesthetic sensibilities.

Direct measures of memory can be further subdivided into two main categories: *recall* and *recognition* (Haist, Shimamura, & Squire, 1992; Hollingworth, 1913; Kintsch, 1968). In a recall test, a person has to produce a response to a question such as an essay question, vocabulary test, or fill-in-the-blank question. For instance, if I ask you what you did last summer, I would be asking you a recall question. In a recognition test, the person doesn't have to produce an answer, but merely choose an answer that is right there in front of him or her, as in a multiple-choice or true-or-false question. For instance, if I were to ask you whether President Bill Clinton was a Democrat or Republican, I would be asking you a recognition question. Recall questions come in two basic flavors depending upon the amount of specificity in the question. In a *free recall* question, the person needs to produce a large amount of information in response to a question. For instance, "Name all the states in the United States" is a free recall question. In a *cued recall* question, the question requires a specific discrete answer, such as "What is the capital of Portugal?" In both cued recall and free recall questions, the individual needs to produce an output on his or her own.

There are also two main flavors of recognition tests. In an *old/ new recognition test*, participants are given a list of items and are asked to indicate, for each item, whether it was presented previously. Each test item is presented one at a time, and for each item, the participants simply answer "old" or "new." For instance, Lampinen, Arnal, and Hicks (2009) stopped customers coming out of a supermarket that contained eight missing child posters. They wanted to see whether customers had paid attention to the posters. So they showed the customers pictures of 16 children. Some of the children had appeared on the posters; others had not. For each picture, the customer simply had to say whether the picture had been in the supermarket. Performance did not exceed chance, indicating that the customers had not paid much attention to the missing child posters.

The other main type of recognition test is called a *forced-choice recognition test*. In a forced-choice test, participants are given a set of options and are asked to indicate which option is correct (as in a multiple-choice test in school). For instance, you might be shown a series of pictures of puppies like the ones shown in

Figure 2.1. Later on, you might be shown three puppies, and you might be asked which puppy you saw. You would then choose your answer from the list. In designing any recognition memory test, there are two types of items. *Targets* are the items that were previously studied. On an old/new recognition test, participants should say "old" to the targets, and on a forced-choice test, participants should choose the target out of the list of options. The other type of item is called a *foil*, or sometimes a *lure* or *distractor*. Foils are items on the test that were not in the materials that were studied. On an old/new recognition test, participants should say "new" to foils, and on forced-choice tests they should not select the foils.

As you might imagine, an important consideration in creating a recognition memory test is to come up with appropriate foils (Wallace, 1982). You have probably taken multiple-choice tests in school in which you've been able to get the correct

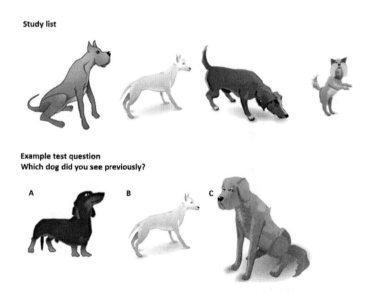

Study list

Example test question
Which dog did you see previously?

A   B   C

FIGURE 2.1 Study list and test list.
Source: Clip art used to create the image obtained from the Open Clipart Library, www.openclipart.org. Clip art image drawn by hrum, https://openclipart.org/detail/191214/dogs-pack-by-hrum-191214.

answer—not because you knew the answer, but because you were able to eliminate the other alternatives. For instance, if we were to ask you, "Which U.S. president had a son who had pet alligators?" and give you the choices "(A) Jim Lampinen, (B) Denise Beike, (C) Herbert Hoover, (D) Napoleon," you could probably get this piece of presidential trivia correct. (Hint: It is not B.) But of course that wouldn't really indicate your memory for the information, merely that you were able to deduce the answer because the other alternatives were not plausible.

Although recall tests and recognition tests are both direct measures of memory, researchers think that they tap slightly different memory processes. One piece of evidence for this is that there are variables that affect recognition memory one way but affect recall memory in a different way. Such differing patterns of results based on the type of test given are called *memory dissociations* (Blaxton, 1989). One example of this are word frequency effects (Kintsch, 1970). Word frequency refers to how often words appear in everyday language. For instance, a word like "cat" is very frequent, whereas a word like "vat" is relatively infrequent. When people study high-frequency word lists versus low-frequency word lists, the typical finding is that people find it easier to recall high-frequency words but easier to recognize low-frequency words. If recall and recognition were measuring the same thing, then the results should turn out the same regardless of which type of test is used. But they don't.

One early account of these word frequency effects was *the generate/test theory of recall* (Bahrick, 1970; Watkins & Gardiner, 1979). According to this theory, when given a recognition memory test, you compare the item's familiarity to some threshold you have for deciding whether the item is old. If it seems familiar enough, you say "old." If it doesn't seem that familiar, you say "new." The reason high-frequency words are difficult to recognize is that they always seem familiar. It's hard for you to tell on a recognition test whether the word "cat" seems familiar because it was on the study list or because it's such a common word. On a recall test, you first mentally generate a list of words you might have seen (i.e., candidate words). You then assess the familiarity of the candidate words just as you would on a recognition test. According to the theory, it's easier to generate high-frequency words such as "cat" than low-frequency words such as "vat." That's why high-frequency words are easier to recall but harder to recognize.

One prediction of this theory is that recall should always be harder than recognition, since recall involves the additional step of generating the alternatives. The problem with this is that some researchers have demonstrated situations in which recall is actually easier than recognition—so-called *recall without recognition* (Tulving & Thomson, 1973). In these experiments participants first study pairs of associated words like *heavy piano*. In a second stage of the experiment participants are given a list of words and are asked to generate associates of that word. Some of the words are meant to evoke one of the previously studied words. For instance, participants might be given the cue *music* and be asked to list the first four words that come to mind, with the thought being that lots of students will generate the word *piano* in response to the word *music*. Once participants have done this for a number of words, they are asked to go through all the words they generated and circle any that they had studied previously. Commonly, people failed to circle words like *piano* that they had previously studied. Nonetheless, when given the word *heavy*, people who couldn't recognize the word *piano* on the recognition test easily recalled it.

This led to an alternative theory of the difference between recall and recognition (Tulving & Thomson, 1973). According to this theory, what makes memory difficult or easy is how closely associated the available cues are to the thing you are trying to remember. Under most circumstances, the cues available in recognition are stronger than the cues available in recall, because in recognition the exact word you are trying to remember is present. However, in the recall without recognition experiment, the design causes participants to think about pianos as *heavy things* when the word is studied but to think of pianos as *musical things* on the recognition test. So the way people are thinking about pianos when studying doesn't match up well with how they are thinking about pianos when being tested. When cued with the word *heavy* on the recall test, the study and test cues match up again, and memory is successful.

In addition to these direct measures of memory, there are also a number of different indirect measures of memory (Merikle & Reingold, 1991). What defines an indirect measure of memory is that, from the participants' perspective, it doesn't seem like a measure of memory at all. Some of the earliest studies looking at indirect tests of memory involved patients with dense amnesias (see Chapter 8 for more detail). In one famous example, Edouard Claparede, a Swiss psychologist, was working with a patient who had Korsakoff's amnesia (Nicolas, 2010). Claparede entered the patient's room and introduced himself, reaching out his hand to shake hands with the patient. Unknown to the patient, the good doctor Claparede had a pin hidden in his hand. When the patient shook the doctor's hand, her hand was pricked by the pin. Ouch! The patient withdrew her hand and, I'm sure, gave the doctor quite a look. On a later day, the patient had no memory of who the doctor was or the whole prior ordeal with the pin. The doctor reached out his hand to shake the patient's hand, but this time she refused to take it, even though she had no conscious recollection of who the doctor was. This finding demonstrated that the patient's memory was preserved in some sense, even though she had no direct recall of the event. Nowadays we'd say she had an *implicit memory* for the episode (Schacter, Chiu, & Ochsner, 1993). Implicit memory is defined memory without awareness, or unconscious memory.

The use of indirect tests of memory is not limited to people with amnesia (Schacter et al., 1993). In fact, a number of standard laboratory techniques have been developed that involve the use of indirect memory tests. One common test is called a *word stem completion test* (Roediger, Weldon, Stadler, & Riegler, 1992). To see how a word stem completion task works, try the following. Find a friend, acquaintance, significant other, archnemesis—whatever. Provide the person with a sheet of paper numbered 1 to 36 and a writing utensil. Have the person read the words in the appendix to this chapter and quickly decide whether each word has exactly two vowels. He or she should write YES if it has exactly two vowels and NO if it has fewer than two vowels or more than two vowels. Your participant should perform the task as quickly as she or he can.

After your participant is done, tell him or her that the first part of the experiment was just a distraction, and that you are moving on to the main part of the experiment now. Provide your participant with a new piece of paper. Put the other one away so the participant can't see it. Show the person the word stems displayed in the following table. For each word stem, your participant should come up with the first five-letter word that comes to his or her mind. For instance, for a word stem like "CHI_ _" he or she might say "CHILL." Your participant should go as quickly as possible, without thinking too much about any particular answer. But remind your participant that the word has to have exactly five letters.

THE_ _	ROB_ _	CRA_ _	THI_ _
COU_ _	GRA_ _	BOO_ _	SWA_ _
SHO_ _	SCO_ _	FLO_ _	PLA_ _
SWI_ _		STR_ _	

Now for scoring your participant's results. The purpose of the word stem completion test is to look for priming (Tulving & Schacter, 1990). Priming happens when a person completes the word stem with a word that he or she saw in the previous part of the experiment, at a rate that is greater than if the person hadn't seen those words previously in the experiment. Go back to the appendix and count how many of the words in the appendix your participant ended up using on the word stem completion test. As a control, we gave those word stems to people who hadn't seen the appendix, and they ended up using an average of 1.7 of the words from the appendix. Three quarters of control participants ended up using 2.25 or fewer words from the appendix, and 95% of control participants ended up using 3 or fewer of the words in the appendix. So if your participant scored higher than that, it's probably because seeing the words in the appendix influenced your participant's responding. In other words, your participant has been primed!

Ask your participant, "When you were completing the test, were you consciously aware of using the words from the back of the chapter?" Your participant might say "Yes," indicating that he or she deliberately used the words from the appendix. If so, ask him or her to indicate which words he or she remembered from the appendix. Or he or she may also say "No," indicating that the priming occurred outside of his or her awareness. Research has shown that people will still show priming effects even if they are explicitly told not to use any of the words they encountered previously (Richardson-Klavehn, Gardiner, & Java, 1994). This finding of priming, even when people are told not to use previously encountered words, is usually taken as evidence of *implicit memory* (Schacter et al., 1993). We will discuss priming effects more in Chapter 8.

ΠOT OΠΕ THIΠG: ΕΠCODIΠG, STORAGE, AND RETRIEVAL

We next turn our attention to the basic mechanisms involved in memory. The first way of thinking about how memory is organized is to consider three basic stages that everybody agrees are involved in memory, regardless of their particular theory of how memory operates (Galotti, 2004). These provide a starting point for our discussion and also some terminology we can share to talk about memory. Imagine yourself taking a walk in the park and seeing a chocolate lab chasing a Frisbee. Your perception of that dog chasing that Frisbee occurs because light from the sun is bouncing off the pooch and the disk and hitting your eyes. When the light hits the eye, the cornea and lens focus the light to a location on the back of your eye called the retina (Enns, 2004).

The retina has little tiny cells called rods and cones that are sensitive to light. When light hits these cells, it causes a bunch of chemical reactions that in turn create a nerve impulse that gets sent to your brain, and—wowza!—you see.

It's generally agreed that to form a memory, this basic perceptual experience needs to get transformed into a code allowing the brain to think about the event, store it, and retrieve it later. This process of transforming the perceptual experience into a memory code is called encoding (Weinstein & Mayer, 1986). Encoding has two major characteristics: First, it is *selective* (Kahneman, 1973). Not everything that you experience perceptually gets selected for encoding, because the amount of attention you have is limited. So the dog and the Frisbee interest you and so get selected for encoding, but maybe you don't even notice the honeybee that is pollinating a nearby flower. Chocolate lab gets encoded; honeybee does not. The second characteristic of encoding is that it involves *elaboration* and interpretation (Bransford, 1979). We don't encode into memory what happens, we encode into memory what we interpret to be happening. Maybe the dog isn't chasing the Frisbee at all. Maybe the Frisbee just happens to be flying in the same direction as the dog is running. Maybe a cat is chasing the dog, and the dog is running from the cat. Who knows? But what you'll store into memory is what you interpret as going on. This, of course, has important implications, because memory obeys a garbage in/garbage out principle. If you never encoded the honeybee, then the honeybee pollinating the flower, even though it happened, isn't a memory for you. If you encoded the dog chasing the Frisbee, but really the dog was running from a ferocious cat, too bad. The dog chasing the Frisbee is the memory you are stuck with. To paraphrase one famous cognitive psychologist, the lie soon enough becomes memory's truth (Loftus, 1992).

The second stage of memory processing is called *storage* (Anderson, 1995). Storage refers to the stage in between encoding an event and later retrieval of the event. It refers to the representation of the memory in your brain when you aren't thinking about the event. People often think of storage as a passive process, as if you were to take a file folder and put it in a file cabinet until you need it again (Simons & Chabris, 2011). As noted in Chapter 3, psychologists have found that memory in storage isn't fixed but rather is labile and subject to change (Loftus, 1979). New information can get into memory and change the memory in storage, and the memory representation itself can fall apart and become less accessible if not retrieved for long periods of time.

The final stage of the memory process is called *retrieval* (Shiffrin & Atkinson, 1969; Tulving & Thompson, 1973). This is where you actually remember the information. Most psychologists believe that retrieval depends on the degree to which the cues present in the environment when you try to remember something match the cues that were available when you originally encoded the information (Tulving & Thomson, 1973). So a good piece of advice when you are trying to remember something is to put yourself back in the same frame of mind you were in when you originally learned the material (more on this later!). But it's arguable that retrieval is the wrong metaphor for how memory operates (Lampinen & Neuschatz, 2008). Retrieval implies that there is some fixed, immutable *thing* residing in some *location* in memory and you just have to go to it and get it, like grabbing a note card out of a card organizer. But most psychologists believe that remembering isn't so much a matter of retrieving as of reconstructing, like when a detective examines clues to make a plausible inference about a crime (Howes & O'Shea, 2014; Lampinen & Neuschatz, 2008; Neisser, 1967; Schacter, 1996). Your memory is just such a detective, as we will discuss later in this book.

NOT ONE THING: MULTIPLE STAGES

The stages we just discussed can be thought of as functional stages that any theory of memory must account for, but they aren't really a theory of memory. We now turn our attention to such theories.

One of the most successful theories of memory was developed by Atkinson and Shiffrin (1968) in the late 1960s and is sometimes called the *modal model* of memory (see Figure 2.2). The model was developed with reference to computer architectures popular at the time and assumes that there are three memory buffers and control processes that move information from buffer to buffer. A memory buffer is simply a storage system that can retain information. The modal model characterizes the memory buffers in terms of their capacity, their duration, their code, and the reason why information is forgotten.

The first memory buffer in the modal model is called the sensory information store (Sperling, 1960). When you look at a scene in front of you, the sensory information store retains everything in that scene for a fraction of a second. The purpose is to

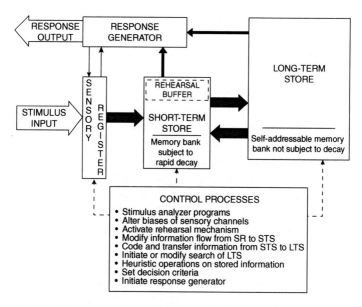

FIGURE 2.2 Stages of the Atkinson and Shiffrin model of memory. LTS, long-term store; SR, sensory register; STS, short-term store. Reprinted from Shiffrin and Atkinson (1969). Copyright 1969, American Psychological Association. Reprinted with permission.

retain information just long enough for you to decide what to do with it next. According to the theory, the capacity of the sensory information store is quite large, but the duration is quite small (a couple of hundred milliseconds). The theory says that the code for the sensory store is unanalyzed sensory features such as colors, shapes, angles, and so on, but nothing as extravagant as a honeybee, a bottle of wine, or Jim Lampinen's face. Information is lost from the sensory information store very quickly and is forgotten due to simple decay.

The second memory buffer is called short-term memory. Imagine that a potential love interest tells you his or her telephone number, but you don't have a piece of paper or an electronic device to record the number. So you walk across the room, where you see a piece of paper that you can write the number on. Meanwhile you are keeping the phone number of your hopefully future paramour in your mind. Short-term memory retains information for about 10 to 20 seconds if you aren't constantly rehearsing it. According to the modal model, people can retain about 7 chunks of information, where a chunk is a meaningful unit of information (Miller, 1956). For instance, the digits 8-1-4-0-2-3-4-2-9 would likely be stored as around nine chunks of information and would be slightly beyond the short-term memory capacity of most people. However, a string of digits like 1-7-7-6-1-4-9-2 might only be stored as two chunks of information as long as you know the significance of the years 1776 and 1492.

According to the theory, forgetting in short-term memory happens due to interference (Waugh & Norman, 1965). If you think about it, this makes a lot of sense. If there are only so many slots in short-term memory for information, then whenever new information is added, it has to push out old information. Let me give an example. Back in college, one of us (Jim) worked as a fast-food manager to make ends meet. At night he'd have to reconcile the money drawers, which involved pulling the drawers, counting the money, entering the totals into a ledger, and so forth. The restaurant made thousands of dollars each shift, so it would take a while. Sometimes in the middle of counting, "5,

10, 15, 20 . . . 425, 430, 435," a crew member came in to ask a question or just to shoot the breeze: "Hey, what are you doing tomorrow?" Jim would answer, "Not much," look down at the pile of money, and realize that he had just lost count. And he'd say, "Aw, shoot," or words to that effect, and have to start over. That's how short-term memory works: It retains information, but it's also very fragile and requires your continued attention lest it be lost very quickly.

The research that first demonstrated some of these basic facts about short-term memory was conducted early in the history of cognitive psychology. Some of the earliest studies were conducted by John Brown (Brown, 1958) and by Lloyd and Margaret Peterson (Peterson & Peterson, 1959). The task they used has been called the Brown–Peterson task in their honor. Participants were given a string of three consonants, such as JML and were asked to repeat the letters after some period of time, say, 5 seconds, or 10, or 30. One problem that had to be overcome was that participants could perform the task perfectly, regardless of time, if they just rotely repeated the letters "J-M-L J-M-L J-M-L J-M-L J-M-L J-M-L" until they had to report the letters. This strategy on the part of participants is called *maintenance rehearsal*. To prevent this kind of rehearsal, participants were given a three-digit number (e.g., 839) and asked to count backward by 3s until they were asked to report the letters. The findings are reproduced in Figure 2.3. When participants were asked to repeat the letters after only a few seconds, they were nearly perfect in reproducing the letters. But when they had to wait 9 seconds or longer to repeat the letters, performance was much worse. By 18 seconds, performance was almost at its floor, indicating that short-term memory lasts about 10 to 20 seconds if participants are prevented from rehearsing the information.

Other early research showed that forgetting in short-term memory was likely due to interference. One demonstration of this was by Nancy Waugh and Donald Norman (1965), who were at Harvard at the time. They compared two ideas of how forgetting could occur. One of these theories was *decay*, which

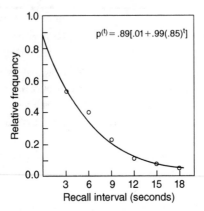

$$p^{(t)} = .89[.01 + .99(.85)^t]$$

FIGURE 2.3 Proportion of items recalled as a function of the delay between encountering items and being asked to recall them in the Brown–Peterson Task.
Reprinted from Peterson and Peterson (1959). Copyright 1959, American Psychological Association. Reprinted with permission.

simply means that the information disappears over time. The other theory is that forgetting occurs due to *retroactive interference*, meaning that new information replaces older information. To test these competing theories, participants were provided with strings of digits one at a time. At the end of the string of digits was a *probe digit*. The participant's task was to indicate what number followed the probe digit during its prior occurrence on the list. For instance, you might be given the digits:

5, 1, 2, 4, 3, 9, 8, 7, 6

If you then hear the probe digit 7, then you should report 6. But if the probe digit is 2, you should report 4, and if the probe digit is 5, you should report 1. The farther back you have to go, the harder the task should be. To determine whether this increased difficulty was due to decay or interference, Waugh and Norman varied both the number of intervening digits and the rate at which the digits were presented. For instance, the total time elapsed is the same if three intervening digits are presented every 4 seconds or if six intervening digits are presented every 2 seconds. If the decay theory is right, all that should matter is the time. If interference theory is correct, then all that should matter is the number of intervening digits. What the Harvard folks found was that all that mattered was the number of digits, not the speed with which they were presented.

The final stage of memory, according to the modal model, is long-term memory. Long-term memory contains information from a minute ago, a week ago, a month ago—all the way out to years and years ago. Some people believe that every piece of information that ever got into long-term memory is still in long-term memory (Shiffrin & Atkinson, 1969; Tulving, 1974). Other researchers believe that information can get lost or distorted and that then the original information no longer exists (Loftus & Loftus, 1980). Resolving this debate is difficult, because even if someone can't remember something, it's always possible that the information still exists in memory but simply isn't accessible. This is because long-term memory is subject to retrieval failure. Retrieval failure is similar to when you know that you stored something on your laptop, but you didn't put it in the right folder and none of your searches are finding it. It still exists on the hard drive of your computer, but you can't retrieve it.

NOT ONE THING: MULTIPLE COMPONENTS IN WORKING MEMORY

By the mid-1970s, people became unhappy with the idea that short-term memory is just a box that holds a limited amount of information for a limited amount of time. This dissatisfaction led Alan Baddeley and Graham Hitch (1974) to propose the working memory model, which has largely supplanted Atkinson and Shiffrin's (1968) idea of short-term memory. There are two big and related ideas in the working memory model. The first is that the memory system that retains information for a short period of time isn't just some passive receptacle for chunks of information. Instead, *working memory* is the active part of memory that is used when we think, solve problems, navigate, read, hold conversations, and so on. Working memory is correlated with fluid intelligence (Engle, Tuholski, Laughlin, & Conway, 1999). It is correlated with reading ability (Daneman & Carpenter, 1980). It is correlated with arithmetic skills (McLean & Hitch, 1999). It is correlated with reasoning using formal logic (Gilhooly, Logie, Wetherick, & Wynn, 1993). In general, working memory is the workhorse of cognition. It is where all the action takes place.

The second big idea is that working memory is a multipart system like the one shown in Figure 2.4. One system retains verbal information for brief periods of time. This part of working memory is called the phonological loop (Baddeley, Gathercole, & Papagno, 1998). Working memory can also process visual information including mental images that exist in the mind's eye. This part of working memory is called the visuospatial sketchpad (Logie, 1995). Controlling these two systems is another system called the central executive (Baddeley, 1996). The central executive is involved in reasoning, decision making, and controlling responses. More recently, a component of working memory

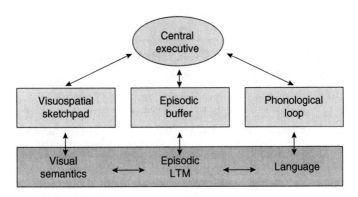

FIGURE 2.4 Working Memory Model.
Reprinted from Baddeley (2000). Copyright 2000, with permission from Elsevier.

called the episodic buffer was proposed (Baddeley, 2000). The episodic buffer combines information from the other buffers into a unified conscious experience. A major assumption of the working memory model is that each of these systems has a limited capacity. So doing two verbal tasks at the same time is difficult, or doing two visual tasks at the same time is difficult, but doing a visual and a verbal task at the same time is not difficult.

NOT ONE THING: MULTIPLE MEMORY SYSTEMS IN LONG-TERM MEMORY

Not only have theorists concluded that short-term memory (or now we would say working memory) is not one thing, but some theorists have also argued that long-term memory is not one thing. The person who made this claim most strongly was Endel Tulving (1984) in his theory of multiple memory systems. In the best known formulation, Tulving (1984) claimed that long-term memory was made up of three partly overlapping systems. The first is called *procedural memory*. Procedural memory is memory for both mental and physical actions that one might take. The other day, the first author went to the batting cage with his stepson James. As a younger man, the first author played an awful lot of baseball—and it remains his favorite sport—but it had been a few years since he had actually swung a bat. So he felt a bit of trepidation as he stood in the batting cage, worried that he would look foolish whiffing at 40 mph baseballs thrown by the batting cage's mechanical arm, while his 12-year-old stepson was knocking the cover off the ball. But what he found was that his procedural memory remembered how to swing, and he was hitting the pitches pretty impressively. Procedural memory can also retain mental procedures, like doing long division. According to Tulving, procedural memories are responsible for implicit memories—that is, memories that occur outside of awareness that are often measured using indirect memory tests. Because procedural memories occur outside of conscious awareness, Tulving (1985a) indicates that they involve anoetic consciousness ("noetic" referring to knowing and "a" meaning "not").

The second memory system outlined by Tulving (1985a) is called semantic memory. Semantic memory refers to memories for facts and details that are not mentally experienced as events in one's life. For instance, a person may know that the Battle of Normandy happened in World War II but probably has no recollection of the experience of learning that fact. Similarly, we all know our names, but we certainly don't have a memory for the experience of learning our name for the first time. These are facts and details but are devoid of an event that the memory is tied to. There are a number of detailed theories of how semantic memories are stored (Anderson, 1996; Collins & Loftus, 1975; Smith, Shoben, & Rips, 1974). The best known of these assume that semantic memories are stored in semantic networks such as the one shown in Figure 2.5 (Collins & Loftus, 1975). Each point in the network represents a concept (e.g., Pyrenees; dog) and links refer to relations between concepts (e.g., kind of). The best known theories

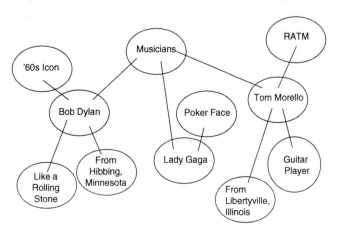

FIGURE 2.5 A very small subsection of a semantic network having to do with musicians. RATM, Rage Against the Machine.

of semantic memory indicate that when a concept is activated, the activation spreads via the links to related concepts. One consequence of this is that it is easier to verify statements that require fewer links (e.g., Is a Pyrenees a type of dog?) than statements that require more links (e.g., Is a Pyrenees a type of animal?) (Collins & Quillian, 1969). Semantic memories are conscious memories of facts about the world, and thus Tulving (1985a) indicates that they involve noetic consciousness (i.e., knowing consciousness).

The last memory system proposed by Tulving is episodic memory. Episodic memory is memory for personally experienced events that occurred at a particular time and place. They involve mentally putting oneself back in an event and in some sense reliving the event in one's mind (e.g., perceptual experiences, emotions, thoughts, contextual details). Thus it has sometimes been said that episodic memory involves a kind of mental time travel (Tulving, 2002). So if you remember your first kiss, the first time you drove a car, or a particularly embarrassing personal experience, those are all episodic memories. But episodic memory is also used to refer to more mundane events, such as remembering that a particular word was on a particular word list in an experiment. Because episodic memory involves putting oneself back in a particular place and time, episodic memories are thought to require at least some degree of self-awareness. Therefore, Tulving (1985a) claimed that they involve autonoetic consciousness (i.e., self-knowing consciousness).

It is important to note that Tulving did not claim that these three systems were entirely independent of each other, or even that they involved entirely distinct brain systems. Instead, he argued that the systems were nested (Tulving, 1985a, 1987). Semantic memory requires and makes use of procedural memory but also involves systems in addition to those involved in procedural memory. Episodic memory requires and makes use of semantic memory but also involves systems in addition to those involved in semantic memory. One consequence of this is that a person might experience brain damage that would impair semantic or episodic memory but leave procedural memory working just fine and dandy, but the reverse should not occur (Tulving, 1987). But not everybody agrees with the idea that there are separate memory systems in the first place. For instance, McKoon, Ratcliff, and Dell (1986) argued that it isn't that there are different kinds of memory, but instead that there are just different types of information all stored in the same memory system. Although not everybody agrees on who is right, most everybody agrees that the episodic, semantic, procedural distinction at least provides a useful heuristic for thinking about long-term memory.

NOT A THING AT ALL: PROCESS-BASED ACCOUNTS OF MEMORY

An alternative way of thinking about memory is not in terms of systems or buffers that contain information, but rather in terms of procedures that are used to process and manipulate information in the mind (Kolers & Roediger, 1984). Thus we can think about memory primarily in terms of what these processes are. The most common distinction is between single process theories and multiple process theories. So let's look at each of these in a little bit of detail.

Single Process Theories—Signal Detection Theory

The best known single process theory of memory is called signal detection theory (Stanislaw & Todorov, 1999). To get a sense of how signal detection theory works, it's first useful to think about an example. Imagine I show you pictures of 20 different kitties and ask you to try to remember the kitty cats for a later test. After 30 minutes delay, I give you an old/new recognition test. The test shows pictures of 40 kitties, 20 of which you've seen before and 20 new, never-before-seen kitties. For each item on the test, you are supposed to say "old" if you saw it before and "new" if you haven't seen it before. Thus there are four possible outcomes.

You can say "old" to a target. When this happens, it is called a hit. You can say "old" to a foil. When this happens it is called a false alarm. You can say "new" to a target. This is called a miss. Or you can say "new" to a foil. This is called a correct rejection.

Dude, your memory stinks

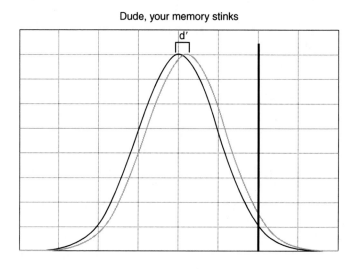

Dude, your memory rocks

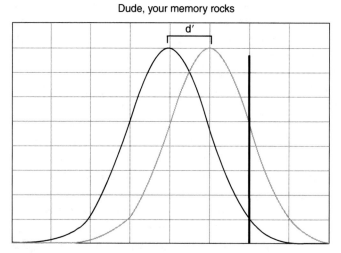

FIGURE 2.6 Illustration of signal detection theory.

You've probably all seen the infamous bell curves like the ones shown in Figure 2.6, probably in the context of people talking about intelligence tests. The idea behind such curves is pretty straightforward. They simply show how common different scores are when those scores fall along some numerical continuum. Recall that there are two types of items on an old/new recognition test: targets and foils. Let's consider the foils first. According to signal detection theory, when you look at a foil on a recognition test, it evokes some sense of familiarity, because you've seen other similar kitties, even though you didn't see that exact kitty. Moreover, if you look at all the foils, the distribution of familiarity values will be a bell-shaped curve. The targets will also evoke some feeling of familiarity, but the familiarity will be greater, on average, than that of the foils, because you just recently saw the targets. The distribution of familiarity for targets will also be a bell-shaped curve. The difference between the peaks of the two bell curves is the measure of memory strength, called d'. Good memory means high d'. Poor memory means low d' (see Figure 2.6).

Because the two bell-shaped curves overlap somewhat, there is no way of knowing for sure whether an item is old or new just based on its familiarity. On average, the old items are more familiar than the new items (by an amount of d'). But there are some old items that aren't that familiar, and there are some new items that are pretty familiar. So according to the theory, what people end up doing is setting a cutoff (i.e., response criterion). If the item is more familiar than the cutoff, they call it old; otherwise, they call it new. The theory says that the cutoff used is pretty much up to the person taking the test. Some people end up being very conservative and setting a very high familiarity cutoff. They end up with very few false alarms but also fewer hits. Some people are very liberal and set a low cutoff. They end up with lots of hits but also more false alarms. Other people are somewhere in the middle.

The hit rate is the proportion of old items that are more familiar than the cutoff. The false alarm rate is the proportion of new items that are more familiar than the cutoff. If you know the proportion of hits and the proportion of false alarms, you can determine the value of d′ with just some basic knowledge of statistics, but doing so is beyond the scope of this book. It's not hard, though, and if you do any research involving memory, it's a good thing to know how to do.

There are variations of signal detection theory that make slightly different assumptions. For instance, a lot of people think that the bell curve for the targets has more variability in it than the bell curve for the foils (Mickes, Wixted, & Wais, 2007; Ratcliff, Sheu, & Gronlund, 1992). As a consequence, the curve for studied items is more spread out than the curve for the unstudied items (see Figure 2.7). This is called *unequal variance signal detection theory*. There is good reason for thinking this might be true. After all, a studied item once had the familiarity of an unstudied item (i.e., back before it was studied it was unstudied). When you study items, you increase their familiarity, but that's probably truer for some items than for others. So for studied items you have the variability that is just because items differ in their familiarity even before you study them, and added on to that is additional variability due to the fact that some items just get more of a boost from study opportunities than others.

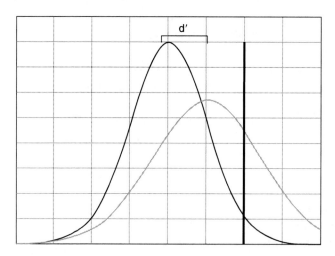

FIGURE 2.7 Illustration of unequal variance signal detection theory.

Dual Process Models

Although signal detection theory, especially the unequal variance version of it, is pretty influential, a lot of memory psychologists believe that it is too simplistic for assuming that recognition memory only occurs in one way (i.e., familiarity). These psychologists have proposed a variety of dual process accounts of memory. One of the most famous examples of this was a theory proposed by George Mandler (1980), who gave the example of being on a bus and seeing someone. The person's face evokes a feeling of familiarity, but you can't quite place where you saw the person. You start to get nervous. What if the person comes over and talks and you have to admit you don't remember where you met the person? "Hi, Marcia, how are you?" To which your response is "Hi . . . um . . . there . . . uhm . . . . Pretty good, how about you?" Talk about a faux pas! Mandler contrasted this with a situation in which you are on the bus, you see a person, and immediately a string of associations dealing with the person comes to mind— this person took part in the science fair in high school, she's named Jordan thanks to her mother's admiration for Michael Jordan, she is a star volleyball player, she likes psychology, and so on.

Mandler (1980) argued, based on this example as well as on experimental evidence, that there were two ways that recognition memory can occur. One, familiarity, involves a sense of prior occurrence but without any context-specifying details. The other, which he called retrieval, but which nowadays is called recollection, involves memory for the item, as well as context-specifying details about the item. To explain this distinction, Mandler argued that two types of details get stored into memory when we encode an event. For instance, a person's face is made up of a nose, two eyes, eyebrows, a mouth, a chin, maybe dimples, maybe hair (maybe not), and so on. Each of those individual features is bound together into a package of associations that represents that individual face. Mandler called these associations *intra-item associations* (associations within the item) and argued that it was these associations that led to a feeling of familiarity. The other type of detail are associations between the item and the context in which the item occurred. So you see a face and associate the face with a name, with where you saw the person, with your assessment of the person's personality, and so on. Mandler called these associations *inter-item associations* (associations between items) and argued that these inter-item associations are responsible for the experience of recollection.

Later researchers took Mandler's basic idea and ran with it. One notable example of this is Larry Jacoby's (1991, 1997) *process dissociation* approach. Like Mandler, Jacoby argued that recognition can occur in two distinct ways—recollection and familiarity. For Jacoby, recollection involves retrieval of contextual details and, importantly, provides people with an opportunity to respond in a way that is contingent upon the context. For instance, if you remember a piece of information but also remember that you got the information from your Aunt Abigail, who is known for telling tall tales, then you might be hesitant to act on the information. If, however, you remember a piece of information and remember that you got the information from Jamie, whose veracity and intelligence are a shining beacon in the world, then you can pretty much take that information to the bank. Additionally, Jacoby made the argument that in at least some cases, feelings of familiarity arise by means of increased *perceptual fluency.* Perceptual fluency means that once you have perceptually analyzed an item, like a person's face, the next time you look at that item, your perceptual system processes it just a tad faster. That increase in processing speed is experienced as a sense of familiarity.

Jacoby (1991) used these ideas to develop a technique for estimating recollection and familiarity using something he called *the process of opposition.* The process of opposition involves answering two types of memory questions: *inclusion questions* and *exclusion questions.* To illustrate, imagine you see a video in which Jamie (who is always reliable and honest) and Abigail (who is not always reliable and honest) make statements about current events. For instance, Jamie might say, "Belgium is experiencing a shortage of turnips" and Aunt Abigail might say, "Iran has halted the import of Twinkies." (*Note:* As of this writing, we do not know if this is actually true. However, we believe the U.S. State Department should make contingency plans to prepare for such an eventuality.) On an *inclusion test* you might be asked, "Did either person say, 'Iran has halted the import of Twinkies'?" This is called an inclusion question, because you are supposed to say yes if either person said it. On an *exclusion test*, you might be asked "Did Jamie say, 'Iran has halted the import of Twinkies'?" (This is called an exclusion question because you are supposed to say yes if Jamie said it but to exclude anything that Abigail said.)

Now think about how inclusion and exclusion questions differ. If you remember the statement about Iran and the Twinkies, but you don't remember the context of who said it, then you have no way of knowing on the exclusion test whether to say yes or to say no. You know it was said, but you don't know *who* said it. So if an item is merely familiar, Jacoby argued, you would respond to it in the same way on exclusion tests and inclusion tests. On the other hand, if you recollect that Abigail said it, then you should say yes on the inclusion test but no on the exclusion test. Thus Jacoby argued that recollection can be measured by taking the difference between yes responses on inclusion tests and yes responses on exclusion tests. Recollection equals inclusion minus exclusion.

While Jacoby used the process of opposition to derive estimates of recollection, Tulving (1985b) proposed a self-report measure to distinguish recollection from familiarity. In the remember/know technique, participants taking a recognition memory test first indicate whether an item is old or new, just like in a standard old/new recognition test (Gardiner, 1988; Gardiner & Java, 1990, 1991; Rajaram, 1993). If they indicate that an item is old, they make an additional judgment indicating their reason for their judgment. If their memory for the item is based on the recollection of specific details of its previous encounter, then they are supposed to indicate that they "remember" the item. If they are sure the item was presented but don't recall any specific details of its occurrence, they are supposed to respond "know."

These different ways of measuring recollection and familiarity each have their own strengths and weaknesses (see Lampinen, Neuschatz, & Payne, 1998), but research has tended to find similar results regardless of which measure is used (Yonelinas, Kroll, Dobbins, Lazzara, & Knight, 1998). This has led Andrew Yonelinas (2001) to summarize the recollection/familiarity distinction with three Cs: consciousness, confidence, and control. Consciousness because in recollection one becomes consciously aware again of some aspect of the item's prior occurrence. Confidence because recollection of event details makes one more certain that the event actually transpired. And control because, as Jacoby pointed out in his process dissociation approach, recollection allows one to respond in a way that is contingent upon the context.

PROOF IS IN THE PUDDING: FUNCTIONAL ACCOUNTS OF MEMORY

So far we have talked about theories of memory that focus on memory stages (e.g., short term versus long term), memory systems (e.g., episodic versus semantic), or memory processes (recollection versus familiarity). Other important work has focused on the relationship between encoding variables and retrieval variables, sometimes just called functional accounts of memory (Payne, Klin, Lampinen, Neuschatz, & Lindsay, 1999). Functional accounts are useful, especially if you are interested in improving your own memory, because they provide guidance for how to improve memory by changing either the encoding dynamics or the retrieval dynamics.

Levels of Processing

Craik and Lockhart (1972) became dissatisfied with the idea of dividing memory into stages. They argued that rather than thinking about memory as having separate stages, it was better to think

41

about how the processing of information at encoding leads to later retention. Short-term memory isn't short term because it is a separate stage in memory processing; it is short term because the information wasn't studied all that well. Long-term memory isn't long-term memory because it is a separate stage of memory, but because the information was studied very well. Although originally conceived as an alternative to the modal model with its various stages, later researchers came to see the levels of processing approach and the modal model as complementary approaches.

The idea behind the levels of processing approach is that when you study information, you can do so in a shallow, superficial manner or in a deeper, more significant manner. Shallow processing focuses on the surface of the item being studied rather than on the meaning. Deep processing focuses on the meaning rather than on the surface structure. The argument of the levels of processing approach is that the deeper the processing at encoding, the better the memory later on.

Think about your own experience reading something for a class. Have you ever had the experience of being midway through a chapter for some class and realizing that you have no idea what the chapter is about? That is, although you read each and every word of each and every sentence, you were just kind of reading the words without really thinking about what they meant. When you read a textbook chapter that way, you are unlikely to retain much information from it later on. You have probably also read things in which you've been totally engrossed, thinking carefully about the examples, working out in your own mind the implications of what is being said. When you process information in that way, later retention is much better.

The classic experiments on the levels of processing approach used an incidental learning technique. In one study, participants were presented with items and were asked to answer focusing questions about the items (Craik & Tulving, 1975). What made the technique *incidental* is that the subjects weren't aware that they were supposed to be memorizing the words; they just thought they were supposed to be answering the questions. Some of the questions were designed to force participants to process the words deeply, and some were designed to force participants to process the words more shallowly. For instance, if the word was "PHONE," participants might be asked one of the following questions:

Structural question: Is the word in capital letters?
Phonemic question: Does the word rhyme with "cone"?
Category question: Is this a communication device?
Sentence question: Does the word fit in the phrase: "The _____ rang, and I answered."

Recognition was best for the items that had been encountered in the context of a category question and worst for items encountered in the context of a structural question. Other research also confirmed that deep processing results in better outcomes than shallow processing (e.g., Bower & Karlin, 1974; Moscovitch & Craik, 1976). However, some critics argued that there wasn't a good way of defining what exactly is deep and what exactly is shallow (Baddeley, 1978). Despite this criticism, the theory provides a good heuristic for guiding one's own study of material.

Encoding Specificity

Another important theory of memory argues that the probability of retrieving an item on a memory test depends on the degree to which the context present while studying the item is also present while taking the test (Tulving & Thomson, 1973). In the best known example of this, participants wearing scuba gear studied groups of items (Godden & Baddeley, 1980). The items were studied either while the person was under water in a pool or while he or she was above ground. The memory test, which occurred either under water or above ground, found that memory was best when the encoding context matched the retrieval context.

These results were instrumental in developing a police interviewing technique known as the cognitive interview (Fisher & Geiselman, 1992; Fisher, Geiselman, & Raymond, 1987; Fisher, McCauley, & Geiselman, 1994; Fisher & Schreiber, 2005). In the cognitive interview, police first establish rapport with the witness to make him or her feel relaxed and at ease. They encourage the witness to report everything he or she is thinking so as to maximize the probability that one memory will cause the retrieval of other memories (i.e., chaining). The police avoid leading questions and focus on open-ended questions and don't interrupt the witness. Most importantly, the interviewer encourages the witness to mentally re-experience the context of the original event. Researchers have found that the cognitive interview can increase recall by close to 50% compared with a standard police interview (Fisher, Geiselman, Raymond, Jurkevich, & Warhaftig, 1987).

CONCLUSIONS

The purpose of this chapter wasn't to cover everything there is to cover about theoretical approaches to the study of memory. Each section could probably be a chapter in its own right. Rather, we wanted to convince you that memory isn't a single thing—or perhaps even a thing at all—but rather a complex collection of skills and abilities that vary depending on the context in which they are being used. Additionally, we wanted to give you some background in terminology, theoretical approaches, and experimental techniques that will allow you to better appreciate the later chapters in the book. The goal of the rest of the book is to take these ideas and run with them, to see how they can help us understand human life in real-world settings and situations when memory skills come to the forefront. Indeed, memory is always at the forefront!

APPENDIX

fight	scrub	right	there	count	swang	piece
birth	awful	sauce	robot	grape	saved	paper
plank	scowl	churn	crude	buses	thigh	other
draft	sugar	drain	candy	cramp	boost	float
stall	shown	swipe	would	strap	scare	whiff
maple						

REFERENCES

Anderson, J. R. (1995). *Cognitive psychology and its implications.* San Francisco, CA: Freeman.

Anderson, J. R. (1996). ACT: A simple theory of complex cognition. *American Psychologist, 51,* 355–365.

Atkinson, R. C., & Shiffrin, R. M. (1968). Human memory: A proposed system and its control processes. In K. W. Spence & J. T. Spence (Eds.), *The psychology of learning and motivation* (Vol. 2, pp. 89–195). New York, NY: Academic Press.

Baddeley, A. D. (1978). The trouble with levels: A reexamination of Craik and Lockhart's framework for memory research. *Psychological Review, 85,* 139–152.

Baddeley, A. D. (1996). Exploring the central executive. *Quarterly Journal of Experimental Psychology, 49A,* 5–28.

Baddeley, A. D. (2000). The episodic buffer: A new component of working memory? *Trends in Cognitive Science, 4,* 417–423.

Baddeley, A., Gathercole, S., & Papagno, C. (1998). The phonological loop as a language learning device. *Psychological Review, 105,* 158–173.

Baddeley, A. D., & Hitch, G. (1974). Working memory. In G. H. Bower (Ed.), *The psychology of learning and motivation: Advances in research and theory* (Vol. 8, pp. 47–89). New York, NY: Academic Press.

Bahrick, H. P. (1970). A two-phase model for prompted recall. *Psychological Review, 77,* 215–222.

Blaxton, T. A. (1989). Investigating dissociations among memory measures: Support for a transfer-appropriate processing framework.

Journal of Experimental Psychology: Learning, Memory, and Cognition, 15, 657–668.

Bower, G. H., & Karlin, M. B. (1974). Depth of processing pictures of faces and recognition memory. *Journal of Experimental Psychology, 103*, 751–757.

Bransford, J. D. (1979). *Human cognition: Learning, understanding, and remembering.* Belmont, CA: Wadsworth.

Brown, J. (1958). Some tests of the decay theory of immediate memory. *Quarterly Journal of Experimental Psychology, 10*, 12–21.

Collins, A. M., & Loftus, E. F. (1975). A spreading-activation theory of semantic processing. *Psychological Review, 82*, 407–428.

Collins, A. M., & Quillian, M. R. (1969). Retrieval time from semantic memory. *Journal of Verbal Learning and Verbal Behavior, 8*, 240–247.

Craik, F. I. M., & Lockhart, R. S. (1972). Levels of processing: A framework for memory research. *Journal of Verbal Learning and Verbal Behavior, 11*, 671–684.

Craik, F. I. M., & Tulving, E. (1975). Depth of processing and the retention of words in episodic memory. *Journal of Experimental Psychology: General, 104*, 268–294.

Daneman, M., & Carpenter, P. A. (1980). Individual differences in working memory and reading. *Journal of Verbal Learning and Verbal Behavior, 19*, 450–466.

Engle, R. W., Tuholski, S. W., Laughlin, J. E., & Conway, A. R. A. (1999). Working memory, short-term memory, and general fluid intelligence: A latent-variable approach. *Journal of Experimental Psychology: General, 128*, 309–331.

Enns, J. T. (2004). *The thinking eye, the seeing brain: Explorations in visual cognition.* New York, NY: W. W. Norton.

Fisher, R. P., & Geiselman, R. (1992). *Memory enhancing techniques for investigative interviewing.* Springfield, IL: Charles Thomas.

Fisher, R. P., Geiselman, R. E., & Raymond, D. S. (1987). Critical analysis of police interview techniques. *Journal of Police Science and Administration, 15*, 177–185.

Fisher, R. P., Geiselman, R. E., Raymond, D. S., Jurkevich, L. M., & Warhaftig, M. L. (1987). Enhancing enhanced eyewitness memory: Refining the cognitive interview. *Journal of Police Science and Administration, 15*, 291–297.

Fisher, R. P., McCauley, M., & Geiselman, R. E. (1994). Improving eyewitness testimony with the cognitive interview. In D. F. Ross, J. D. Read, & M. P. Toglia (Eds.), *Adult eyewitness testimony: Current trends and developments* (pp. 245–269). New York, NY: Cambridge University Press.

Fisher, R. P., & Schreiber, N. (2005). Forensic psychiatry and forensic psychology: Forensic interviewing. In J. Payne-James, R. Byard, T. Corey, & C. Henderson (Eds.), *Encyclopedia of forensic and legal medicine* (pp. 371–378). Oxford, UK: Elsevier Science.

Flory, P., & Pring, L. (1995). The effects of data-driven and conceptually driven generation of study items on direct and indirect measures of memory. *The Quarterly Journal of Experimental Psychology A: Human Experimental Psychology, 48A*, 153–165.

Galotti, K. M. (2004). *Cognitive psychology: In and out of the lab.* Belmont, CA: Wadsworth.

Gardiner, J. M. (1988). Functional aspects of recollective experience. *Memory and Cognition, 16*, 309–313.

Gardiner, J. M., & Java, R. I. (1990). Recollective experience in word and nonword recognition. *Memory and Cognition, 18*, 23–30.

Gardiner, J. M., & Java, R. I. (1991). Forgetting in recognition memory with and without recollective experience. *Memory and Cognition, 19*, 617–623.

Gilhooly, K. J., Logie, R. H., Wetherick, N. E., & Wynn, V. (1993). Working memory and strategies in syllogistic reasoning tasks. *Memory and Cognition, 21*, 115–124.

Godden, D., & Baddeley, A. (1980). When does context influence recognition memory? *British Journal of Psychology, 71*, 99–104.

Haist, F., Shimamura, A. P., & Squire, L. R. (1992). On the relationship between recall and recognition memory. *Journal of Experimental Psychology: Learning, Memory, and Cognition, 18*, 691–702.

Hollingworth, H. L. (1913). Characteristic differences between recall and recognition. *American Journal of Psychology, 24*, 532–544.

Howard, D. V., Fry, A. F., & Brune, C. M. (1991). Aging and memory for new associations: Direct versus indirect measures. *Journal of Experimental Psychology: Learning, Memory, and Cognition, 17*, 779–792.

Howes, M. B., & O'Shea, G. (2014). *Human memory: A constructivist view.* Waltham, MA: Academic Press.

Jacoby, L. L. (1991). A process dissociation framework: Separating automatic from intentional uses of memory. *Journal of Memory and Language, 30*, 513–541.

Jacoby, L. L. (1997). Invariance in automatic influences of memory: Toward a user's guide for the process-dissociation procedure. *Journal of Experimental Psychology: Learning, Memory and Cognition, 24*, 3–26.

Kahneman, D. (1973). *Attention and effort*. Englewood Cliffs, NJ: Prentice Hall.

Kintsch, W. (1968). Recognition and free recall of organized lists. *Journal of Experimental Psychology, 78*, 481–487.

Kintsch, W. (1970). *Learning, memory, and conceptual processes*. New York, NY: Wiley.

Kolers, P. A., & Roediger, H. L. (1984). Procedures of mind. *Journal of Verbal Learning and Verbal Behavior, 23*, 425–449.

Lampinen, J., Arnal, J., & Hicks, J. (2009). The effectiveness of supermarket posters in helping to find missing children. *Journal of Interpersonal Violence, 24*, 406–423.

Lampinen, J. M., & Neuschatz, J. S. (2008). Reconstructive memory. In B. Cutler (Ed.), *Encyclopedia of psychology and the law*. Thousand Oaks, CA: Sage.

Lampinen, J. M., Neuschatz, J. S., & Payne, D. G. (1998). Memory illusions and consciousness: Exploring the phenomenology of true and false memories. *Current Psychology, 16*, 181–224.

Light, L. L., & LaVoie, D. (1993). Direct and indirect measures of memory in old age. In P. Graf & M. J. Masson (Eds.), *Implicit memory: New directions in cognition, development, and neuropsychology* (pp. 207–230). Hillsdale, NJ: Lawrence Erlbaum Associates.

Light, L. L., LaVoie, D., Valencia-Laver, D., Albertson Owens, S. A., & Mead, G. (1992). Direct and indirect measures of memory for modality in young and older adults. *Journal of Experimental Psychology: Learning, Memory, and Cognition, 18*, 1284–1297.

Loftus, E. F. (1979). The malleability of human memory. *American Scientist, 67*, 312–320.

Loftus, E. F. (1992). When a lie becomes memory's truth: Memory distortion after exposure to misinformation. *Current Directions in Psychological Science, 1*, 121–123.

Loftus, E. F., & Loftus, G. R. (1980). On the permanence of stored information in the human brain. *American Psychologist, 35*, 400–420.

Logie, R. H. (1995). *Visuo-spatial working memory*. Hove, UK: Lawrence Erlbaum.

Lorsbach, T. C., & Morris, A. K. (1991). Direct and indirect testing of picture memory in second and sixth grade children. *Contemporary Educational Psychology, 16*, 18–27.

Mander, G. (1980). Recognizing: The judgment of previous occurrence. *Psychological Review, 87*, 252–271.

McKoon, G., Ratcliff, R., & Dell, G. S. (1986). A critical evaluation of the semantic-episodic distinction. *Journal of Experimental Psychology: Learning, Memory, and Cognition, 12*, 295–306.

McLean, J. F., & Hitch, G. J. (1999). Working memory impairments in children with specific arithmetic learning difficulties. *Journal of Experimental Child Psychology, 74*, 240–260.

Merikle, P. M., & Reingold, E. M. (1991). Comparing direct (explicit) and indirect (implicit) measures to study unconscious memory. *Journal of Experimental Psychology: Learning, Memory, and Cognition, 17*, 224–233.

Mickes, L., Wixted, J. T., & Wais, P. E. (2007). A direct test of the unequal-variance signal detection model of recognition memory. *Psychonomic Bulletin and Review, 14*, 858–865.

Miller, G. A. (1956). The magical number seven, plus or minus two: Some limits on our capacity for processing information. *Psychological Review, 63*, 81–97.

Moscovitch, M., & Craik, F. I. M. (1976). Depth of processing, retrieval cues, and uniqueness of encoding as factors in recall. *Journal of Verbal Learning and Verbal Behavior, 15*, 447–458.

Neisser, U. (1967) *Cognitive psychology*. New York, NY: Appleton-Century-Crofts.

Nicolas, S. (2010). Experiments on implicit memory in a Korsakoff patient by Claparede (1907). *Cognitive Neuropsychology, 13*, 1193–1199.

Payne, D. G., Klin, C. M., Lampinen, J. M., Neuschatz, J. S., & Lindsay, D. S. (1999). Memory applied. In F. T. Durso, R. Nickerson, R. W. Schvaneveldt, S. T. Dumais, D. S. Lindsay, & M. T. H. Chi (Eds.), *The handbook of applied cognition* (pp. 83–113). New York, NY: John Wiley and Sons.

Peterson, L. R., & Peterson, M. J. (1959). Short-term retention of individual verbal items. *Journal of Experimental Psychology, 58*, 193–198.

Rajaram, S. (1993). Remembering and knowing: Two means of access to the personal past. *Memory and Cognition, 21,* 89–102.

Ratcliff, R., Sheu, C. F., & Gronlund, S. D. (1992). Testing global memory models using ROC curves. *Psychological Review, 3,* 518–535.

Richardson-Klavehn, A., & Bjork, R. A. (1988). Measures of memory. *Annual Review of Psychology, 39,* 475–543.

Richardson-Klavehn, A., Gardiner, J. M., & Java, R. I. (1994). Involuntary conscious memory and the method of opposition. *Memory, 2,* 1–29.

Roediger, H. L., Weldon, M. S., Stadler, M. L., & Riegler, G. L. (1992). Direct comparison of two implicit memory tests: Word fragment and word stem completion. *Journal of Experimental Psychology: Learning, Memory, and Cognition, 18,* 1251–1269.

Schacter, D. L. (1996). *Searching for memory: The brain, the mind, and the past.* New York, NY: Basic Books.

Schacter, D. L., Chiu, C. Y. P., & Ochsner, K. N. (1993). Implicit memory: A selective review. *Annual Review of Neuroscience, 16,* 159–182.

Shiffrin, R. M., & Atkinson, R. C. (1969). Storage and retrieval processes in long-term memory. *Psychological Review, 76,* 179–193.

Simons, D. J., & Chabris, C. F. (2011) What people believe about how memory works: A representative survey of the U.S. population. *PLoS ONE, 6*(8), e22757.

Smith, E. E., Shoben, E. J., & Rips, L. J. (1974). Structure and process in semantic memory: A featural model for semantic decisions. *Psychological Review, 81,* 214–241.

Sperling, G. (1960). The information available in brief visual presentations. *Psychological Monographs: General and Applied, 74,* 1–29.

Stanislaw, H., & Todorov, N. (1999). Calculation of signal detection theory measures. *Behavior Research Methods, Instruments, and Computers, 31,* 137–149.

Tulving, E. (1974). Cue-dependent forgetting. *American Scientist, 62,* 74–82.

Tulving, E. (1984). Multiple learning and memory systems. In K. M. J. Lagerspetz & P. Niemi (Eds.), *Psychology in the 1990s* (pp. 163–184). London, UK: Elsevier.

Tulving, E. (1985a). How many memory systems are there? *American Psychologist, 40,* 385–398.

Tulving, E. (1985b). Memory and consciousness. *Canadian Psychology/ Psychologie Canadienne, 26,* 1–12.

Tulving, E. (1987). Multiple memory systems and consciousness. *Human Neurobiology, 6,* 67–80.

Tulving, E. (2002). Episodic memory: From mind to brain. *Annual Review of Psychology, 53,* 1–25.

Tulving, E., & Schacter, D. (1990). Priming and human memory systems. *Science, 247,* 301–306.

Tulving, E., & Thomson, D. M. (1973). Encoding specificity and retrieval processes in episodic memory. *Psychological Review, 80,* 352–373.

Wallace, W. P. (1982). Distractor-free recognition tests of memory. *American Journal of Psychology, 95,* 421–440.

Watkins, M. J., & Gardiner, J. M. (1979). An appreciation of generate-recognize theory of recall. *Journal of Verbal Learning and Verbal Behavior, 18,* 687–704.

Waugh, N. C., & Norman, D. A. (1965). Primary memory. *Psychological Review, 72,* 89–104.

Weinstein, C., & Mayer, R. (1986). The teaching of learning strategies. In M. Wittrock (Ed.), *Handbook of research on teaching* (3rd ed.). New York, NY: Macmillan.

Yonelinas, A. P. (2001). Consciousness, control, and confidence: The 3 Cs of recognition memory. *Journal of Experimental Psychology: General, 130,* 361–379.

Yonelinas, A. P., Kroll, N. E. A., Dobbins, I., Lazzara, M., & Knight, R. T. (1998). Recollection and familiarity deficits in amnesia: Convergence of remember-know, process dissociation, and receiver operating characteristic data. *Neuropsychology, 12,* 323–339.

Zajonc, R. B. (1968). Attitudinal effects of mere exposure. *Journal of Personality and Social Psychology, 9,* 1–27.

Memory Illusions

One of the best known psychologists of the 20th century was Jean Piaget (Beilin, 1992; Flavell, 1967; Singer & Revenson, 1996). Piaget was a Swiss developmental psychologist who revolutionized our understanding of children's thinking. To give you a sense of the man's intellect, Piaget was publishing scientific papers in the biological sciences at age 10 (Plucker, 2012). At the age of 22, Piaget received his PhD at the University of Neuchâtel. Showoff! In 1951, he published his treatment of symbolic thought in children, *Play, Dreams, and Imitation in Childhood* (Piaget, 1951). In it, he described one of his own earliest memories. The memory he described was from when he was about 2 years old. He describes a kidnapping attempt in which his nurse tried to protect him. The memory he described was vivid and detailed. He recalled being able to see scratches on his nurse's face. He remembered a crowd coming up to see what had happened. He remembered his attacker escaping.

Piaget was in his mid-50s when he published this, and he was recalling an event that happened when he was just a little kid. Yet it is clear from his description that his memory for the kidnapping is perceptually vivid, narratively detailed, and emotional in content. Wow!

THE STOREHOUSE METAPHOR

Examples of vivid and detailed memories such as this one have convinced many people that human memory is largely reproductive in nature. Psychologists sometimes call this the *storehouse metaphor* (see Draaisma, 2001, and Roediger, 1980, for a discussion of this and other metaphors). According to the storehouse metaphor, memory is kind of a warehouse. When events happen in your life, they are packed up, maybe put in some bubble wrap, and stored away, like the inventory in a large warehouse. Considering all the things that happen in a person's life, it would be a large warehouse indeed, comprising shelf after shelf of stored information. When one remembers an event from one's life, one looks through this warehouse. Sometimes the memory one is looking for is found. Sometimes it isn't found—it's a big warehouse, after all. Nonetheless, all the events that you have ever encountered are stored away in memory and are still in that storehouse one way or another. At least, that's the claim of the storehouse metaphor.

Lots of people believe that the storehouse metaphor—or something like it—is a good description of human memory. For instance, one recent representative survey found that close to two thirds of people agree with the sentiment that "human memory works like a video camera, accurately recording the events we see and hear so that we can review and inspect them later" (Simons & Chabris, 2011). The same survey indicated that nearly half of people believe that "Once you have experienced an event and formed a memory of it, that memory does not change."

Why do so many people believe that the storehouse metaphor is true? There are probably multiple reasons. We've all grown up with a dizzying array of devices that can be used to store information: notebooks, scrapbooks, notecards, audiotapes, VHS, floppy drives, CDs, DVDs, hard drives, flash drives, smartphones, tablets, the so-called cloud—and the list goes on and on. Considering our daily interactions with these systems, it's natural that we would analogize between these human-made information storage devices and the information storage device that resides between our two ears. In each of the human-made storage devices, unless there is some sort of physical damage, the information that is put into storage is retained in storage for an indefinite period of time, in more or less the same format as it was originally encountered. Sometimes you can't find the information you're looking for, like when the first author is looking for pretty much anything in the piles of junk on his desk. But that doesn't mean that the information isn't there. Why shouldn't the human brain show the same felicity?

As Loftus and Loftus (1980) point out, we have also all had the experience of not being able to remember something—a person's name, the answer on a test, a person's birthday, the definition of Stanislavski's method—only to later recall the information in response to a suitable reminder (Tulving, 1974). Those experiences are suggestive. They create an impression that the information that we could not retrieve for some period of time was still locked away in pristine form within the storehouse of human memory. Perhaps it's the case, then, that whenever we fail to remember something, it is due to an imperfection in locating the answer in memory, not a limitation or inaccuracy in what's stored in memory.

Loftus and Loftus (1980) also point to a number of empirical findings that have led some to believe that memory is indeed like a storehouse. For instance, some have pointed to the success of hypnosis in aiding in the recovery of previously unrecoverable memories (Reiser & Nielson, 1980) as evidence that information gets stored in memory in pristine form and that the inability to recall a fact stems from a difficulty in finding the information in memory, not from a failure in storing the information. Others have pointed to the pioneering work of neurosurgeon Wilder Penfield (1969). Penfield was attempting to cure the seizures caused by epilepsy by identifying the part of the brain responsible for the seizure and then severing those connections. His technique involved operating on conscious patients while under local anesthetic. You might think that's kind of a freaky thing to do—poking around in the brain of a fully awake patient. But the brain doesn't have any pain receptors, so it doesn't hurt. And because the patient is awake, he or she is able to tell the surgeon what he or she is experiencing during the surgery—which is useful. While he was mucking about in a patient's brain, Penfield would apply weak electrical currents to different parts of the brain to see which locations induced the seizure. He would then perform targeted surgery on those sections in the hope of limiting future seizures. During the course of these surgeries, Penfield discovered something really extraordinary. Sometimes when he stimulated the temporal lobe of his patients, they would experience vivid and convincing memories of long-forgotten events. These memories were sometimes almost like reliving the events. These experiments by Penfield convinced many people that the brain retains tremendous details of past events, consistent with the storehouse metaphor.

CONSTRUCTIVE/RECONSTRUCTIVE THEORIES OF MEMORY

Despite the appeal of the storehouse metaphor, modern-day memory psychologists put very little stock in the idea. In fact, a survey of memory experts by Simon and Chabris (2011) found that 0% of memory experts agreed with the statement, "Human memory works like a video camera, accurately recording the events we see and hear so that we can review and inspect them later," and 0% agreed with the statement, "Once you have experienced an event and formed a memory of it, that memory does not change." Why the disconnect between what memory experts believe and what the general public and some nonmemory psychologists believe? Well, first off, the evidence provided for the storehouse metaphor is really kind of weak when looked at closely (Loftus & Loftus, 1980). It is true that people sometimes recall things under hypnosis that they did not recall prior to hypnosis. But these are mostly just anecdotal accounts. When careful scientific studies of the effects of hypnosis on memory are carried out, it has generally been found that the amount of information that people report under hypnosis increases, but a lot of the reported information is incorrect (Mazzoni & Lynn, 2007). In other words, hypnosis increases willingness to report information but doesn't improve the accuracy of the information recalled. Similarly, although Penfield's patients appeared to be retrieving pristine memories of long forgotten events, there was no evidence presented that these events ever happened (Loftus & Loftus, 1980; Neisser, 1967). The memories could have just been confabulated.

The second reason so few memory psychologists believe the storehouse metaphor is true is because there is very convincing evidence that it is the wrong metaphor. Just because your laptop computer has a memory and human beings have memories does not mean that human memory is like the memory on your laptop (Chatham, 2007). The designs of the two devices are very different—massive but relatively slow parallel processing vs. extremely rapid serial processing. The representations are different—analog vs. digital. The manner of development is different—evolution vs. human engineering. And the devices serve different functions—specific survival functions versus general-purpose computation. In fact, our best understanding is that brains are massively parallel simulation devices (Barsalou, 1999). Brains take a set of assumptions and simulate likely outcomes. This process of simulating the world came in very handy in evolutionary times. For instance, if an ancient human had the thought that it might be fun to pet a crocodile on the nose, he or she could run a mental simulation of what might happen and decide against such foolishness. Remembering a past event is also a kind of simulation, a simulation of what happened in the past, rather than a veridical reproduction of the past (Glenberg, 1997). Theories of memory as a simulation of the past are called constructive/reconstructive theories. Constructive theories deal with filling in gaps at encoding as the event transpires, whereas reconstructive theories deal with filling in gaps at retrieval as one tries to remember the event. They are the dominant approach to understanding human memory.

To better understand memory construction/reconstruction, let's start with some assumptions that are common to these theories (Lampinen & Neuschatz, 2008). The first assumption is that memory is far from perfect. Information stored in memory is partial and incomplete. We fail to notice crucial details. We assume details are true that aren't really true. So the record stored in memory is partial, incomplete, and only partially accurate. Moreover, information available at retrieval is only a small fraction of what was originally available in the cognitive, emotional, and perceptual representations of the original events. The second assumption is that we make up for these limitations by making reasonable inferences in order to reconstruct or simulate the past. In the words of Sir Frederic Bartlett (1932), "It is fitting to speak of every human cognitive reaction—perceiving, imagining, remembering, thinking and reasoning—as an effort after meaning." That is, memory is part and parcel of trying to figure out and adapt to the world around us, not a passive recorder of information. Gaps in memory are filled in with a number of different types of details, including other past events (Reinitz, Lammers, & Cochran, 1992), general knowledge of what typically happens (Brewer & Nakamura, 1984), information gained after an event (Loftus, 1979), and a variety of intuitive reasoning strategies (Johnson, Hashtroudi, & Lindsay, 1993). The process is so swift, and in many cases so effortless, that it is often impossible for us to distinguish between details that were in the original event and the details that were added to create a coherent simulation.

Now you might be asking how we know this view of memory is true and that the storehouse metaphor is wrong. The most obvious answer to that question is that the storehouse model predicts that the errors we make should be primarily errors of omission, whereas the constructive/reconstructive models predict that we should experience a combination of errors of omission and errors of commission. Errors of omission refer to situations in which we leave out details that were in the original event. Errors of commission refer to situations in which details are remembered that were not part of the original event. Both theories predict that errors of omission will occur. However, the storehouse model has no easy way of predicting errors of commission. Constructive/reconstructive models, on the other hand, predict that errors of commission will be common, because the process of filling in gaps in memory involves considerable guesswork.

The scientific research on all this is really very clear. Errors of commission are quite common and can occur under a variety of circumstances for a variety of different reasons. Not only that, these errors of commission come to mind as full-blown memories—not merely hunches or guesses (Lampinen, Neuschatz, & Payne, 1998). The brain is involved in guesswork when it simulates a past event, but the simulation can seem at times as if it is nothing more than a veridical replay of the past event. Because of their convincing experiential nature, these memory errors have sometimes been called "memory illusions" or, more commonly, "false memories." Here's an example. Remember when we were talking about Piaget's memory for having been kidnapped on the Champs-Elysees and all that? As it turned out, that never happened! Nor did anything like it happen. Piaget's caretaker concocted the story out of whole cloth to obtain a reward. She wrote a letter to Piaget's parents after a religious conversion with the Salvation Army. Here's how Piaget described it:

> She wanted to confess her past faults, and in particular to return the watch she had been given as a reward on this occasion. She had made up the whole story, faking the scratches.

Score 1 for the Salvation Army! We think you'll agree that the account is fascinating. The memory Piaget had was false, yet it was perceptually vivid and detailed and seemed as real to Piaget as any other memory. Indeed, even as an older man, having come to understand that the memory was false, Piaget said, "I can still see most clearly . . . ." So how are such false memories formed? That's what we're about to find out.

HOW MEMORY ILLUSIONS ARE CREATED

Schemas

A good place to start any discussion is at the beginning. When it comes to the systematic study of memory distortion, that involves traveling to jolly old England in the first half of the 20th century. It was there, at Cambridge University, that Sir Frederic Bartlett conducted his pioneering work on the reconstructive nature of memory. Bartlett was born October 20, 1886. Back then, memory research, such as existed, was dominated by the nonsense-syllable paradigm developed by Ebbinghaus (1885/1913). Ebbinghaus chose to study nonsense syllables because he wanted to study memory in a pure form, uncontaminated by people's prior experiences, knowledge, beliefs, stereotypes, or expectations. Bartlett thought this way of thinking about memory was completely wrong-headed. In particular, Bartlett thought the idea of separating memory from meaning was impossible. According to Bartlett, the process of imposing meaning on the past just *is* memory. Here's how he put it:

> [R]emembering is not the re-excitation of innumerable fixed, lifeless and fragmentary traces. It is an imaginative reconstruction,

or construction, built out of the relation of our attitude towards a whole active mass of organised past reactions or experience, and to a little outstanding detail which commonly appears in image or in language form. (Bartlett, 1932)

In explaining how memory works, Bartlett latched on to an idea that had been used previously to help explain muscular coordination—the idea of a schema. A schema is an organized representation in your long-term memory of the typical state of affairs for an object, person, or event. For instance, if you're like us, you know what a dog is. Dogs have fur, tails (mostly), long noses (mostly), floppy ears (often), pointy ears (sometimes), chase stuff (almost always), can do tricks (often), bark (almost inevitably), are slobbery (sometimes), and so on. The mental representation of this interrelated set of facts that you and I have about dogs is an example of a schema. Schemas have a number of functions. For instance, they allow us to predict the future. If you're with your dog and a squirrel runs across the path, you might well predict that the dog is going to chase the squirrel. If you pet your dog on the head, you can be pretty sure that your dog won't purr. Schemas also help you store information in memory. In particular, we tend to store in memory details that are relevant to our schema— that is, dog-related stuff. Schemas can also help us by allowing us to *constructively* store inferences into memory. For instance, imagine your dog is out of sight and around the corner you hear barks and growls. When you peer around the corner, you see your dog and a Billy goat. You're likely to infer, based on your schemas, that your dog was barking at the goat, not that the goat was barking at the dog. This inference, because it's so reasonable given your schema, is likely to be encoded into your memory even though you didn't directly experience it. Later on, you might remember having *seen* your dog barking at a goat even though that's not precisely what happened. Schemas also allow people to actively *reconstruct* past events at time of retrieval. For instance, when fondly recalling a puppy play date, you might recall that your dog sniffed another dog's backside, even if that didn't happen.

Bartlett's (1932) study of schemas didn't involve dogs or goats or puppy play dates. Rather, his most famous study involved a Native American folktale called "The War of the Ghosts." Bartlett deliberately chose these materials because they were quite unlike anything his participants had ever heard before, both in form and content. Given that, he wanted to see if his participants would try to impose meaning on the story by making use of their preexisting schemas. Bartlett's participants were typically able to recall the general idea of the story, but the details were changed, sometimes dramatically. The style of the story tended to change when participants recalled it, making it more like stories they had heard in the past. Participants tended to omit unfamiliar details that they couldn't really make sense of. Details were changed to match the participants' prior experiences. Bartlett concluded that these changes happened because memory is reconstructive and guided by schemas. Bartlett's book, in which he describes this research, is a classic in psychology and is well worth the read.

Bartlett's research was very influential, especially when cognitive psychologists got hold of it in the 1970s. For instance, John Bransford and colleagues conducted a series of experiments in which they demonstrated how important schemas were for making sense of and remembering events (Bransford, Barclay, & Franks, 1972; Bransford & Franks, 1971; Bransford & Johnson, 1972). In one study, participants listened to the following somewhat confusing narrative (Bransford & Johnson, 1972):

> If the balloons popped, the sound wouldn't be able to carry since everything would be too far away from the correct floor. A closed window would also prevent the sound from carrying, since most buildings tend to be well insulated. Since the whole operation depends on a steady flow of electricity, a break in the middle of the wire would also cause problems. Of course, the fellow could shout, but the human voice is not loud enough to carry that far. An additional problem is that a string could break

on the instrument. Then there could be no accompaniment to the message. It is clear that the best situation would involve less distance. Then there would be fewer potential problems. With face to face contact, the least number of things could go wrong.[1]

Now really, what the heck is that all about? When people were asked to rate how comprehensible the passage was, they gave it very low ratings. When asked to recall the passage, people were able to recall very few details.

Now turn to page 64 and carefully study the picture shown in Figure 3.1. Once you've done so, return to this page. We'll wait.... Okay, now having seen the picture, read the passage again. What do you think? A lot easier, right? That's what Bransford and Johnson (1972) found. Participants who were presented with the story along with the accompanying drawing rated the story as much more comprehensible than those who were presented with the story without the drawing. Moreover, those who had the drawing were better able to recall the details. Bransford and Johnson concluded that this was because the drawing activated participants' prior knowledge—that is, schemas—about things like romance and musical instruments and balloons and electrical current and so on. Those schemas helped participants to make sense of and remember the story.

Lots of other interesting studies have been conducted on schemas. For instance, important research showed that schemas can influence both memory construction (i.e., inferences being stored in memory) and memory reconstruction (i.e., gaps being filled when the memory is recalled). For example, Dooling and Christiaansen (1977) provided participants with the following story:

Gerald Martin strove to undermine the existing government to satisfy his political ambitions. Many of the people of his country supported his efforts. Current political problems made it relatively easy for Martin to take over. Certain groups remained loyal

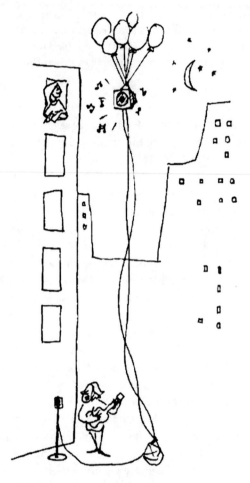

FIGURE 3.1 Illustration used as context in Bransford and Johnson (1972).
Reprinted from Bransford and Johnson (1972). Copyright 1972, with permission from Elsevier.

to the old government and caused Martin trouble. He confronted these groups directly and so silenced them. He became a ruthless, uncontrollable dictator. The ultimate effect of his rule was the downfall of his country.[2]

Some people heard this story. Other people heard the exact same story, except that the name Gerald Martin was replaced with the name Adolph Hitler. The participants then took an old/new recognition test. Right before the old/new recognition test, some of the participants who heard the Gerald Martin version of the story were told that the story had actually been about Adolph Hitler. So there were three conditions:

No Schema: People heard the story was about Gerald Martin and never learned any different.

Schema Early: When people heard the story, the character was identified as Hitler, therefore allowing people to activate their Hitler schema. Thus, people could use the Hitler schema constructively while processing the passage to make inferences, or reconstructively at the time of the test to fill in gaps in their memories.

Schema Late: When people read the story, the character was identified as Gerald Martin. But right before taking the test, people were told that the story was actually about Hitler. Thus, people could activate their Hitler schema while taking the test and use it reconstructively.

The test included some sentences that really were in the passage, as well as sentences that were not in the passage, but that matched the Hitler schema (e.g., he persecuted Jewish people). For each sentence the participant's job was to indicate whether or not it was explicitly stated in the story. The results strongly supported the use of reconstructive memory processes. The participants in the *no schema* condition falsely recognized the Hitler-related foils less than 5% of the time. The participants in the *schema early* condition falsely recognized the Hitler-related foils around 30% of the time. For participants in the *schema late* condition, false recognition of the Hitler-related foils was around 22%.[3] These results demonstrated that people reconstruct their memory at the time of retrieval, using schemas to fill in gaps in their memories.

Studies like this have been conducted in a variety of domains and it turns out that there is very good evidence that we have schemas for just about everything. Smith and Studebaker (1996) found that jurors have schemas about typical crime categories and will often misremember testimony in a way that confirms their crime schemas. Lodge and Hamill (1986) found that voters have schemas about politicians from different political parties and show a bias toward remembering details that match the politician's political party orientation. People have schemas about racial and ethnic groups—that is, stereotypes—and these can influence memory for members of those groups (Sherman, Stroessner, Loftus, & Deguzman, 1997). People have schemas for the typical items that are in a room, and this can cause people to misremember how a room is configured (Brewer & Treyens, 1981; Lampinen, Copeland, & Neuschatz, 2001; Pezdek, Whetstone, Reynolds, Askari, & Dougherty, 1989). And these are just a few examples of specific ways in which schemas guide memory for everyday events.

Scripts

One widely studied type of schema is a schema for a stereotypical event like washing one's car, going to a restaurant, or taking your pet to the vet (Bower, Black, & Turner, 1979). These event schemas are called *scripts* because they are thought to guide behavior in ways that are similar to how theatrical scripts guide actors on the stage. The concept of a script was originally developed by the computer scientist Roger Schank (Schank & Abelson, 1977). Schank wanted to come up with a way for computer programs to draw conclusions from stories. He realized that most stories we read leave out a lot of information that is merely common knowledge. So the challenge was to figure out how this common knowledge is represented and then to give that common knowledge to a computer. Scripts consist of a sequential series of actions that are causally connected—that is, the later actions depend on earlier actions. For instance, in a restaurant script, the action of paying the bill depends on the server's having brought you some food. The server's bringing you food depends on your having ordered food. Your ordering food depends on your having looked at the menu. And so on.

According to Schank, scripts guide our actions when we find ourselves in situations that are similar to situations we have been in before. As Schank and Abelson (1995) put it:

> [Scripts] make clear what is supposed to happen and what various acts on the part of others are supposed to indicate. They make mental processing easier, by allowing us to think less, in essence. You don't have to figure out every time you enter a restaurant how to convince someone to feed you.

Scripts also guide memory construction and reconstruction. They guide memory construction because scripts guide predictions we make as we go through an event. When we order something from the menu, we predict ahead of time that food will be forthcoming. Scripts also guide learning, primarily by causing us to analyze expectancy violations—cases where the prediction doesn't turn out as expected (Schank, 1983). Schank (1999) gives the example of a person who is used to going to sit-down restaurants, in which the server brings a menu and the customer orders the meal. If that person goes to a fast-food burger joint and sits at the table waiting for a server to bring a menu, he or she will likely go hungry. The person's script predicts that sitting at a table will be followed shortly by a waiter or waitress with a menu—but that's not how fast-food restaurants work. This violation of the expectation generated by the script results in learning—memory is updated with exceptions to the general script the person had been relying on.

The script concept was very appealing to psychologists and served as the basis for a lot of research (e.g., Bower et al., 1979; Graesser, Woll, Kowalski, & Smith, 1980; Holst & Pezdek, 1992; Lampinen, Faries, Neuschatz, & Toglia, 2000; Rizzella & O'Brien,

2002). One early psychological theory based on Schank's ideas was the script pointer + tag hypothesis, championed by Arthur Graesser (Graesser, Gordon, & Sawyer, 1979; Graesser et al., 1980). The hypothesis goes like this: When you encounter an event, you first figure out what script is relevant. Perhaps the script is washing your car. At that point you instantiate—that is, make active in memory—your washing the car script. You then go about the process of washing your car following the script. Occasionally, as you do so, something unexpected will happen—for example, you forget the window was open when you spray the car with the hose. These cases are tagged as violations of the expectancy generated by the script. What ultimately gets stored in memory is a pointer to the script that was active as well as tags identifying any unexpected occurrences (e.g., WashingCar$ + LeftWindowOpen). That's it. The expected actions (e.g., turning on the water for the hose) are not uniquely stored in memory, because they are already part of the script that was activated.

Graesser et al. (1979) tested the script pointer + tag hypothesis by presenting people with stories about common, everyday events. The stories include a series of actions that derived from a set of scripted activities. Say, for instance, that you are reading a story about a guy eating at a restaurant. Some of the actions in the story match the underlying script (e.g., looked at the menu) while other actions violate the underlying script (e.g., spilled a glass of water). After reading several such stories, participants were given a recognition memory test. Each item on the test was an action that might have happened in one of the stories. The participant's job was to say whether the action was explicitly mentioned in the story. Some of the test statements were mentioned in the story—that is, targets. Half of these were consistent with the script (e.g., looked at the menu), and half of were inconsistent with the script (e.g., spilled a glass of water). Other test statements were not explicitly mentioned in the story—that is, foils. Half of these were consistent with the script (e.g., left a tip) and half of were inconsistent with the script (e.g., forgot his wallet).

For script-consistent actions, the number of targets recognized was not much different from the number of foils recognized. This finding matches the script pointer + tag hypothesis. According to the hypothesis, people don't save to memory specifics that match one's script. Rather, they just store a pointer to the relevant script and assume everything in the script is likely to have happened. For script-inconsistent actions the story is different. People recognize a large proportion of the script-inconsistent targets but rarely falsely recognize script-inconsistent foils. This is because inconsistent actions are explicitly tagged in memory as unique events. False recognition of foils occurs only when the foils match the script, and this, of course, isn't the case for script-inconsistent actions.

The concept of a script is powerful and important. Scripts explain how we interact with the world and how we can organize and recall complex events. They often lead us to correctly simulate the past, although sometimes they cause us to make inferences that are reasonable but nonetheless mistaken.

Postevent Information

Imagine you're hosting a party at your palatial mansion. Your favorite musical artist, Justin Bieber, is playing on the sound system, and there are about 20 people there, laughing and dancing and having a good time. About 11 p.m., a man comes in wearing a ski mask, brown leather gloves, a lime-green hoodie, and jorts. He pulls out a steak knife and proceeds to steal your entire Justin Bieber collection. He grabs a handful of Chex party mix before crashing through the plate glass window and jumping from the second-floor balcony into the swimming pool below. When the police arrive, they begin to question witnesses and analyze the crime scene. You hear your best friend Stan describe the assailant as being mid-20s, muscular, with a Boston accent, and wearing a yellow hoodie and jorts. When the police question you, you are still distraught. You, too, describe a man with a muscular build, yellow hoodie, and Boston accent. The police ask you,

"About how long was the blade on this hunting knife the fella had?" You say, "Five inches, give or take." The next day, you are browsing your favorite blog, and they describe the bizarre robbery that happened at your party. The ski mask, the black leather gloves, the scar on his neck, the priceless Justin Bieber collection. You call up your parents and tell them all about the crazy neck-scarred Bostonian who robbed you with a hunting knife while wearing a yellow hoodie, jorts, and black gloves.

The preceding story is apocryphal. But it illustrates another way in which memories can become distorted—postevent information (Ayers & Reder, 1998). Postevent information is information that is encountered after an event and that can become incorporated into one's memory for the event. Research on postevent information began in earnest in the 1970s with a technique developed by Elizabeth Loftus (1979) at the University of Washington. The technique is simple enough and illustrated in the high-quality artist rendition in Figure 3.2. First, participants witness an event. The event may be staged or shown on slides or videotape. After a delay, participants are exposed to information about the event. This postevent information may be presented as a presupposition in a question (e.g., "About how long was the blade on this hunting knife the fella had?") or as part of a narrative description of the event (e.g., like the blog post in the example). Sometimes the postevent information is misleading—that is, it contains false information. Other times the postevent information is neutral—that is, it contains no false information. After another delay (retention interval) participants are asked memory questions about the original event. Findings show that witnesses will often incorporate misleading postevent information into their memories, creating false memories based on suggestion.

Consider first a classic study by Loftus and Palmer (1974). Participants viewed a public safety film designed to show the consequences of automobile accidents. Following the film, participants were asked to describe what happened and were asked to estimate the speed of the vehicles. Some participants were asked "About how fast were the cars going when they hit

PHASE I	PHASE II	PHASE III

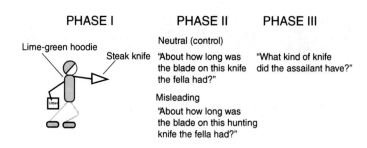

Neutral (control)

"About how long was the blade on this knife the fella had?"

"What kind of knife did the assailant have?"

Misleading

"About how long was the blade on this hunting knife the fella had?"

Lime-green hoodie

Steak knife

FIGURE 3.2 The postevent information paradigm.

each other?" For other participants, the word "hit" was replaced with another word—"smashed," "collided," "bumped," or "contacted." When the word "smashed" was used, people provided higher estimates of the speed of impact than when "contacted" or "hit" was used, showing that changing a single word in a sentence can dramatically affect people's memory of the event. In a second study, Loftus and Palmer showed that the "smashed" version of the question led people to mistakenly report having seen broken glass when in fact no broken glass was shown in the film. The creation of false memories in this manner has been called the *misinformation effect*.

Loftus and colleagues went on to examine a number of different types of false memories that can be created by postevent information. One kind of false memory involves *replacing* one detail in an event with a different inconsistent detail. In one study, participants saw a slide presentation in which a car came to a corner, turned right, and then plowed into a pedestrian in the crosswalk (Loftus, Miller, & Burns, 1978). For some participants, the slides showed a *stop sign* at the corner. For other participants the slides showed a *yield sign* at the corner (see Figure 3.3). After a delay, participants were asked a series of questions, including a critical question about what happened while the car was at the corner. There were three versions of the critical question:

Neutral: "Did another car pass the red Datsun while it was stopped at the intersection?"

FIGURE 3.3 Critical slides.
Source: Loftus, Miller, and Burns (1978). Copyright 1978, American Psychological Association. Reprinted with permission.

Misleading: Participants who saw the yield sign were asked: "Did another car pass the red Datsun while it was stopped at the stop sign?" Participants who saw the stop sign were asked: "Did another car pass the red Datsun while it was stopped at the yield sign?"

Consistent: Participants who saw the yield sign were asked: "Did another car pass the red Datsun while it was stopped at the yield sign?" Participants who saw the stop sign were asked: "Did another car pass the red Datsun while it was stopped at the stop sign?"

After another delay, participants were shown two slides, one showing the car at the stop sign and one showing the car at the yield sign and they were asked which slide they saw. The results are shown in Figure 3.4. As you can see, misleading information led to a substantial decrease in accuracy on the crucial question.

Another kind of false memory that can be created by post-event information involves supplanting a memory with additional information. In this kind of false memory, the misleading information does not contradict anything in the original event; it simply adds information that wasn't there. In Loftus (1975) participants watched a film of an automobile accident and then

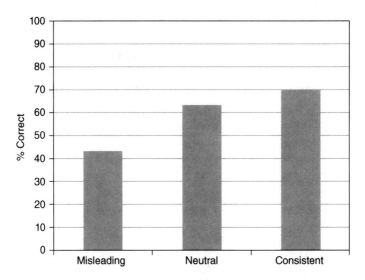

FIGURE 3.4 Percent correct in Loftus, Miller, and Burns (1978).
Source: This figure created by authors based on tabled values in Loftus, Miller, and Burns (1978). Copyright 1978, American Psychological Association. Used with permission.

answered 10 questions about the film. One question in particular asked, "How fast was the white sports car going when it passed the barn while traveling along the country road?" There wasn't really a barn in the film at all. Nevertheless, when later asked, more than 17% of participants indicated that they had seen a barn. Participants in the control condition were asked, "How fast was the white sports car going when while traveling along the country road?" Less than 3% of these participants later reported seeing a barn.

In addition to these kinds of memory distortions, postevent information can also produce subtle changes along continuous dimensions like speed, height, weight, number, and hue. These changes have sometimes been called *memory blends* (Belli, 1988; Metcalfe, 1990). Consider, for instance, what happened in Loftus (1977). Participants saw a slide presentation showing a car hitting a pedestrian. In one slide, a green car was shown driving past the accident scene. Participants then answered 12 questions about the slides, including a critical misleading question: "Did the blue car that drove past the accident have a ski rack on the roof?" For participants in the control condition, the question was "Did the car that drove past the accident have a ski rack on the roof?" After 20 minutes, the participants were presented with color chips and were asked to indicate the color of the car that had driven by. Participants who had been asked the control question generally remembered the car as being green in hue—as it was. However, participants who had been asked the misleading question tended to select a color that was a bluish-green, a blend between what had actually been seen (green) and the suggested color (blue).

In the 1980s, two sets of criticisms were leveled against this work, both leading to contentious debates in the memory community. The first was leveled by McCloskey and Zaragoza (1985) and it went like this: In most of the early work on the misinformation effect, people see an event (stop sign) and are then presented with postevent information that is either misleading (yield sign) or neutral (intersection). They then take a test in which they are asked to choose between the correct answer and the false suggested answer (was it a stop sign or yield sign?). That people do worse on this test when they received misleading postevent information was taken to indicate that the false information either replaced the original information in memory (Loftus, 1979), or interfered with its retrieval (Christiaansen & Ochalek, 1983). McCloskey and Zaragoza reasoned that there was a much simpler explanation: Maybe some people in the experiments would not have remembered the original information in the first place. Maybe they weren't paying attention to the slides, or maybe the queried detail slipped their mind at the time of the test. Whatever. When those participants were in the control condition, their only option on the final test would be to guess. So they should be correct about 50% of the time on average on a two-alternative multiple-choice test. But when those participants were in the experimental condition, there is some possibility that when they are asked the critical question on the final test, they will remember the information from the misleading question (e.g., "I don't remember what was in the slides, but I do remember the experimenter mentioning a yield sign"). Because the postevent information those participants encountered is false, they should be correct less than 50% of the time on average. In other words, it's possible that memory wasn't distorted at all, but that people quite reasonably assumed the experimenter knew what he or she was talking about, and the participants deliberately used that information to answer the question.

To test this hypothesis, McCloskey and Zaragoza (1985) developed what they called a *modified recognition test*. The modified recognition test includes two options, the original item from the slides or film and a new item that was not in the original event and that was also not suggested in the postevent information. If you had been in one of their studies, you might have seen some slides in which a worker enters an office and fixes a chair and then steals twenty bucks and a fancy-looking calculator. In one version of the slides, he uses a screwdriver to fix the chair. Participants then read a narrative that includes some postevent information. In the misleading postevent information condition, the narrative might say that they worker used a *wrench* to fix the chair. In the control condition, the narrative simply said that the worker fixed the chair—no specific tool was mentioned. In the standard memory test, participants would ordinarily be asked to decide between the original item and the suggested item. ("Was it a screwdriver or a wrench?") In the modified test used by McCloskey and Zaragoza, participants were asked to distinguish between the original item and a new, never before mentioned item ("Was it a screwdriver, or was it a hammer?").

To see why this approach appealed to McCloskey and Zaragoza, consider the following examples. Imagine that misleading postevent information really does impair memory. If this were true, then some percentage of people who would have correctly remembered the screwdriver from the slides won't be able to remember the screwdriver when they are exposed to the misleading information that it was a wrench. Those people should perform poorly on the standard memory test (i.e., screwdriver or wrench?), and they should also perform poorly on the modified memory test (e.g., screwdriver vs. hammer?). Alternatively, misleading information may only affect people who would not have remembered the original event anyway. If this were true, then people would do worse on items they had been misled about on the standard memory test, because they would be biased to choose the suggested alternative. This wouldn't happen on the modified test, because the misleading alternative isn't an option on the modified test. As you can see in Figure 3.5, McCloskey and Zaragoza found no evidence of a misinformation effect on the modified test even though they did find evidence of a misinformation effect using the standard test. McCloskey and Zaragoza's critique was largely seen as sound and reasonable. However, later researchers provided evidence that there are circumstances in which misinformation impairs memory, using the modified recognition test suggested by McCloskey and Zaragoza (e.g., Belli, 1989).

A second major critique of the misinformation effect concerned whether participants really believe they have a memory for the suggested item, or whether they are just relying on what the experimenter said in order to answer the question. Zaragoza and Koshmider (1989) phrased this objection as, "Misled subjects may know more than their performance implies." To understand this criticism, consider what the experiment is like from the participant's point of view. Imagine you are in the Loftus (1975) study and you view a videotape of a car traveling down a country road. Later on you are asked the question, "How fast was the white sports car going when it passed the barn while traveling along the country road?" You don't remember a barn, but you do remember a white sports car, and you provide an estimate of its speed. Later on you are asked, "Did you see a barn?" Now let's say you don't remember seeing a barn, but you do remember that there was a question that mentioned a barn. Might you not

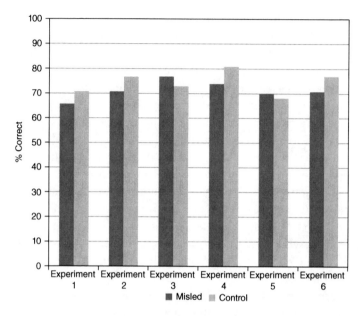

FIGURE 3.5 Accuracy on the modified recognition test in McCloskey and Zaragoza (1985).
Source: This figure created by authors based on tabled values in McCloskey and Zaragoza (1985). Copyright 1985, American Psychological Association. Used with permission.

reason as follows: (1) The experimenter said there was a barn in the film, so there must have been one. (2) I saw the whole film, so (3) I must have seen the barn; I just don't remember it.

To address this possible explanation, Zaragoza and Koshmider (1989) showed participants slides of the workman in the office again. After viewing the slides, participants were exposed to postevent information. For instance, if they saw a screwdriver, they were told it was a wrench. They then took either a standard forced-choice memory test (e.g., "Was it a wrench or a screwdriver?") or a specially designed source memory test. On the source memory test, participants were presented with items and for each item participants were told to respond "saw" if they explicitly remembered seeing the item in the slides. They were told to respond "read" if they did not explicitly remember the item from the slides but did remember reading about it in the narrative. Participants were also able to select "consistent" if they remembered the item but didn't remember the source and "inconsistent" if they remembered something inconsistent with the item's presentation. When tested with the standard test, evidence of memory impairment was found. However, when the source test was used, there was no evidence that participants really thought they remembered the suggested items.

A short time later, researchers demonstrated that misleading information can sometimes produce false memories as measured by the source monitoring test (Zaragoza & Lane, 1994). They found that this was especially true when the misleading information was embedded as a presupposition in a question and especially for misinformation that supplants, rather than contradicts, information in the original event. In other work, Lindsay (1990) used the process of opposition that we described in Chapter 2. In his research, participants viewed an event and then read a narrative that contained misleading information that was inconsistent with the item shown in the slides. The final memory test included a set of cued recall questions, half of which dealt with items that had been mentioned in the narrative. Participants were given a hard and fast decision rule: If you remember something being explicitly mentioned in the narrative, you can be certain that it was not in the original event. For example, imagine in the slides you see a particular brand of cigarettes. In the narrative, you might hear that it was a different brand of cigarettes. On the final memory test, you would then be asked, "What brand of cigarettes was shown in the slides?" Given the instructions, if you could explicitly remember what was mentioned in the narrative, you could be certain that brand of cigarettes was *not* in the slides. Lindsay found that even with the explicit warning, people still often falsely recalled details that had been suggested in the misleading narrative, indicating that participants believed the suggested items had been part of the original event.

Postevent information is very common and can come in many forms. People who witness crimes may read newspaper articles about the crime, may get information from police investigators, or may hear what other witnesses say about the event (Paterson & Kemp, 2006). Each of these sources of information can result in a person inserting false information into their memory for the event.

Other Sources of False Memories

Classically, schemas, scripts and postevent information have formed the basis of most constructive and reconstructive theories of memory. However, there are a number of other ways in which false memories can and do form, and we want to describe three of those briefly.

Imagination. When people mentally imagine an event, it can activate many of the same brain regions that become active when a person actually experiences an event (Gonsalves & Paller, 2000; Gonsalves, Reber, Gitelman, Parrish, Mesulam, & Paller, 2004). Consequently, when recalling an imagined event, one might mistakenly attribute the imagined event to an actual experience (Johnson & Raye, 1981). Such errors are described in detail in the *source monitoring framework* developed by Yale University's Marcia Johnson (Johnson, Hashtroudi, & Lindsay, 1993; Mitchell & Johnson, 2009). According to Johnson's theory, when people remember an event it is often necessary to attribute the source of the memory. Did the event really happen to me, or did I dream it? Did Jamie tell me that joke, or did Julia tell me that joke? Did I turn off the teapot, or did I only intend to turn off the teapot? In each case, one is attempting to determine the source of the information. Johnson argues that in so doing, we make use of qualitative characteristics that are typically associated with particular sources of memories, as well as a set of decision strategies for judging source. For instance, imagined events result in less vivid perceptual details being stored in memory than do experienced events, whereas imagined events lead to memories being formed for details of the cognitive operations used to create the mental image. These kinds of details can be used to make reasonably good judgments about the source of a memory, but these judgments aren't perfect, and source monitoring errors can and do occur (Mitchell & Johnson, 2000). Indeed, the misinformation effect is a kind of source monitoring error, typically involving confusing details that were suggested to you with details that you directly experienced (Frost, Ingraham, & Wilson, 2002; Lindsay & Johnson, 1989; Mitchell, Johnson, & Mather, 2003).

One way that the effect of imagination on memory has been studied is via the imagination inflation paradigm (Garry, Manning, Loftus, & Sherman, 1996). Participants were given a "life events inventory" that asked about 40 events that might have occurred in the person's early childhood (e.g., "Won a stuffed animal at a carnival game"; "Broke a window with your hand"). For each item, participants provided a rating of whether or not the event happened using an 8-point scale (1 = definitely did not happen; 8 = definitely did happen). Then, 2 weeks later, participants came back and they were asked to imagine a set of four events. These four events had been previously rated by participants, but no mention was made of this fact. The experimenter then feigned distress and indicated that he or she had misplaced the questionnaire from 2 weeks earlier and asked participants to fill out the questionnaire again. When the Life Event Inventories were examined, an interesting result was found. Participants tended to increase their ratings across the 2-week period, and this was more likely to occur for the imagined items than for items that had not been imagined. This study showed that when you imagine an event, it increases the chances that you will believe the event happened. Later research showed that imagination not only increases the belief that the event happened but can actually lead people to explicitly remember events that hadn't happened (Garry & Polaschek, 2000).

Imagination inflation has also been demonstrated for complex actions. In Goff and Roediger (1998), participants listened to lists of actions. For some of the actions, participants were to engage in the action. For instance, a participant would hear "Tug your ear lobe" and would tug his or her ear lobe. For other actions, participants were to imagine engaging in the action. For instance, a participant would hear "Touch your knee" and would imagine touching his or her knee. In a second session, participants imagined sets of actions. Some of the actions were imagined once, some three times, and some five times. Some of these actions were the same as those that had occurred in the original session, and some were new actions. Participants then took a test. They were presented with actions and were asked whether they had encountered an action during the first session. If they said "yes," they were to indicate whether they had imagined the action, enacted the action, or just heard the action. The more often the action was imagined, the more likely it was that participants believed they had actually engaged in the action. So imagining touching one's knee can lead to actually remembering touching one's knee. Other researchers have confirmed this finding (Lampinen, Odegard, & Bullington, 2003; Thomas, Bulevich, & Loftus, 2003). Imagination is a powerful source for creating false memories and undoubtedly Piaget's memory was created partly by imagining the story of the kidnapping throughout childhood.

Association. A very rich and very old tradition in cognitive psychology is called associationism (Hothersall, 2003). Associationism is the idea that concepts in the mind are connected together by links, such that one concept tends to activate another concept in the mind. For instance, you hear the word "dog," you think the word "cat." You see the word "fork," you think the word "knife." Associations of this type are produced every time two concepts co-occur in our experience. Notice that these kinds of mental associations are different from schemas because they aren't necessarily produced by any sort of complex organized representation of the world. Rather, they are simple binary connections produced by the co-occurrence of concepts in our experience.

These kinds of associations can be used to create false memories using a very simple procedure called the DRM paradigm. The paradigm is named for James Deese (1959), who invented the paradigm in the 1950s, and for Henry Roediger and Kathleen McDermott (1995), who popularized it again in the 1990s. Participants are presented with a list of items (e.g., hot, snow, warm, winter) that are all semantically associated with a nonpresented critical lure (e.g., cold). Participants then take a memory test for these items. Participants show very high rates of false recall or recognition for the nonpresented critical lure. The DRM effect is very powerful. False recall and recognition of the critical lures approach the level at which people correctly recall or recognize actual targets from the lists. Not only that, but the critical lures are recognized or recalled with high degrees of confidence (Payne, Ellie, Blackwell, & Neuschatz, 1996), and the effect occurs even when people are warned about the nature of the effect (Gallo, Roberts, & Seamon, 1997; Neuschatz, Payne, Lampinen, & Toglia, 2001). We have included some DRM lists in Table 3.1. To try out the study, get a friend and read him or her the words written in lowercase letters at a rate of one word every 2 seconds. Don't read the underlined word; that one is the critical lure. After you read each list, give your friend a number between 50 and 100 and ask your friend to count backward for 30 seconds. Then ask your friend to recall as many items as he or she can from the list. Then proceed to the next list. See how many of the critical lures your friend mistakenly recalls.

Two main theories have been proposed for the DRM effect. One theory is called activation monitoring (Roediger, Watson, McDermott, & Gallo, 2001). According to this theory, every time you study an item from the DRM list, it activates related concepts in your mind. Since each word on the DRM list is related to the critical lure, the critical lure receives a great deal of activation. When your memory is tested, this high degree of activation makes it seem as if you've encountered the critical lure previously. A monitoring process then tries to determine why the item seems familiar—that is, did I encounter it previously or did I merely think of it because of all the other items? The monitoring process

TABLE 3.1 LISTS THAT CAN BE USED TO DEMONSTRATE THE DRM FALSE MEMORY EFFECT

Anger	Black	Bread	Chair	Cold	Doctor	Foot	Fruit
mad	white	butter	table	hot	nurse	shoe	apple
fear	dark	food	sit	snow	sick	hand	vegetable
hate	cat	eat	legs	warm	lawyer	toe	orange
rage	charred	sandwich	seat	winter	medicine	kick	kiwi
temper	night	rye	couch	ice	health	sandals	citrus
fury	funeral	jam	desk	wet	hospital	soccer	ripe
ire	color	milk	recliner	frigid	dentist	yard	pear
wrath	grief	flour	sofa	chilly	physician	walk	banana
happy	blue	jelly	wood	heat	ill	ankle	berry
fight	death	dough	cushion	weather	patient	arm	cherry
hatred	ink	crust	swivel	freeze	office	boot	basket
mean	bottom	slice	stool	air	stethoscope	inch	juice
calm	coal	wine	sitting	shiver	surgeon	sock	salad
emotion	brown	loaf	rocking	Arctic	clinic	smell	bowl
enrage	gray	toast	bench	frost	cure	mouth	cocktail

(continued)

TABLE 3.1 **LISTS THAT CAN BE USED TO DEMONSTRATE THE DRM FALSE MEMORY EFFECT** *(continued)*

Girl	High	King	Man	Mountain	Music	Needle	River
boy	low	queen	woman	hill	note	thread	water
dolls	clouds	England	husband	valley	sound	pin	stream
female	up	crown	uncle	climb	piano	eye	lake
young	tall	prince	lady	summit	sing	sewing	Mississippi
dress	tower	George	mouse	top	radio	sharp	boat
pretty	jump	dictator	male	molehill	band	point	tide
hair	above	palace	father	peak	melody	prick	swim
niece	building	throne	strong	plain	horn	thimble	flow
dance	noon	chess	friend	glacier	concert	haystack	run
beautiful	cliff	rule	beard	goat	instrument	thorn	barge
cute	sky	subjects	person	bike	symphony	hurt	creek
date	over	monarch	handsome	climber	jazz	injection	brook
aunt	airplane	royal	muscle	range	orchestra	syringe	fish
daughter	dive	leader	suit	steep	art	cloth	bridge
sister	elevate	reign	old	ski	rhythm	knitting	winding

(continued)

TABLE 3.1 LISTS THAT CAN BE USED TO DEMONSTRATE THE DRM FALSE MEMORY EFFECT *(continued)*

Rough	Sleep	Slow	Soft	Spider	Sweet	Thief	Window
smooth	bed	fast	hard	web	sour	steal	door
bumpy	rest	lethargic	light	insect	candy	robber	glass
road	awake	stop	pillow	bug	sugar	crook	pane
tough	tired	listless	plush	fright	bitter	burglar	shade
sandpaper	dream	snail	loud	fly	good	money	ledge
jagged	wake	cautious	cotton	arachnid	taste	cop	sill
ready	snooze	delay	fur	crawl	tooth	bad	house
coarse	blanket	traffic	touch	tarantula	nice	rob	open
uneven	doze	turtle	fluffy	poison	honey	jail	curtain
riders	slumber	hesitant	feather	bite	soda	gun	frame
rugged	snore	speed	furry	creepy	chocolate	villain	view
sand	nap	quick	downy	animal	heart	crime	breeze
boards	peace	sluggish	kitten	ugly	cake	bank	sash
ground	yawn	wait	skin	feelers	tart	bandit	screen
gravel	drowsy	molasses	tender	small	pie	criminal	shutter

To try out the DRM false memory effect, read the words to a volunteer at a rate of approximately one word every 2 seconds in the order provided. Don't read the very top word (e.g., Anger, Black, Bread, etc.). Those are the critical lures. After each list, ask your participant to recall all the items on the list. Then move on to the next list. See how often your volunteer mistakenly recalls the critical lure.

Reprinted from Roediger and McDermott (1995). Copyright 1995, American Psychological Association. Reprinted with permission.

is simply the process described in the source monitoring framework that we discussed earlier in this chapter.

One source of evidence for the activation monitoring account comes from correlational research looking at which DRM lists produce the most false memories (Roediger, Watson, McDermott, & Gallo, 2001). This research has found that the lists that have the highest mean backward associative strength (MBAS) produce the most false memories. Backward associative strength refers to the probability that you will think of the critical lure given that you are presented with one of the study items. For instance, if I ask you what is the first word you think of when you hear the word "HOT"—how likely is it that you'll say "COLD"? If you do that for all of the study items on a DRM list and then take the average, that is MBAS. So that provides pretty good evidence for the activation part of the activation monitoring account. There is also evidence for the monitoring account. For instance, slow presentation of DRM lists (e.g., one item every 4 seconds) decreases the number of false memories relative to fast presentation (e.g., one item every 1 second). This is because slower presentation makes it easier for you to recall later which items were presented and which were only thought of.

The other main theory offered to explain the DRM effect is known as fuzzy trace theory (Reyna & Brainerd, 1995). Fuzzy trace theory started as a theory of memory development but has since become very popular in studying memory and reasoning in both children and adults. According to fuzzy trace theory, every time you study an item, you store two types of representations: verbatim and gist. A verbatim representation is an exact record of the item that was presented including its perceptual details. Gist, on the other hand, refers to overall patterns and meanings. When studying a DRM list, a verbatim representation is stored for each item, but also a gist representation is extracted that represents what each word means and how all the words are related to each other. At the time of the test, retrieval of a verbatim trace leads to the correct acceptance of targets and the correct rejection of critical lures. However, retrieval of a gist trace will tend to lead to acceptance of targets and acceptance of critical lures. Both targets and critical lures match the gist of what was presented, but only targets match the verbatim of what was presented.

One important difference between verbatim and gist is that gist is forgotten more slowly than verbatim. Consistent with this prediction, many researchers have found that false memories persist over time (McDermott, 1996; Payne, Elie, Blackwell, & Neuschatz, 1996; Toglia, Neuschatz, & Goodwin, 1999). Another important characteristic of gist is that it is more influenced by organizational strategies than is verbatim memory. For instance, when DRM lists are randomly intermixed, false memories are lower than if the DRM lists are presented in a blocked format (Brainerd et al., 2003; McDermott, 1996; Toglia et al., 1999).

The jury is still out on which of these theories provides a better explanation of the DRM effect. Each theory can accommodate the set of findings that exist to date and both theories make interesting and informative predictions. Perhaps the most interesting thing about the DRM effect is how powerful it is. And this is an issue that we turn to next: the conscious experience of false memories.

MEMORY ILLUSIONS AND CONSCIOUSNESS

Early into psychologists' study of false memories, the emphasis was simply on whether participants made errors of commission on the memory tests researchers gave them. Any such errors of commission were treated as false memories when the psychologists analyzed their data. But in the late 1990s, researchers came to the realization that participants can make errors of commission on memory tests for a variety of different reasons. Lampinen, Neuschatz, and Payne (1998) made the following analogy. There is a phenomenon in perception known as *apparent motion*

(Ramachandran & Anstis, 1986). In one type of apparent motion experiment, you see a bright dot at one location on a computer screen. The dot is erased and the screen is blank for around 60 milliseconds. Then another dot appears at a nearby location. From the participant's point of view, it appears as if there is a single dot that moves continuously from one location to the next. Most people would agree that this is a perceptual illusion. The true state of the world is that there are two stationary dots, separated in time. But the perception is of a single dot that moved continuously. But now imagine that a participant sees a single dot on a screen. The participant is then asked to close his or her eyes. The experimenter then presses a button to advance to a new slide in which the dot is in a different location. The participant then opens his or her eyes and is asked what just happened. The participant says, "It looks like the dot moved." Lampinen et al. argued that no reasonable person would conclude that this was a perceptual illusion. Rather, it is a deliberate inference from correctly perceived facts.

When thinking about memory illusions it is important to make a similar distinction. Imagine, for instance, I read you the DRM list "hot, snow, warm, winter, ice, etc." and then I ask you, "Did you hear the word COLD?" You might answer that question affirmatively, not because you have a memory for the word "COLD," but because you reason as follows: (1) I don't remember hearing the word "COLD," but (2) I do remember hearing the words "HOT, SNOW, WARM, WINTER," and (3) all those words are related to the word "COLD," (4) so I bet I did hear the word "COLD." In this case, it would be correct to say that you have a *false belief* that you heard the word *cold*, but it would be wrong to say you have a *false memory* of having heard the word *cold*. Hypothetical cases like these lead inexorably to the conclusion that the study of false memories requires examining the *phenomenology of memory* (Lampinen et al., 1998). Phenomenology roughly means the subjective first-person experience of the participant.

Since the 1990s, a number of studies have been conducted examining the phenomenology of false memories. These studies lead to the following generalizations. First, when people make errors of commission on memory tests, they are sometimes making deliberate inferences and are not experiencing false memories at all, while at other times the error of commission is caused by a subjective experience that is similar to the subjective experience one has when having an actual memory (Payne, Neuschatz, Lampinen, & Lynn, 1997). Second, on average, false memories are somewhat less vivid and detailed than are true memories, but these differences are small in magnitude (Mather, Henkel, & Johnson, 1997; Norman & Schacter, 1997). One consequence of this is that it is difficult to tell if any particular memory is a true or false memory based only on its phenomenological characteristics. Third, there is a subset of false memories that are extremely vivid and detailed. These false memories have been called phantom recollections (Brainerd, Payne, Wright, & Reyna, 2003; Brainerd, Wright, Reyna, & Mojardin, 2001).

Let us briefly describe simple ways that the phenomenology of false memories has been studied. One approach has been to use the remember/know procedure described in Chapter 2 (Tulving, 1985). Recall that in the remember/know procedure, participants study a set of items and are then given a recognition memory test. The test includes some previously studied items (OLD) and some previously unstudied items (NEW). Participants say whether each item was studied previously. If they say "yes" in response to this question, they are asked to indicate the basis of their judgment by either saying "remember" or "know." Participants are told to say "remember" if their judgment is based on recalling one or more particular detail about the presented item— for example, the tone of voice it was said in, where it was on the list, a thought they had when they heard the item (Rajaram, 1993). Participants are told to say "know" if they are sure the item was presented, but they can't recall any particular details about its presentation. A number of studies have now shown that a substantial proportion of the errors of commission that occur in false-memory experiments are false "remember" judgments (Anastasi, Rhodes, & Burns, 2000; Dewhurst, 2001; Dewhurst & Anderson, 1999; Holmes, Waters, & Rajaram, 1998; Hyman, Gilstrap, Decker,

& Wilkinson, 1998; Lampinen, Copeland, & Neuschatz, 2001; Lampinen, Faries, Neuschatz, & Toglia, 2000; Reinitz et al., 1992; Roediger & McDermott, 1995). Now that is really very striking, because it shows not only that participants inferred that something occurred that didn't occur, but they are also convinced that they can recall particular details of its presentation.

A particular example of the types of details people claim to recall was first demonstrated by David Payne and his colleagues (Payne, Ellie, Blackwell, & Neuschatz, 1996). Participants in this experiment listened to DRM lists that were presented by two speakers, a male speaker and a female speaker. After listening to a number of such lists, the participants were asked to recall the lists three times. After the final recall attempt, participants were asked to go back through the items they recalled and indicate which speaker said each word. Participants were cautioned not to guess, but only to write a speaker if they specifically remembered that that person said the word. Astonishingly, participants assigned a specific speaker to the critical nonpresented words (e.g., COLD) more than 80% of the time on average. So not only did participants think they remembered hearing the nonpresented word, they thought they could remember who said it. In a follow-up experiment, Lampinen, Neuschatz, and Payne (1999) told participants that 25% of their judgments of who the speaker was were wrong, and that they should go back and change 25% of their answers. Participants were no more likely to change their wrong answers than their right answers!

These results show that false memories are often experienced in a subjectively compelling fashion—that is, as phantom recollections. But what explains this effect? Two major explanations have been provided. One possibility is that as people study material in false-memory experiments, or as they retrieve the information later on, they create mental images of the experience (see Gallo, 2006, for a discussion). So even though you don't hear the word "COLD," when the word "COLD" pops into your head, you imagine what it would sound like if spoken by one of the speakers. The other possibility is called content borrowing (Lampinen, Meier, Arnal, &

Leding, 2005; Lampinen, Ryals, & Smith, 2008). According to the content borrowing account, the nonpresented item seems familiar to the participant because related items have been experienced. Because of that familiarity, participants search their memory for details that might tend to corroborate their memory. They then take details from actual presented items and glue them together (feature binding is the technical term) to create a vivid and detailed but false memory. The extant literature suggests that phantom recollections can be produced by both of these mechanisms.

CONCLUSIONS

The evidence that we reviewed in this chapter demonstrates that memory can't always be trusted. The first author has sometimes quipped that he studies false memories so that when he's an old man he'll be able to remember a life much more interesting than it actually was. There's some truth to that, we imagine. Each of us actively constructs our reality. We don't passively perceive information and we don't passively store or retrieve memories. And although there are objective truths in the world, the world as remembered is filtered by our own preconceptions, beliefs, and experiences. Most of the time this is alright, because the function of memory is not typically to be able to produce verbatim details of the past, but rather to be able to ponder and convey the lessons learned from events—the gist of the story. There are cases, however, where accurate recollection of specific details is vitally important. And it is to these kinds of cases that we turn next.

NOTES

1. Reprinted from Bransford and Johnson (1972). Copyright 1972, with permission from Elsevier.

2. Reprinted from Dooling and Christiaansen (1977). Copyright 1977, American Psychological Association. Used by permission.
3. These values are not exact. They are estimates based on eyeballing the graphs in the original published article.

REFERENCES

Anastasi, J. S., Rhodes, M. G., & Burns, M. C. (2000). Distinguishing between memory illusions and actual memories using phenomenological measurements and explicit warnings. *The American Journal of Psychology, 113*, 1–26.

Ayers, M. S., & Reder, L. M. (1998). A theoretical review of the misinformation effect: Predictions from an activation-based memory model. *Psychonomic Bulletin and Review, 5*, 1–21.

Barsalou, L. W. (1999). Perceptual symbol systems. *Behavioral and Brain Sciences, 22*, 577–660.

Bartlett, F. C. (1932). *Remembering: A study in experimental and social psychology.* New York, NY: Macmillan.

Beilin, H. (1992). Piaget's enduring contribution to developmental psychology. *Developmental Psychology, 28*, 191–204.

Belli, R. F. (1988). Color blend retrievals: Compromise memories or deliberate compromise responses? *Memory and Cognition, 16*, 314–326.

Belli, R. F. (1989). Influences of misleading postevent information: Misinformation interference and acceptance. *Journal of Experimental Psychology: General, 118*, 72–85.

Bower, G. H., Black, J. B., & Turner, T. J. (1979). Scripts in memory for text. *Cognitive Psychology, 11*, 177–220.

Brainerd, C. J., Payne, D. G., Wright, R., & Reyna, V. F. (2003). Phantom recall. *Journal of Memory and Language, 48*, 445–467.

Brainerd, C. J., Wright, R., Reyna, V. F., & Mojardin, A. H. (2001). Conjoint recognition and phantom recollection. *Journal of Experimental Psychology: Learning, Memory, and Cognition, 27*, 307–327.

Bransford, J. D., Barclay, J., & Franks, J. J. (1972). Sentence memory: A constructive versus interpretive approach. *Cognitive Psychology, 3*, 193–209.

Bransford, J. D., & Franks, J. J. (1971). The abstraction of linguistic ideas. *Cognitive Psychology, 2*, 331–350.

Bransford, J. D., & Johnson, M. K. (1972). Contextual prerequisites for understanding: Some investigations of comprehension and recall. *Journal of Verbal Learning and Verbal Behavior, 11*, 717–726.

Brewer, W. F., & Nakamura, G. V. (1984). The nature and functions of schemas. In R. S. Wyer & T. K. Srull (Eds.), *Handbook of social cognition* (Vol. 1, pp. 119–160). Hillsdale, NJ: Erlbaum.

Brewer, W. F., & Treyens, J. C. (1981). Role of schemata in memory for places. *Cognitive Psychology, 13*, 207–230.

Chatham, C. (2007). *Ten important differences between brains and computers.* Developing Intelligence. Science Blogs. Retrieved from http://scienceblogs.com/developingintelligence/2007/03/27/why-the-brain-is-not-like-a-co

Christiaansen, R., & Ochalek, K. (1983). Editing misleading information from memory: Evidence for the coexistence of original and postevent information. *Memory and Cognition, 11*, 467–475.

Deese, J. (1959). On the prediction of occurrence of particular verbal intrusions in immediate recall. *Journal of Experimental Psychology, 58*, 17–22.

Dewhurst, S. A. (2001). Category repetition and false recognition: Effects of instance frequency and category size. *Journal of Memory and Language, 44*, 153–167.

Dewhurst, S. A., & Anderson, S. J. (1999). Effects of exact and category repetition in true and false recognition memory. *Memory and Cognition, 27*, 664–673.

Dooling, D. J., & Christiaansen, R. E. (1977). Episodic and semantic aspects of memory for prose. *Journal of Experimental Psychology: Human Learning and Memory, 3*, 428–436.

Draaisma, D. (2001). *Metaphors of memory: A history of ideas about the mind.* Cambridge, UK: Cambridge University Press.

Ebbinghaus, E. (1885/1913). *Memory: A study in experimental psychology.* New York, NY: Columbia University Press.

Flavell, J. (1967). *The developmental psychology of Jean Piaget.* New York, NY: D. Van Nostrand.

Frost, P., Ingraham, M., & Wilson, B. (2002). Why misinformation is more likely to be recognized over time: A source monitoring account. *Memory, 10*, 179–185.

Gallo, D. A. (2006). *Associative illusions of memory: False memory research in DRM and related tasks.* New York, NY: Psychology Press.

Gallo, D. A., Roberts, M. J., & Seamon, J. G. (1997). Remembering words not presented in lists: Can we avoid creating false memories? *Psychonomic Bulletin and Review, 4,* 271–276.

Garry, M., Manning, C. G., Loftus, E. F., & Sherman, S. J. (1996). Imagination inflation: Imagining a childhood event inflates confidence that it occurred. *Psychonomic Bulletin and Review, 3,* 208–214.

Garry, M., & Polaschek, D. L. L. (2000). Imagination and memory. *Current Directions in Psychological Science, 9,* 6–10.

Glenberg, A. M. (1997). What memory is for. *Behavioral and Brain Sciences, 20,* 1–55.

Goff, L. M., & Roediger, H. (1998). Imagination inflation for action events: Repeated imaginings lead to illusory recollections. *Memory & Cognition, 26,* 20–33.

Gonsalves, B., & Paller, K. A. (2000). Neural events that underlie remembering something that never happened. *Nature Neuroscience, 3,* 1316–1321.

Gonsalves, B., Reber, P. J., Gitelman, D. R., Parrish, T. B., Mesulam, M., & Paller, K. A. (2004). Neural evidence that vivid imagining can lead to false remembering. *Psychological Science, 15,* 655–660.

Graesser, A. C., Gordon, S. E., & Sawyer, J. D. (1979). Recognition memory for typical and atypical actions in scripted activities: Tests of a script pointer + tag hypothesis. *Journal of Verbal Learning and Verbal Behavior, 18,* 319–332.

Graesser, A. C., Woll, S. B., Kowalski, D. J., & Smith, D. A. (1980). Memory for typical and atypical actions in scripted activities. *Journal of Experimental Psychology: Human Learning and Memory, 6,* 503–515.

Holmes, J. B., Waters, H., & Rajaram, S. (1998). The phenomenology of false memories: Episodic content and confidence. *Journal of Experimental Psychology: Learning, Memory, and Cognition, 24,* 1026–1040.

Holst, V. F., & Pezdek, K. (1992). Scripts for typical crimes and their effects on memory for eyewitness testimony. *Applied Cognitive Psychology, 6,* 573–587.

Hothersall, D. (2003). *History of psychology* (4th ed.). New York, NY: McGraw-Hill.

Hyman, I., Gilstrap, L. L., Decker, K., & Wilkinson, C. (1998). Manipulating remember and know judgements of autobiographical memories: An investigation of false memory creation. *Applied Cognitive Psychology, 12,* 371–386.

Johnson, M. K., Hashtroudi, S., & Lindsay, D. (1993). Source monitoring. *Psychological Bulletin, 114,* 3–28.

Johnson, M. K., & Raye, C. L. (1981). Reality monitoring. *Psychological Review, 88,* 67–85.

Lampinen, J. M., Copeland, S. M., & Neuschatz, J. S. (2001). Recollections of things schematic: Room schemas revisited. *Journal of Experimental Psychology: Learning, Memory and Cognition, 27,* 1211–1222.

Lampinen, J. M., Faries, J. M., Neuschatz, J. S., & Toglia, M. P. (2000). Recollections of things schematic: The influence of scripts on recollective experience. *Applied Cognitive Psychology, 14,* 543–554.

Lampinen, J. M., Meier, C., Arnal, J. A., & Leding, J. K. (2005). Compelling untruths: Content borrowing and vivid false memories. *Journal of Experimental Psychology: Learning, Memory and Cognition, 31,* 954–963.

Lampinen, J. M., & Neuschatz, J. S. (2008). Reconstructive memory. In B. Cutler (Ed.), *Encyclopedia of psychology and the law.* Thousand Oaks, CA: Sage.

Lampinen, J. M., Neuschatz, J. S., & Payne, D. G. (1998). Memory illusions and consciousness: Exploring the phenomenology of true and false memories. *Current Psychology, 16,* 181–224.

Lampinen, J. M., Neuschatz, J. S., & Payne, D. G. (1999). Source attributions and false memories: A test of the demand characteristics account. *Psychonomic Bulletin and Review, 6,* 130–135.

Lampinen, J. M., Odegard, T. N., & Bullington, J. (2003). Qualities of memories for performed and imagined actions. *Applied Cognitive Psychology, 17,* 881–893.

Lampinen, J. M., Ryals, D. B., & Smith, K. (2008). Compelling untruths: The effect of retention interval on content borrowing and vivid false memories. *Memory, 16,* 149–156.

Lindsay, D. S. (1990). Misleading suggestions can impair eyewitness's ability to remember event details. *Journal of Experimental Psychology: Learning, Memory, and Cognition, 16,* 1077–1083.

Lindsay, D. S., & Johnson, M. K. (1989). The eyewitness suggestibility effect and memory for source. *Memory and Cognition, 17,* 349–358.

Lodge, M., & Hamill, R. (1986). A partisan schema for political information processing. *American Political Science Review, 80,* 505–519.

Loftus, E. F. (1975). Leading questions and the eyewitness report. *Cognitive Psychology, 7,* 560–572.

Loftus, E. F. (1977). Shifting human color memory. *Memory and Cognition, 5,* 696–699.

Loftus, E. F. (1979). The malleability of human memory. *American Scientist, 67,* 312–320.

Loftus, E. F., & Loftus, G. R. (1980). On the permanence of stored information in the human brain. *American Psychologist, 35,* 409–420.

Loftus, E. F., Miller, D. G., & Burns, H. J. (1978). Semantic integration of verbal information into a visual memory. *Journal of Experimental Psychology: Human Learning and Memory, 4,* 19–31.

Loftus, E. F., & Palmer, J. C. (1974). Reconstruction of automobile destruction: An example of the interaction between language and memory. *Journal of Verbal Learning and Verbal Behavior, 13,* 585–589.

Mather, M., Henkel, L. A., & Johnson, M. K. (1997). Evaluating characteristics of false memories: Remember/know judgments and memory characteristics questionnaire compared. *Memory and Cognition, 25,* 826–837.

Mazzoni, G., & Lynn, S. J. (2007). Using hypnosis in eyewitness memory: Past and current issues. In M. P. Toglia, J. D. Read, D. F. Ross, & R. C. L. Lindsay (Eds.), *The handbook of eyewitness psychology,* Vol. 1. *Memory for events* (pp. 321–338). Mahwah, NJ: Lawrence Erlbaum Associates.

McCloskey, M., & Zaragoza, M. (1985). Misleading postevent information and memory for events: Arguments and evidence against memory impairment hypotheses. *Journal of Experimental Psychology: General, 114,* 1–16.

McDermott, K. B. (1996). The persistence of false memories in list recall. *Journal of Memory and Language, 35,* 212–230.

Metcalfe, J. (1990). Composite Holographic Associative Recall Model (CHARM) and blended memories in eyewitness testimony. *Journal of Experimental Psychology: General, 119,* 145–160.

Mitchell, K. J., & Johnson, M. K. (2000). Source monitoring: Attributing mental experiences. In E. Tulving & F. I. M. Craik (Eds.), *The Oxford handbook of memory* (pp. 179–195). New York, NY: Oxford University Press.

Mitchell, K. J., & Johnson, M. K. (2009). Source monitoring 15 years later: What have we learned from fMRI about the neural mechanisms of source memory? *Psychological Bulletin, 135*, 638–677.

Mitchell, K., Johnson, M., & Mather, M. (2003). Source monitoring and suggestibility to misinformation: Adult age-related differences. *Applied Cognitive Psychology, 17*, 107–119.

Neisser, U. (1967). *Cognitive psychology.* New York, NY: Appleton-Century-Crofts.

Neuschatz, J. S., Payne, D. G., Lampinen, J. M., & Toglia, M. P. (2001). Assessing the effectiveness of warnings and the phenomenological characteristics of false memories. *Memory, 9*, 39–51.

Norman, K. A., & Schacter, D. L. (1997). False recognition in younger and older adults: Exploring the characteristics of illusory memories. *Memory and Cognition, 25*, 838–848.

Paterson, H. M., & Kemp, R. I. (2006). Comparing methods of encountering post-event information: The power of co-witness suggestion. *Applied Cognitive Psychology, 20*, 1083–1099.

Payne, D. G., Elie, C. J., Blackwell, J. M., & Neuschatz, J. S. (1996). Memory illusions: Recalling, recognizing, and recollecting events that never occurred. *Journal of Memory and Language, 35*, 261–285.

Payne, D. G., Neuschatz, J. S., Lampinen, J. M., & Lynn, S. (1997). Compelling memory illusions: The qualitative characteristics of false memories. *Current Directions in Psychological Science, 6*, 56–60.

Penfield, W. (1969). Consciousness, memory, and, man's conditioned reflexes. In K. Pribram (Ed.), *On the biology of learning* (pp. 127–168). New York, NY: Harcourt, Brace & World.

Pezdek, K., Whetstone, T., Reynolds, K., Askari, N., & Dougherty, T. (1989). Memory for real-world scenes: The role of consistency with schema expectation. *Journal of Experimental Psychology: Learning, Memory, and Cognition, 15*(4), 587–595.

Piaget, J. (1951). *Play, dreams and imitation in childhood.* London, UK: Heinemann.

Plucker, J. (2012). Jean Piaget—Biographical profiles. *Human Intelligence.* Retrieved from www.indiana.edu/~intell/piaget.shtml

Rajaram, S. (1993). Remembering and knowing: Two means of access to the personal past. *Memory and Cognition, 21*, 89–102.

Ramachandran, V. S., & Anstis, S. M. (1986). The perception of apparent motion. *Scientific American, 254*(6), 102–109.

Reinitz, M. T., Lammers, W. J., & Cochran, B. P. (1992). Memory-conjunction errors: Miscombination of stored stimulus features can produce illusions of memory. *Memory and Cognition, 20,* 1–11.

Reisner, M., & Nielson, H. (1980). Investigative hypnosis: A developing specialty. *The American Journal of Clinical Hypnosis, 23,* 75–77.

Reyna, V. F., & Brainerd, C. J. (1995). Fuzzy-trace theory: An interim synthesis. *Learning and Individual Differences, 7,* 1–75.

Rizzella, M. L., & O'Brien, E. J. (2002). Retrieval of concepts in script-based texts and narratives: The influence of general world knowledge. *Journal of Experimental Psychology: Learning, Memory, and Cognition, 28,* 780–790.

Roediger, H. L. (1980). Memory metaphors in cognitive psychology. *Memory and Cognition, 8,* 231–246.

Roediger, H. L., & McDermott, K. B. (1995). Creating false memories: Remembering words not presented in lists. *Journal of Experimental Psychology: Learning, Memory, and Cognition, 21,* 803–814.

Roediger, H. L., Watson, J. M., McDermott, K. B., & Gallo, D. A. (2001). Factors that determine false recall: A multiple regression analysis. *Psychonomic Bulletin and Review, 8,* 385–407.

Schank, R. C. (1983). *Dynamic memory: A theory of reminding and learning in computers and people.* New York, NY: Cambridge University Press.

Schank, R. C. (1999). *Dynamic memory revisited.* New York, NY: Cambridge University Press.

Schank, R. C., & Abelson, R. P. (1977). *Scripts, plans, goals and understanding: An inquiry into human knowledge structures.* Hillsdale, NJ: Erlbaum.

Schank, R. C., & Abelson, R. P. (1995). Knowledge and memory: The real story. In R. S. Wyer (Ed.), *Knowledge and memory: The real story* (pp. 1–85). Hillsdale, NJ.: Lawrence Erlbaum Associates.

Sherman, J. W., Stroessner, S. J., Loftus, S. T., & Deguzman, G. (1997). Stereotype suppression and recognition memory for stereotypical and nonstereotypical information. *Social Cognition, 15*(3), 205–215.

Simons, D. J., & Chabris, C. F. (2011). What people believe about how memory works: A representative survey of the U.S. population. *PLoS ONE, 6*(8), e22757. doi:10.1371/journal.pone.0022757

Singer, D. G., & Revenson, T. A. (1996). *A Piaget primer: How a child thinks.* New York, NY: Plume.

Smith, V. L., & Studebaker, C. A. (1996). What do you expect? The influence of prior knowledge of crime categories on fact-finding. *Law and Human Behavior, 20,* 517–532.

Thomas, A. K., Bulevich, J. B., & Loftus, E. F. (2003). Exploring the role of repetition and sensory elaboration in the imagination inflation effect. *Memory and Cognition, 31,* 630–640.

Toglia, M. P., Neuschatz, J. S., & Goodwin, K. (1999). Recall accuracy and illusory memories: When more is less. *Memory, 7,* 233–256.

Tulving, E. (1974). Cue-dependent forgetting. *American Scientist, 62,* 74–82.

Tulving, E. (1985). Memory and consciousness. *Canadian Psychology/Psychologie Canadienne, 26,* 1–12.

Zaragoza, M. S., & Koshmider, J. W. (1989). Misled subjects may know more than their performance implies. *Journal of Experimental Psychology: Learning, Memory, and Cognition, 15,* 246–255.

Zaragoza, M. S., & Lane, S. M. (1994). Source misattributions and the suggestibility of eyewitness memory. *Journal of Experimental Psychology: Learning, Memory, and Cognition, 20,* 934–945.

Who Done It? Memory and Eyewitness Identification

et's say you're telling a friend about a Milwaukee Brewers game you went to with your dad. Maybe you remember eating a hot dog when you were at this big game. But really you bought the hot dog for your dad, not for yourself. Your memory was inaccurate, but so what? Harmless error—good memory, good story—what really matters is spending time with your dad. But sometimes the accuracy of memory becomes a matter of the utmost importance. Such is the case when eyewitnesses are asked to testify in criminal court about the things they witnessed. In this chapter we are focusing on one particular type of eyewitness memory— the memory of an eyewitness for the face of the perpetrator. This is typically called *eyewitness identification*.

Eyewitness identifications are crucial evidence in upward of 80,000 criminal cases per year (Wells et al., 1998). This being the case, making sure those identifications are accurate and reliable is tremendously important. Victims of crimes deserve to have justice done in their cases. Accurate eyewitness memory can help police catch criminals and can help prosecutors bring solid cases against those criminals. The person accused of a crime also deserves to have justice done—to not be falsely accused or wrongfully imprisoned. There are actually two reasons why this is important (Wells, 1978). First, if a person is mistakenly identified due to a memory error on the part of a witness, that person may go to prison and spend time in prison for a crime he or she did not commit (Scheck, Neufeld, & Dwyer, 2000). Because liberty is precious, and time lost can never be regained, when an innocent person goes to prison, it is a tragedy. But that is only part of the problem. If a crime has occurred and the wrong person goes to prison, it means that the guilty party is still free to commit additional crimes (Huff, 2003). Mistaken identifications thus risk the individual liberty of the innocent and the collective safety of the public. We hope that these arguments convince you that eyewitness memory is an important and interesting topic and one worth reading about. Eyewitness memory is also interesting because it is a multifaceted topic (Lampinen, Neuschatz, & Cling, 2012). To understand eyewitness memory, one has to understand perceptual psychology, cognitive psychology, social psychology, motivation, emotion, reasoning, personality—just about every kind of psychology you can imagine.

MISTAKEN IDENTIFICATIONS

Back in the 1984 an assailant broke into 22-year-old Jennifer Thompson's home in North Carolina (Hansen, 2001). He restrained her. He put a knife to her throat. Then he sexually assaulted her. The whole crime lasted for more than an hour, and the victim was hurt pretty badly. A few days later, the police developed a potential suspect—a man named Ronald Cotton. They put Mr. Cotton's picture in a photographic lineup and showed the lineup to the victim, Jennifer Thompson. She identified him with a great deal of confidence as the man who had terrorized her, the man who had raped her. You can imagine the feeling of relief that she must have felt. The person who attacked her in this horrible manner had been apprehended and was in custody. He wasn't going to hurt anybody anymore. Mr. Cotton protested his innocence throughout the trial, but a jury of his peers convicted him in January 1985. He was put in prison, sentenced to life.

Approximately 10 years later, people in the United States were transfixed with the murder trial of a former NFL football star—O.J. Simpson was accused of the murder of his former wife Nicole Brown Simpson and her friend Ronald Goldman. The trial was widely televised, and it just so happens that Ronald Cotton watched the trial on TV in prison. It was here that he learned about the advances that had been made in DNA testing of forensic evidence. He realized that there were potential biological samples in his case that could be tested using this technology. DNA could set him free. His attorneys convinced a judge to allow the rape kit to be tested. The tests excluded Mr. Cotton as the rapist and implicated another man, Bobby Poole. Cotton was released—a free man—after spending 11 years in prison for a crime he didn't commit.

An interesting twist to this story is that after Ronald Cotton was released from prison, he and Jennifer Thompson became fast friends. They began touring the country together talking about the problem of wrongful conviction. They even wrote a book together (Thompson-Cannino, Cotton, & Torneo, 2009). There are probably a lot of people in such a circumstance who would be angry with the person who had made the mistaken identification. But Mr. Cotton didn't feel that way. After all, the identification made by Jennifer Thompson was not done out of malice or spite. She made the identification because in her mind, she was sure her identification was correct. But her memory was faulty.

This example illustrates quite well the fragility of eyewitness memory. Mr. Cotton was not the attacker. But Jennifer Thompson's memory didn't know any different.

We know that Ronald Cotton is not alone. It seems as if every couple of weeks, the news has a story about another person who was wrongfully convicted of committing, and who subsequently served time for, a crime the he or she did not really commit (Innocence Project, 2014). In some cases the person who is eventually exonerated has spent time on death row—awaiting the hangman's noose, so to speak. There have now been 300+ DNA exoneration cases in which people have been released from prison after serving up to 3 decades in prison (Innocence Project, 2014). Each of these cases is an individual tragedy. Because most cases do not have biological evidence that can be used to exonerate the convicted person, these 300 exonerations likely represent only a portion of all wrongful convictions. In 75% of DNA exoneration cases, mistaken eyewitness memory is a contributing cause for why the person was convicted. In a third of those cases, there were two or more witnesses who both identified the same person—incorrectly!

Mistaken identifications are a memory problem. They involve a person retrieving details from memory but being mistaken in the recollection of those details. It will probably never be the case that we can entirely eliminate these errors. The good news is that cognitive and social psychologists have been hard at work since the 1970s in developing science-based approaches that can reduce the problem.

THE NATURE OF THE IDENTIFICATION TASK

Before we get into the specifics of how eyewitness errors can be reduced, it is useful first to know something about the procedures police use to obtain eyewitness identifications (Lampinen et al.,

2012). Police lineups are similar to a multiple-choice test, with an explicit or implicit "none of the above" or "I'm not sure" option. In the standard police lineup, there are two kinds of people. The *suspect* is the person that the police believe (suspect) may have committed the crime. In addition to the suspect, a good police lineup also includes a number of *foils*.[1] Foils are people who the police know for sure are innocent, but who match the same general description as the suspect. The purpose of including foils in a lineup is to protect innocent suspects. In a fair lineup, if the suspect is innocent, an errant witness should be no more likely to mistakenly identify the innocent suspect than he or she is to mistakenly identify one of the foils. Although picking a foil is a mistake, it is a relatively harmless mistake, because the police know all the foils are innocent. Picking an innocent suspect, on the other hand, is a dangerous mistake. The suspect is already believed by police to be guilty of the crime, and an identification by a witness confirms that suspicion in the eyes of law enforcement. Thus a witness who selects an innocent suspect is making a *dangerous error*—an error in which an innocent person may be subjected to wrongful conviction.

In the United States, the stereotypical police lineup contains one suspect and five foils—although this can vary from jurisdiction to jurisdiction and case to case. Other countries require that the lineup contain more foils (Malpass, Tredoux, & McQuiston-Surrett, 2007). Lineups can be presented live, called corporeal lineups. They can also be presented by showing the witness a series of photographs, sometimes called photoarrays. In the United States, most lineups are presented in the form of a photoarray (Fulero & Wrightsman, 2009). Photoarrays are much easier to construct, since all you need are photographs, not actual live individuals. Any time a witness views a lineup, there are two possible states of affairs. Sometimes the police have the right person, and the suspect is guilty of the crime. A lineup with a guilty suspect is called a *target-present lineup*. Sometimes the police have the wrong person—the suspect is innocent. A lineup with an innocent suspect is called a *target-absent lineup*.

The correct choice in a target-present lineup is to select the suspect. The correct choice in a target-absent lineup is to reject the lineup altogether.

In practice, police don't know for sure if they are showing a witness a target-present or target-absent lineup. If the police knew definitively that the suspect was guilty, there would be no point in presenting the lineup at all. However, researchers can set up experiments in which it is known for sure whether the suspect is guilty or innocent. To give you a flavor of these experiments, consider a study by Pigott, Brigham, and Bothwell (1990). The study took place at banks in Florida. On a number of occasions at a number of different banks, a confederate—that is, a person working with the experimenters—entered the bank and walked up to the center aisle and acted as if he was filling out a deposit slip. He then walked up to a teller and handed the teller an obviously forged U.S. postal money order. The forgery was really bad—the researchers had taken a $10 money order and added a 1 in blue ink pen so that it said $110. Of course, none of the tellers cashed the money order. When the teller refused, the confederate acted angry, grabbed the money order, and then left. Tellers contacted their bank manager—who we should note, was in on the experiment. The manager indicated that she or he would call the police. A few hours later, a researcher posing as a police detective arrived. She interviewed the teller and showed the teller either a target-present or target-absent lineup. So how accurate were the witnesses? When witnesses viewed a target-present lineup, they picked the correct person a bit under 50% of the time. When witnesses viewed a target-absent lineup, they incorrectly picked *someone* from the lineup close to 40% of the time. This is a pretty high rate of mistaken identifications, especially given that the tellers were under the impression that this was a real crime. We should note that examination of data from actual lineups indicates that 30% to 40% of all lineup identifications are identifications of innocent fillers (Slater, 1994—37.93%; Valentine, Pickering, & Darling, 2003—30.16%; Wells, Steblay, & Dysart, 2011—41%; Wright & McDaid, 1996—33.73%).

SYSTEM VARIABLES AND ESTIMATOR VARIABLES

In 1978, Iowa State University's Garry Wells wrote an important article that would guide eyewitness researchers for more than 3 decades. In it, he argued that there are basically two types of variables that influence identification accuracy. He called these variables *system variables* and *estimator variables*. A system variable is some factor that can influence the accuracy of an eyewitness and that is under the control of the criminal justice system—for example, the police. For instance, the police can decide how many foils to put in a lineup. They can decide what instructions to give the witness. And so forth. An estimator variable, on the other hand, is a factor that can influence the accuracy of an eyewitness, but that isn't under the control of the police. For instance, the police have no control over whether the crime occurred at night or during the day, but certainly the amount of lighting at the time of the crime can influence the accuracy of the witness when viewing a lineup. Wells (1978) argued that psychologists would be better off focusing most of their attention on system variables rather than estimator variables. Here's how Wells put it in his seminal paper:

> But, whatever the approach, estimator variable research has a natural restriction in its application to criminal justice: Estimator-variable research cannot alter the accuracy of a given witness's account of a real crime; it can only reduce or increase the court's reliance on the witness's testimony. (Wells, 1978, p. 1548)

His logic was that system variables offered psychologists with an opportunity to be proactive—coming up with procedures that would decrease wrongful convictions on the front end. Estimator variables, on the other hand, were seen by Wells (1978) as reactive—allowing psychologists to estimate the likely reliability of a witness, but not allowing psychologists to improve the accuracy of those witnesses. In our own view, both types of variables are extremely important to understand. And moreover, they are

107

likely to interact with each other. For instance, age of the witness is an estimator variable. Manner of lineup presentation is a system variable. But what type of lineup presentation is best may depend on the age of the witness (Pozzulo & Lindsay, 1998). In the next sections, we'll describe some of the best known system variables and estimator variables that have been studied by psychologists. We'll then talk about how society can use this information to decrease the odds of wrongful convictions.

ESTIMATOR VARIABLES

We'll start our description with estimator variables. One can broadly think about estimator variables as falling into three main classes: characteristics of the witnessing situation, characteristics of the witness, and characteristics of the person being witnessed. Let's start with characteristics of the situation.

Situational Variables

Opportunity to View. As we talked about in previous chapters, your ability to accurately remember an event depends on forming an accurate perceptual representation of the event at the get go— at encoding. Memory follows the old computer science adage of "garbage in, garbage out." If the initial perceptual representation is impoverished or inaccurate, then obviously your ability to retrieve accurate details from the crime will also be impoverished. The factors that influence this initial perceptual representation can be thought of as the "opportunity to view" the perpetrator. There are three main factors that influence opportunity to view. These are lighting, distance, and duration.

Consider first the effects of lighting on your ability to form an accurate representation of a person's face. Every image that we see is caused by light reflecting off of the surface of the object, entering our eyes, and activating photoreceptors on a thin sheet of cells in the back of the eye called the retina (Enns, 2004; Foley & Matlin, 2010; Goldstein, 2007). Two kinds of light-sensitive cells exist in the retina: cones and rods. Cones are *photopic*, which means that they are designed to function best in conditions in which there is a lot of light. Rods are *scotopic*, which means that they are designed to function in dim lighting conditions. At intermediate lighting conditions, both rods and cones are active. Such conditions are called *mesopic* (Yurov, 1967). Cones are heavily concentrated in the center of the retina, an area called the fovea (Foley & Matlin, 2010). They have fantastic spatial resolution—they can be used to perceive very fine details. However, they are less sensitive to light than rods. In dim lighting conditions, cones respond only minimally. Rods are distributed more evenly throughout the retina, although they are entirely absent from the fovea. Rods are extremely sensitive to light—that is, they function even in dim lighting conditions. However, rod-based vision is not very good at seeing fine details. Consequently the ability to see fine details is best under photopic conditions and is worst under scotopic conditions. The ability to see details is at an intermediate level under mesopic conditions.

We think you can see where this is going. Lots of criminal activity occurs at night. For instance, about half of armed robberies in one study occurred after 8 p.m. (Felson & Poulsen, 2003). In another study, 25% of all lineups involved situations in which the lighting at the time of the crime was judged by police to be "poor" (Valentine et al., 2003). In bright lighting conditions, our initial memory representation is likely to include fine details of a person's face because vision is based on the cones. But under dim lighting conditions, our initial memory representation of a person's face is likely to be much less detailed, because vision is based primarily on rods. Studies have tended to confirm this prediction. For instance, DiNardo and Rainey (1991) showed participants photographs of faces under either dim or bright illumination. Participants were then shown a set of test photographs and for each one had to indicate if the person in the photograph had been seen previously. Correct identifications of previously seen photographs decreased from 90% to 76% when going from bright to dim illumination conditions. False identifications of new photographs increased from 23% to 53%. In other research, participants have been asked to view individuals at night who are illuminated by standard street lights (Fotios & Cheal, 2007; Knight, 2010; Raynham & Saksvikronning, 2003; Rea, Bullough, & Akashi, 2009). The participants started a long distance away and then walked toward the person until they were sure they could identify the person. The typical finding in these studies is that people need to be between 5 and 12 meters before they feel confident that they can make an identification. These findings confirm the idea that lighting is extremely important in identification, because the degree of lighting influences the adequacy of the memory representation that is initially stored.

A second factor that goes into the opportunity to view is the distance the witness is from the perpetrator. Many crimes occur when the perpetrator is relatively close to the witness, as is the case when someone is robbed or assaulted. But in other cases, for instance a driveby shooting, the perpetrator may be a considerable distance away from the witness. Distance has a big effect on the quality of the initial perceptual representation that is formed, because although the retina has a lot of photoreceptors, it doesn't have an *infinite number* of photoreceptors (Goldstein, 2007). We know that sounds like common sense, but it has important implications for eyewitness memory. The farther away the perpetrator is from the witness, the smaller the image of the perpetrator on the retina. The smaller the image on the retina, the fewer photoreceptors there are to process that image. So faces that are farther away are represented in a much less detailed form than faces that are close to the witness. One way of thinking about this is that when you see someone from far away, the representation is equivalent to seeing a picture that is highly pixelated. For instance, the picture shown in Figure 4.1 shows the approximate amount of visual detail one would have in viewing the first author from 80 feet away.

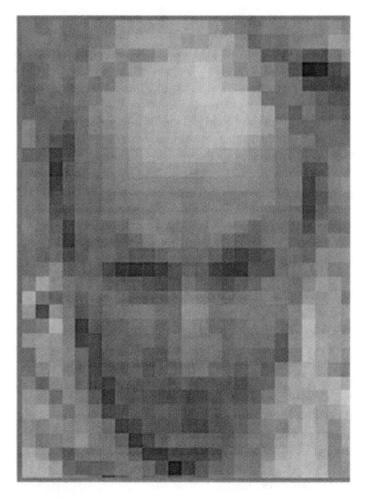

FIGURE 4.1 Distance results in an image that has less visual detail.

The effects of distance on face recognition have basically been studied in two ways. In one type of study, the researchers take pictures of faces and size them so that the image produced on the participant's retina is equivalent to the retinal image of a face seen from that distance. For instance, Loftus and Harley

(2005) took faces of celebrities sized to correspond to particular distances and had participants try to name the celebrities. Participants were very good at naming the faces when they were sized to correspond to short distances. However, at farther and farther distances, performance got worse and worse. Naming accuracy dropped to about 50% when the faces were sized to be equivalent to a face seen from approximately 55 feet away. Naming accuracy was essentially zero when the faces were sized to be equivalent to viewing a face from approximately 128 feet away.

Other studies have examined face recognition for actual people viewed at various distances. Lampinen, Erickson, Moore, and Hittson (2014) had undergraduate students view targets at a variety of distances from 5 yards to 40 yards away. Each person was viewed for 10 seconds. Participants were then shown photographs of individuals and asked to pick the ones that they had seen. Distance had a large effect on recognition. When the viewing occurred at 5 yards away, the average accuracy was around 80%. When the viewing occurred at 40 yards away, accuracy was just over 60%. Keep in mind that this was an old/new recognition test, so accuracy based on chance alone was 50%.

A final aspect of the opportunity to view a face concerns the duration for which the face is visible. Most theories of perception assume that when we examine a visual scene we sample information (Lamberts & Freeman, 1999). Because less information can be sampled from a face that has been studied for a short period of time than a face that has been studied for a long period of time, it is not surprising that some studies have found that faces that are seen only briefly are less likely to be recognized accurately. Earlier we told you about a study by DiNardo and Rainey (1991) in which they varied the lighting when people were viewing pictures of faces. In that same study, they also studied how long participants had to view the faces. Each picture was shown for either 1.5 seconds or 5 seconds. Under bright lighting conditions, faces that were studied for 5 seconds were correctly recognized 90% of the time. Faces that were studied for 1.5 seconds were correctly recognized 86% of the time, which isn't much different. However, the test also included some new, previously unseen faces. These were falsely recognized 23% of the time by people in the 5-second condition and 53% of the time for participants in the 1.5-second condition. Thus, decreasing viewing time from 5 seconds to 1.5 seconds more than doubled the number of false identifications.

The effect of viewing time has also been examined in situations that more closely approximate an actual eyewitness event. In one study, participants watched a film of a bank robbery in which the robber was visible for either 12 seconds or 45 seconds (Memon, Hope, & Bull, 2003). Participants then saw either a target-present or target-absent lineup. For target-present lineups, 95% of the young adult participants correctly identified the robber in the long exposure condition compared to 29% in the brief exposure condition.[2] For the target-absent lineup, 90% of participants in the brief exposure condition made a mistaken identification, compared to 41% in the long exposure condition. We think you'll agree that these differences are quite dramatic and are consistent with the claim that longer viewing times lead to better memory representations being formed.

Although these studies suggest that long exposure conditions lead to better eyewitness memory, it may surprise you to know that there are some exceptions. In one study, confederates visited convenience stores and remained in the store for either a brief period of time or a long period of time (Read, 1995). After the confederate left, an experimenter arrived and asked the store clerk to view either a target-present or target-absent lineup. In half of the lineups of each type, all the members of the lineup wore glasses and their hair up, just like how the confederate looked when she visited the store. Thus everyone, in both the target-present and target-absent lineup, bore at least a superficial similarity to the confederate's appearance in the store. For the other half of the lineups, all the lineup members wore their hair down and did not wear glasses. Thus everyone, in both the target-present and target-absent lineup, was superficially dissimilar from how the confederate looked when she visited the store.

In the condition where the appearance was different from the confederate's appearance in the store, worked out just as you might expect. Participants who got to view the woman for a longer period of time did better than people who got to view the woman for a shorter period of time. However, in the condition where everyone's appearance superficially matched the confederate's appearance in the store, something freaky happened. People who got to view the confederate for a longer period of time were more likely to correctly pick her out of the target-present lineup than people who got to view her for a shorter period of time. However, they were also more likely to incorrectly pick a foil from the target-absent lineups. You might be asking yourself how this could be. To understand Read's hypothesis, it's important to remember that recognition judgments depend both on the memory record and on the decision criteria witnesses set (see Chapter 2). According to the explanation offered by the authors, when there is a superficial match in similarity, participants become convinced one of the members of the lineup must be the person who had visited the store. Furthermore, participants in the long viewing time condition feel like they should be able to make the identification. So they are more likely to pick someone from both the target-present and target-absent lineups.

The general lesson so far is that opportunity to view can strongly affect recognition accuracy. This is because each of these factors—lighting, distance, viewing time—is likely to affect the amount of detail that can be stored in a memory representation. The amount of detail available at retrieval, of course, is limited by what was processed by the visual system in the first place. We now turn to another situational variable that can strongly affect eyewitness memory.

Stress. So far we've talked about characteristics of events that are likely to affect people's ability to extract perceptual details from a face—lighting, duration, and distance. Because the memory record that is formed is ultimately limited by the details that are originally perceived, these factors place important limitations on eyewitness memory. However, eyewitness events have not only a perceptual content but also an emotional content. Observing a crime is an unpleasant experience. Being a victim of a crime is an even worse experience. And if the crime is violent, like the one experienced by Jennifer Thompson, then the emotional experience may be traumatic. Emotion and memory are very tightly linked, as we'll discuss in more detail later in the book. However, for now we should note that there has been a fair amount of research by scientists on how stressful events impact perception and memory for faces.

One of the earliest of these studies used a very simple procedure (Brigham, Maass, Martinez, & Whittenberger, 1983). Participants were brought into an experiment room and were attached to a shock generator. They were given a sample shock so that they knew what to expect. The amount of shock was enough to be extremely unpleasant, but not enough to produce any serious or longlasting physical damage. Participants were then shown a series of photographs of people's faces. On half the trials, they received a shock shortly after the presentation of the face. They didn't know in advance which faces would be associated with the shock and which would not be associated with the shock. Participants in a control condition were also hooked up to the shock generator and given a sample shock. However, the shock generator was then disconnected, and they viewed the photographs without any risk of getting shocked. Participants were then asked to complete a memory test. They saw a series of pictures and were asked to indicate, for each picture, whether they had seen in before. How did this experiment turn out? First, as you might imagine, the participants hooked up to the shock generator reported experiencing more stress during the study period. More importantly, memory for the photographs was much more accurate among participants in the low-stress condition. The authors concluded that memory for faces is likely to be poor when people encounter those faces under high stress.

Memory psychologists who study the relationship between stress and face memory have offered three main theories to explain why memory for faces can be impaired by stress. The first of these is called the Yerkes–Dodson Law and was originally proposed back in 1908 (Yerkes & Dodson, 1908). Stress is associated with physiological arousal—increased heart rate, sweaty palms, and the like. Yerkes and Dodson proposed that at low levels of arousal, performance should be poor because you need a certain level of arousal just to function. Consider, for example, a person who isn't much of a morning person trying to function at a meeting before he or she has his or her first cup of coffee. As arousal increases, performance gets better, because the person is aroused enough to focus attention on the task at hand. At very high levels of arousal, performance suffers again, because the system becomes overloaded and breaks down. For instance, a lot of people, when they need to speak in public, or when they are out on a first date, have difficulty because they become so nervous that they have trouble thinking of what to say. So eyewitness researchers who subscribe to the Yerkes–Dodson Law argue that the relationship between stress and eyewitness memory should be an upside down U function (see Figure 4.2). When arousal is low, memory will be poor. When arousal is too high, memory will be poor. At some intermediate level of arousal, memory will be best.

The second main theory of how stress and eyewitness memory are related is called the cue utilization hypothesis. According

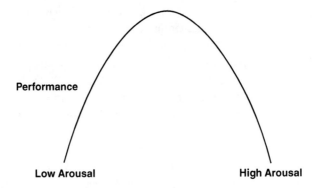

Performance

Low Arousal   High Arousal

FIGURE 4.2 Yerkes–Dodson Law.

to this hypothesis, the effect of stress is to focus attention on a smaller range of features (Easterbrook, 1959) in the environment. Features that are seen as being absolutely essential to survival receive a great deal of attention and should be remembered well. Features that are incidental to survival receive hardly any attention and shouldn't be remembered well. Some researchers have argued, for instance, that when a perpetrator uses a weapon, attention is drawn to the weapon and away from the face, resulting in poor memory for the face. This has been called the *weapon focus effect* (Erickson, Lampinen, & Leding, 2014; Hope & Wright, 2007; Kramer, Buckhout, & Eugenio, 1990; Loftus, Loftus, & Messo, 1987; Pickel, 2007; Tooley, Brigham, Maass, & Bothwell, 1987).

Kenneth Deffenbacher (1994) has argued that eyewitness memory can be understood in terms of a theory called the catastrophe model of stress (Fazey & Hardy, 1988). This theory is similar to the Yerkes–Dodson Law in that it says that very low arousal and very high arousal can be associated with poor memory. However, there are also a couple of important differences. First, the theory says that high levels of arousal can lead to an orienting response that should increase memory for the event. However, when high arousal is associated with high levels of cognitive anxiety—that is, worry—performance will suffer a catastrophic decline. This decline is seen as being much more sudden and dramatic than the slow gradual decline in performance envisioned by the Yerkes–Dodson Law.

Regardless of the particular theory one believes, the bulk of the research on stress and face perception has found that high levels of stress are associated with declines in memory for faces (Deffenbacher, Bornstein, McGorty, & Penrod, 2008). In one recent study, Charles Morgan of Yale University and his colleagues (2004) studied military personnel undergoing survival training. As part of the survival training, they underwent a simulated capture by enemy personnel and underwent mock interrogations. Some interrogations used harsh interrogation tactics that had been shown in prior research to produce stress levels similar to those soldiers' experience in combat. In other interrogations the interrogation tactics were not stress inducing, but instead involved trying to befriend the soldiers and trick them into revealing information (think good cop/bad cop). After the ordeal of the mock capture and mock interrogations was over, the soldiers viewed lineups and were asked to identify their captors. When shown target-present photospreads, the high-stress condition resulted in correct identifications of the interrogator 34% of the time, compared to 76% for the low-stress interrogations. False identifications occurred 68% of the time in the high-stress condition compared to 12% of the time in the low-stress condition. These results support the idea that high stress decreases the accuracy of eyewitness memory, and these results have been confirmed when researchers have conducted systematic meta-analyses of research on the relationship between stress and eyewitness identification.

Characteristics of the Witness. In the movie *My Cousin Vinny*, Joe Pesci plays inexperienced lawyer Vinny Gambini, attempting to win his first murder trial on behalf of his cousin Bill, played by Ralph Macchio. One of the witnesses against Bill Gambini is a sweet-looking, gray-haired lady named Constance Riley (Paulene Myers), who testifies that she saw Bill Gambini. The punch line becomes apparent when Ms. Riley puts on her glasses while on the witness stand—the lenses are as thick as the bottoms of Coke bottles. Gambini then walks to a distance that is about half as far from Ms. Riley as she says she witnessed the two young men and holds up two fingers. He asks her how many fingers he's holding up. She says four. The testimony concludes with Ms. Riley indicating that she thinks she needs thicker glasses. As is illustrated with this example, witnesses vary in terms of their ability to remember people and events. Differences can arise from something as simple as eyesight or from personality differences, alcohol intoxication, drug use, and so on.

Child Witnesses. It is not unusual for children to testify in criminal trials. It used to be the case that courts acted under the assumption that children were inherently unreliable witnesses

(Ceci & Bruck, 1993). Children were only allowed to testify if they could pass muster in a competency hearing. Many jurisdictions had rules that said children's testimony would only be allowed if there was other corroborating evidence that backed up the child's story. And in many courts, the jury heard an instruction that children's testimony was prone to error. In the 1980s many of those rules changed with the realization that children were often the victims to crimes and the only witness.

Children are more suggestible than adults, especially preschool-age children (Ceci & Bruck, 1993). So it's important that police not ask children leading questions. With regard to lineups, the general finding has been that children are especially likely to make false identifications in target-absent lineups (see the meta-analysis by Pozzulo & Lindsay, 1998). For instance, in a study by Joanna Pozzulo and Rod Lindsay (1999), adults and children, 10 to 14 years old, watched a videotape showing a man named Mike. After viewing the video, they were asked to describe Mike and where then shown either a target-present or target-absent lineup. Children were correct 65% of the time on the target-present lineup, compared to 80% of the time for adults. In the target-absent lineups children falsely identified someone 46% of the time, compared to only 13% of the time for adults. Not only that, but children tend to be extremely overconfident in their judgments. For instance, Keast, Brewer, and Wells (2007) found that children who indicated that they were more than 90% certain in their selection of a person from a lineup were correct less than 30% of the time.[3]

Elderly Witnesses. The past several decades have seen major demographic shifts in the United States and many other countries around the world. In the 1950s, roughly 1 in 10 Americans was over the age of 65, whereas it is projected that by 2020, 1 in 6 Americans will be 65 or older (Moody & Sasser, 2014). These trends are a function of the large surge of births that followed World War II as well as increased life expectancy. As a consequence of increased life expectancy, not only is the proportion of the elderly increasing, but the proportion of the elderly population that is older than 80 is also steadily rising. These changing demographic trends suggest that the proportion of elderly individuals who come into contact with the criminal justice system will increase in the coming years. Fear of becoming a victim of crime is a major concern for many elderly persons.

As people get older, it's normal for them to experience some increased difficulty in their ability to remember things (Verhaeghen & Marcoen, 1993; Verhaeghen, Marcoen, & Goossens, 1993). An implication of this is that elderly witnesses might have more trouble remembering people and events. Two kinds of experiments have been conducted to test these hypotheses. In some experiments, participants—young adults and older adults—study pictures showing faces of people (e.g., Bartlett & Leslie, 1986; Mason, 1986; Smith & Winograd, 1978). After a retention interval, they then see another set of photos. Some of the photos are of people that were shown previously, and some are completely new pictures (i.e., an old/new recognition test of the type we talked about in Chapter 2). For each picture, the participant's job is to say whether he or she saw that person previously. Recall that correctly recognizing a previously seen person is called a "hit," and mistakenly saying you recognize someone you've never seen before is called a "false alarm." In a review of these studies, Searcy and colleagues (1999) found that the hit rate for younger and older adults was about the same, but false alarms were about 20% higher for older adults than younger adults.

Other studies comparing young adults with older adults have presented participants with mock crimes and then presented participants with target-present or target-absent lineups. For instance, Wilcock and Bull (2009) showed older and younger adults a videotape of a man stealing a car. About half an hour later, participants were shown either a target-present or target-absent lineup. In the target-present lineup, young adults correctly selected the car thief from the lineup about 75% of the time, compared to 62.5% of the time for the elderly participants. In the target-absent lineup, young adults mistakenly selected someone

31.3% of the time, compared to 75% for the elderly participants. Thus, young adults did a little bit better in the target-present lineup than elderly adults, but in target-absent lineups, elderly participants were more than twice as likely to mistakenly identify an innocent person than were young adult participants. This pattern has been replicated in a number of different studies (Erickson, Lampinen, & Moore, 2014).

Characteristics of the Perpetrator. In addition to characteristics of the eyewitness, characteristics of the perpetrator may influence the ability to remember a face. Perhaps the most studied of these characteristics is the distinctiveness of the face (Light, Kayra-Stuart, & Hollander, 1979). Distinctiveness may sound a bit like an amorphous "in the eye of the beholder" kind of construct, but it actually has a fairly precise meaning that can be operationalized. A person with a distinctive face is basically a person whose face is atypical when compared to the average face. Some studies have found that previously studied distinctive faces are more likely to be correctly recognized on a later memory test than are less distinctive faces (Bartlett, Hurry, & Thorley, 1984; Cohen & Carr, 1975; Going & Read, 1974; Light, Kayra-Stuart, & Hollander, 1979; Sheperd, Gibling, & Ellis, 1991; Valentine, 1991; Valentine & Bruce, 1986; Wickham, Morris, & Fritz, 2000; Winograd, 1981). Moreover, previously unseen distinctive faces are less likely to be mistakenly recognized than are less distinctive faces.

Another characteristic of the perpetrator that may influence recognition is whether the perpetrator was wearing a disguise or changed his or her appearance after the crime. For instance, consider the two images of the first author shown in Figure 4.3. It is likely that if you saw the person in the left panel you might not be able to recognize him when his appearance is changed to that in the right panel. Studies have shown that even slight variations of this sort can have dramatic effects on the accuracy of later recognition (Cutler, Penrod, & Martens, 1987a, 1987b; Krouse, 1981). To think about why this is, recognize that for people you know well, basic theories of face perception suggest that you develop

FIGURE 4.3 Effects of change of appearance/disguise on recognition. *Note:* Both of these are pictures of the first author. Obviously, the hat in the picture on the right is an especially good disguise.

a viewpoint-independent representation of that person's face (Bruce & Young, 1986). That is, you are able to recognize someone you know well across a broad range of possible transformations: The person changes hair style, the person loses weight, the person is wearing makeup, the person grows a beard—for people you know well, you can still recognize them despite these kinds of changes. On the other hand, for a person you've only seen one time, the representation stored into memory is viewpoint-dependent. It is specifically tied to the precise details of how the person looked during that particular instance when you saw the person. So it is difficult to generalize to what the person looks like in other circumstances.

Interactions Between Witness and Perpetrator. So far we've talked about characteristics of the witness and characteristics of the perpetrator that might influence eyewitness memory. But perhaps the best known finding in eyewitness testimony research involves how witness characteristics and perpetrator characteristics interact. The effect is called the *own race bias* (Meissner & Brigham, 2001). It's the finding that people are more accurate in identifying members of their own racial or ethnic group than they are at identifying members of other racial or ethnic groups. To give you just one example of the research on this topic, consider a study by Platz and Hosch (1988). White, Black, and Hispanic confederates entered local convenience stores in Texas in which the store clerk was either White, Black, or Hispanic. Each confederate acted out a script that was designed to draw attention to himself. For instance, in one script the confederate would walk up to the counter with a product. When told the price he would fumble around in his pockets looking for change. He'd then leave the store, explaining that he didn't have enough money. Shortly thereafter he would return to the store with the money, but would ask for a brand of beer that the store doesn't carry. You could imagine that this set of behaviors would be memorable to the store clerks! There were three scripts like this, and the three confederates switched off who enacted each script as they went from store to store. Then, 2 hours after the three confederates visited the store, an experimenter came by claiming to represent a law firm. The experimenter showed the clerk three target-present lineups—one for the Black confederate, one for the White confederate, and one for the Hispanic confederate. The clerks were most accurate in identifying the confederate who matched them in terms of race/ethnicity.

Dozens of studies like these have been done over the years and the findings have been summarized quite nicely by Meissner and Brigham (2001). Across the studies they found that when people are shown a picture of a person that they have previously seen, people are about 1.4 times more likely to identify that person if he or she is a member of their own race or ethnicity than if they are a member of a different race or ethnicity. When shown a picture of previously unseen person, participants are about 1.56 times more likely to falsely identify that person if he or she is a member of a different race or ethnicity.

Different views have been offered for why the own race bias occurs. According to one view, it's because people have more experience, on average, with members of their own race than members of other races (Cross, Cross, & Daly, 1971). Other researchers have suggested that racial animus plays a role in the own race bias, although the evidence for this view is mixed (Ferguson, Rhodes, Lee, & Sriram, 2001). Perceptual psychologists have argued that own race faces are processed holistically, as a gestalt, whereas other race faces are more likely to be processed as independent features (Michel, Rossion, Han, Chung, & Caldara, 2006). Each of these views has some evidence in support. Perhaps most amazing, there is evidence that the own race bias develops in the first year of life (Kelly et al., 2007).

The own race bias is just one of a number of cross categorization effects that have been shown in face memory. For instance, young adults are better at recognizing other young adults than they are at recognizing children or older adults (Anastasi & Rhodes, 2006). Studies have even been conducted showing that people are better at recognizing people who they believe support the same sports team they do, than they are at recognizing people who support a different sports team (Bernstein, Young, & Hugenberg, 2007).

System Variables

There's an old saying that everybody talks about the weather, but nobody does anything about it. The same can be said about estimator variables. When thinking about how it comes about that witnesses make false identifications, estimator variables are an important set of factors to consider. And these variables can be used retrospectively to make an estimate of how accurate a witness is likely to be. But they can't be used proactively to make witnesses more accurate. That's where system variables come in. In this section we review some of the most important system variables known to influence identification accuracy.

Instruction Bias. Imagine that you're the victim of a crime. You're walking down the street, just minding your own darn business, when a man jumps out from a car, takes you down with a leg sweep, and absconds with your iPhone. You immediately decide to call the police, but then realize that you don't have your iPhone. So you go into a shop and ask them to call the police for you. When the police arrive they take a report and get a description of the assailant. After a couple of weeks of not hearing anything, you give up. But then one day, a detective calls you and asks you to come down to the police station to look at a lineup. What are you likely to think at that very moment? If you're like most people, you will probably conclude that the police must have caught the assailant. After all, why would they take the time to conduct a lineup unless they had good reason to believe they had the person who did it? The problem with this assumption is that it is likely to cause the witness to view the lineup task as one where (1) the perpetrator is in the lineup and (2) the witness's job is to pick the suspect out of the lineup.

Now it's true, of course, that when the police construct a lineup, they have a suspect in mind. But as we've already discussed, sometimes the suspect is guilty and sometimes the suspect is innocent. The reason for the lineup is to provide addition information about which of those hypotheses is true. If the suspect is innocent, the job of the witness is not to pick the suspect out of the lineup—it is to say that the suspect is not there. Because witnesses are likely to make these kinds of assumptions, the U.S. Department of Justice advises that it is extremely important that police provide unbiased lineup instructions (Technical Working Group, 1999). Unbiased lineup instructions minimally advise the witness that the perpetrator may or may not be in the lineup.

One of the earliest studies to establish the importance of lineup instructions was conducted by Roy Malpass and Patricia Devine (1981). The study was conducted in a large classroom where the instructor was doing a biofeedback demonstration. During the middle of the demonstration, a student entered the classroom. The instructor told the student to wait because a class was in session. The student stood by the side of the biofeedback machine and started messing with the dials. The instructor asked him to stop. The student messed with the dials on the gizmo some more. The instructor, getting angry, asked him to stop again. He messed with the dials one more time, but this time when the instructor asked him to stop, he yelled an obscenity at the instructor and ran of the room. The instructor pretended to chase after him, but then came back into the room and pretended to call campus security. A bit later, campus security arrived. Students were then told it was just a study and they were given the opportunity to play the role of witness in the rest of the experiment. Those who wanted to participate were shown a lineup 1 to 3 days after the "crime." Some participants were shown a target-present lineup, and some were shown a target-absent lineup. In those two groups, some participants were told that the perpetrator may or may not be in the lineup. These were the unbiased instructions. Other participants were given biased instructions, "Which of these is the person you saw push over the equipment?" In target-absent lineups, witnesses who received biased lineup instructions mistakenly identified an innocent person from the lineup 78% of the time, compared to 33% among witnesses who received unbiased lineup instructions. There was no significant effect of lineup instructions on target-present lineups. Later studies confirmed these results (Steblay, 1997). Unbiased instructions are one of the most important things police can do to limit mistaken identifications.

Composition Bias. Imagine that when you are interviewed by the police, you describe the thief as a White male with blonde, thinning hair, in his late 40s. One day, the first author of this book is walking down the street and the police nab him, owing to his devious appearance and his matching your description. To construct the lineup, the police obtain a photograph of the first author (i.e., the suspect) as well as five foils. The five foils the police select are the second author (a Caucasian female), an 80-year-old African American female, a 12-year-old Hispanic male, a 25-year-old punk rocker, and Honey Boo Boo. The police are careful to present the pictures to you in a random order and ask you whether you can identify the person who assaulted you.

Do you think this would be a fair lineup? Hopefully your answer is no. The purpose of including foils in a lineup is to provide a degree of protection to innocent suspects. In a fair target-absent lineup, if the witness makes a mistake and picks someone, it should be just as likely that the witness will pick one of the foils as the witness will pick the suspect. But in the lineup fancifully described earlier, there's only one reasonable choice—the suspect—in light of what the witness's description is. Eyewitness researchers would say that the *nominal size* of the lineup is six—that is, there are six people in the lineup—but the *functional size* is one, because there is only one reasonable choice.

You might wonder how often these kinds of biased lineups occur. The answer is *more often than you might think*. Wells (n.d.) for instance, described a case in 1995 where the perpetrator was described as a young African American male. When the police conducted the lineup, it included an African American male suspect and five Hispanic male suspects. Now if you're the witness, it's pretty obvious in a case like that who the police think committed the crime. Undoubtedly, that may influence your choice.

In some cases, lineup bias is more subtle than the cases just described. In these cases researchers can measure lineup bias using a mock witness paradigm (Wells et al., 1979). In the mock witness paradigm, the researchers recruit participants who did not witness the original crime. These participants are provided with the description provided by the witness and are shown the lineup. They are asked to pick the person that they believe is the best match to the description. Considering that the participants didn't see the actual perpetrator, if the lineup is fair, the participant should be no more likely to pick the suspect than any of the foils. For instance, in a six-person lineup, mock witnesses should pick the suspect no more than one sixth of the time.

Valentine and Heaton (1999) tested this assumption by obtaining photographs of 25 actual lineups, along with the descriptions of the perpetrator that had been given by the witness. The study was conducted in the UK, where the typical lineup includes nine people (one suspect and eight foils). Thus, in a fair lineup, a mock witness who is given only the witness description should select the suspect no more than one time out of nine (approximately 11% of the time). When mock witnesses were shown these lineups, along with the description of the culprit given by the actual witnesses, they chose the suspect approximately one quarter of the time, suggesting that the lineups were biased against the suspect.

Two different methods of selecting the foils for a lineup have been suggested (Luus & Wells, 1991). The *match to suspect* approach involves selecting foils due to their similarity to the suspect. The police investigator visually inspects a picture of the suspect, then looks through collections of photos trying to find people who look similar to the suspect. A problem with the match to suspect approach is that it doesn't really say how similar is similar enough. For instance, imagine you had a suspect and five doppelgangers—exact duplicates. Clearly, that wouldn't be helpful because even if the suspect is guilty, and even if the witness has a perfect memory, the witness would still be unable to pick the guilty suspect from the lineup.

The *match to description* approach gets around this problem. It involves selecting foils due to their similarity to the description given by the witness without regard to how similar they are to the suspect. In most cases, this is the better way to select foils for a lineup. To see why, imagine a witness describes the perpetrator as a slim Caucasian male with short brown hair. The police pick up a suspect who matches that description. The police also obtain pictures of five men. Each of the men is slim, Caucasian, and has short brown hair. Imagine now that the suspect is innocent. If that is true, then there is no particular reason to think that the suspect is going to look any more like the perpetrator than are any of the foils. All the police know about the suspect is based on the description, and everybody in the lineup is an equally good match to the description. If, however, the suspect is guilty, the fact that there is some variability in the appearance of the targets and foils will make it easier for the witness to pick out the guilty suspect. Consequently, description-matched lineups result in more correct identifications of guilty people without affecting the false identification of innocent people.

Interviewer Bias. Social psychologists have known for decades that when an interviewer has a particular hypothesis, he or she can sometimes inadvertently influence the responses he or she gets from a participant. These are known as interviewer expectancy effects (Rosenthal, 1994). In one study, Rosenthal and Fode (1961) had research assistants conduct a picture rating experiment. Each of 10 researchers tested 10 participants. The task involved showing the participants pictures of individuals and obtaining ratings of how successful the participant thinks the person is likely to be. Half of the experimenters were told that previous research had found that the pictures were rated high on success, whereas the other half were told that the pictures had previously been rated low on success. The results were fascinating and somewhat alarming. When the interviewer believed that the pictures had previously been rated high on success, ratings obtained from participants tended to be high on success. When the interviewer believed that the pictures had previously been rated low on success, ratings obtained from participants tended to be low on success.

So how could this happen? To understand it, one needs to keep in mind that the process of obtaining information from people in an interview is a social phenomenon (Rosenthal, 1976). It's true that the interviewee is providing information to the interviewer, but the interviewer is also providing information to the interviewee. It's a two-way street. Interviewers can influence respondents by their tone of voice, by the follow-up questions they choose to ask, by body language, and so on. These cues can often be subtle, but people are pretty good at picking up on them and responding accordingly. For this reason, whenever possible, scientists conduct studies in a double-blind manner (Meyers & Hanseen, 2012). That is, the participant does not know the hypothesis, and the researcher does not know the hypothesis, or at least doesn't know what condition the participant is in. Double-blind research is standard practice in most research involving people—psychological research, medical research, sociological research—because it is known how strong interviewer expectancy effects can be.

A while back, Gary Wells and colleagues at Iowa State University pointed out that a police lineup is, in many ways, like a psychology experiment (Wells & Luus, 1990). The police investigator has a hypothesis—the suspect is guilty. He or she conducts an experiment to test that hypothesis—that is, the lineup. The experiment includes certain controls—unbiased lineup instructions, description matched foils. If the witness selects the suspect, it makes the hypothesis that the suspect is guilty more credible. If the witness fails to select the suspect, it makes the hypothesis that the suspect is guilty less credible. There's a problem though. In most police lineups, the investigator knows who the suspect is. Police investigators are people, and just like any other people, they could inadvertently tip the witness to their hypothesis—that is, that the suspect is guilty. For that reason, the American Psychology Law Society (Wells et al., 1998) recommends that all lineups be conducted in a double-blind manner by someone who does not know who the suspect is (see Douglas, Smith, & Fraser-Thill, 2005; Greathouse & Kovera, 2009; Haw & Fisher, 2004; Phillips, McAuliff, Kovera, & Cutler, 1999, for experiments testing the effectiveness of double-blind lineups).

Manner of Presentation. The typical way of presenting a lineup is to present all of the lineup members at the same time and ask the witness if he or she identifies the culprit from among the lineup. For over 3 decades, however, researchers have been experimenting with different ways of presenting lineups, with a goal of increasing accuracy. One early method that was advocated is called a blank lineup (Wells, 1984). Blank lineups are designed to weed out witnesses who are prone to making false identifications. In this procedure, a witness is told that he or she will view a lineup. The lineup is shown and the witness is asked whether he or she can identify the perpetrator from the lineup. Unbeknownst to the witness, the lineup is entirely made up of foils—that is, people who the police know to be innocent. If the witness chooses someone from this lineup, then the police know that the witness may be unreliable. If the witness rejects the lineup, the witness is shown the lineup that contains the suspect. Wells (1984) showed that the blank lineup technique can substantially decrease false identifications.

A short time later, Lindsay and Wells (1985) suggested a radical change to how lineups are conducted. They recommended that the individuals in a lineup be shown to witnesses one at a time, rather than all at once. They called this approach a sequential lineup. As the witness views each person, the police ask for an absolute judgment—for example, "Is this the person you saw?" If the witness says "no," the next individual is shown. The process is continued until the suspect and all the foils are shown. The idea behind the sequential lineup is to decrease the use of relative judgment strategies in which people compare and contrast lineup members. Early studies found that sequential lineups decreased false identifications, with little effect on correct identifications (Lindsay & Wells, 1985). However, later studies found that sequential presentations decrease both false and true identifications (Carlson, Gronlund, & Clark, 2010). Currently, there is considerable debate among eyewitness experts as to which approach is better.

A third approach that has been suggested is called an elimination lineup (Pozzulo & Lindsay, 1999). In an elimination lineup, the witness first decides which member of the lineup comes closest to his or her memory of the perpetrator. Importantly, this is done without asking the witness to commit to that particular person. Once the witness reduces the lineup to a single person who is most similar to the perpetrator, the witness next makes an absolute judgment: "Is this the person who committed the crime?" Elimination lineups have been found to be particularly helpful for children in reducing false identifications.

Each of these approaches is designed to reduce false identifications of innocent suspects, while still allowing correct identifications of guilty suspects. These approaches continue to be studied by eyewitness experts.

Manner of Presentation (Lineup vs. Showup). A final approach that is sometimes used by law enforcement isn't a lineup at all—at least not in the traditional sense. Instead it's called a showup (Steblay, Dysart, Fulero, & Lindsay, 2001). In a showup, the police come up with a person who they think may have committed the crime, and they show that person and that person alone to the witness. See why we said it's not a lineup? You need at least two points to make a line! Showups are used in somewhere between 30% and 70% of all identifications (Lampinen, Neuschatz, & Cling, 2012). They are especially likely if there are exigent circumstances and the police feel there isn't enough time to create a lineup. However, it's widely agreed in legal circles that showups can be suggestive. There are two reasons that showups can be problematic. The first is that if the police show a witness a single person, and only that person, it's pretty clear who the police think the culprit is. The fact that the witness knows who the police suspect of the crime may increase the jeopardy faced by an innocent suspect who might have some resemblance to the actual culprit, whomever he or she may be.

The second problematic aspect of showups is that they lack the procedural safeguards that are inherent in lineups. Recall that in a lineup, the foils serve as a kind of control to protect innocent suspects from being mistakenly identified. In a fair target-absent lineup, if a witness makes a mistake and chooses someone, it is more likely that he or she will choose one of the foils than that he or she will pick the suspect. Think of it this way: If you're an innocent suspect, and there are five other people in the lineup who match the description of the witness just as well as you do, your chances of being misidentified aren't any greater than are theirs. So if the witness does mistakenly pick somebody, there's only 1 chance in 6 that he or she will pick you. In a showup, on the other hand, the cards are stacked against you. The witness likely believes that you are being shown by the police because you are as guilty as all get out. And if the witness makes a mistake and picks someone, the only person he or she can pick is you.

The research tends to support these concerns. A statistical review of studies comparing lineups to showups (Steblay et al., 2001) found that on average the probability of a mistaken identification of a suspect in a showup is approximately twice as high as the chances of a mistaken identification of a suspect in a lineup. Correct identifications of guilty suspects were not significantly affected by whether a lineup or showup was used. Frankly, if we were ever falsely accused of a crime, we'd be much more comfortable in a fair lineup than we would be in a showup. Wouldn't you?

MAKING A DIFFERENCE

As we noted at the outset, eyewitness identification is one area in which precise and accurate memories are very important. Sadly, errors in eyewitness identification are all too common, and jurors may place an undue emphasis on identifications. However, a great deal of progress has been made in psychological science over the last several decades. Memory psychologists have learned a lot about how eyewitness memory works and the things that can be done to improve eyewitness accuracy. Even more importantly, the criminal justice system has taken notice. In the late 1990s, the U.S. Department of Justice issued a set of guidelines for interviewing eyewitnesses, guidelines based largely on the research of psychologists (Technical Working Group, 1999). Many individual states have followed suit by promulgating their own standards based on the best scientific research available (Florida Department of Law Enforcement, 2011; New York State Justice Task Force, 2011; Office of the Attorney General, New Jersey, 2001; Office of Attorney General, State of Wisconsin, 2010). More recently, the New Jersey Supreme Court developed a set of jury instructions specifically designed to inform the jury of many of the factors we reviewed in this chapter in cases that involve eyewitness testimony (Weiser, 2012). So although much needs to be done, including better promulgation of these findings to investigating officers, the scientific study of eyewitness identifications has been a real success story for psychology.

NOTES

1. Foils are sometimes called fillers, but we will stick with the use of the term *foil* in this chapter.
2. There was also an elderly adult condition, but for the present purposes, we focus on the results for young adults.
3. Exact numbers were not reported by Keast et al. (2007), and these estimates are based on visual inspection of Figure 1 of their article.

REFERENCES

Anastasi, J. S., & Rhodes, M. G. (2006). Evidence for an own-age bias in face recognition. *North American Journal of Psychology, 8*, 237–253.

Bartlett, J. C., Hurry, S., & Thorley, W. (1984). Typicality and familiarity of faces. *Memory and Cognition, 12*, 219–228.

Bartlett, J. C., & Leslie, J. E. (1986). Aging and memory for faces versus single views of faces. *Memory and Cognition, 14*, 371–381.

Bernstein, M., Young, S. G., & Hugenberg, K. (2007). The cross-category effect: Mere social categorization is sufficient to elicit an own-group bias in face recognition. *Psychological Science, 18*, 706–712.

Brigham, J. C., Maass, A., Martinez, D., & Whittenberger, G. (1983). The effect of arousal on facial recognition. *Basic and Applied Social Psychology, 4*, 279–293.

Bruce, V., & Young, A. (1986). Understanding face recognition. *British Journal of Psychology, 77*, 305–327.

Carlson, C., Gronlund, S. D., & Clark, S. E. (2010). Lineup composition, suspect position, and the sequential lineup advantage. *Journal of Experimental Psychology: Applied, 14*, 118–128.

Ceci, S. J., & Bruck, M. (1993). Suggestibility of the child witness: A historical review and synthesis. *Psychological Bulletin, 113*, 403–439.

Cohen, M. E., & Carr, W. J. (1975). Facial recognition and the von Restoff effect. *Bulletin of the Psychonomic Society, 6*, 383–384.

Cross, J. F., Cross, J., & Daly, J. (1971). Sex, race, age, and beauty as factors in recognition of faces. *Perception and Psychophysics, 10*, 393–396.

Cutler, B. L., Penrod, S. D., & Martens, T. (1987a). Improving the reliability of eyewitness identification: Putting context into context. *Journal of Applied Psychology, 72*, 629–637.

Cutler, B. L., Penrod, S. D., & Martens, T. (1987b). The reliability of eyewitness identification: The role of system and estimator variables. *Law and Human Behavior, 11*, 233–258.

Deffenbacher, K. A. (1994). Effects of arousal on everyday memory. *Human Performance, 7*, 141–161.

Deffenbacher, K. A., Bornstein, B. H., McGorty, K., & Penrod, S. D. (2008). Forgetting the once-seen face: Estimating the strength of an eyewitness's memory representation. *Journal of Experimental Psychology: Applied, 14*, 139–150.

DiNardo, L., & Rainey, D. W. (1991). The effects of illumination level and exposure time on facial recognition. *Psychological Record, 41*, 329–334.

Douglas, A. B., Smith, C., & Fraser-Thill, R. (2005). A problem with double-blind photospread procedures: Photospread administrators use one eyewitness's confidence to influence the identification of another eyewitness. *Law and Human Behavior, 29*, 543–562.

Easterbrook, J. A. (1959). The effect of emotion on cue utilization and the organization of behaviour. *Psychological Review, 66*, 183–201.

Enns, J. T. (2004). *The thinking eye, the seeing brain: Explorations in visual cognition*. New York, NY: W. W. Norton.

Erickson, W. B., Lampinen, J. M., & Leding, J. K. (2014). The weapon focus effect in target-present and target-absent line-ups: The roles of threat, novelty and timing. *Applied Cognitive Psychology, 28*, 349–359.

Erickson, W. B., Lampinen, J. M., & Moore, K. (2014). *A verdict on elderly eyewitness identification: A meta-analysis and discussion*. Manuscript submitted for publication.

Fazey, J. A., & Hardy, L. (1988). *The inverted-U hypothesis: A catastrophe for sport psychology* (British Association for Sports Sciences Monograph No. 1). Leeds, UK: National Coaching Foundation.

Felson, M., & Poulsen, E. (2003). Simple indicators of crime by time of day. *International Journal of Forecasting, 19,* 595–601.

Ferguson, D., Rhodes, G., Lee, K., & Sriram, N. (2001). "They all look alike to me": Prejudice and cross-race face recognition. *British Journal of Psychology, 92,* 567–577.

Florida Department of Law Enforcement. (2011). *Standards for Florida state and local law enforcement agencies in dealing with photographic or live lineups in eyewitness identification.* Retrieved from www.fdle.state.fl.us/Content/getdoc/327876c5-0464-4ecb-832a-79962c5e09a9/GuidelinesEyewitnessID.aspx

Foley, H. J., & Matlin, M. W. (2010). *Sensation and perception* (5th ed.). Boston, MA: Allyn & Bacon.

Fotios, S. A., & Cheal, C. (2007). Lighting for subsidiary streets: Investigation of lamps of different SPD. Part 1—Visual performance. *Lighting Research and Technology, 39,* 215–232.

Fulero, S. M., & Wrightsman, L. S. (2009). *Forensic psychology.* Belmont, CA: Wadsworth.

Going, M., & Read, J. D. (1974). Effects of uniqueness, sex of subject, and sex of photograph on facial recognition. *Perceptual and Motor Skills, 39,* 109–110.

Goldstein, E. B. (2007). *Sensation and perception* (7th ed.). Belmont, CA: Thomson Wadsworth.

Greathouse, S., & Kovera, M. B. (2009). Instruction bias and lineup presentation moderate the effects of administrator knowledge on eyewitness identification. *Law and Human Behavior, 33,* 70–82.

Hansen, M. (2001). Forensic science: Scoping out eyewitness IDs. *American Bar Association Journal, 87,* 39.

Haw, R. M., & Fisher, R. P. (2004). Effects of administrator-witness contact on eyewitness identification accuracy. *Journal of Applied Psychology, 89,* 1106–1112.

Hope, L., & Wright, D. (2007). Beyond unusual? Examining the role of attention in the weapon focus effect. *Applied Cognitive Psychology, 21,* 951–961.

Huff, C. R. (2003). Wrongful convictions: The American experience. *Canadian Journal of Criminology and Criminal Justice, 46,* 107–120.

Innocence Project. (2014). *The Innocence Project*. Retrieved from www .innocenceproject.org

Keast, A., Brewer, N., & Wells, G. L. (2007). Children's metacognitive judgments in an eyewitness identification task. *Journal of Experimental Child Psychology, 97,* 286–314.

Kelly, D., Quinn, P., Slater, A., Lee, K., Ge, L., & Pascalis, O. (2007). The other-race effect develops during infancy: Evidence of perceptual narrowing. *Psychological Science, 18,* 1084–1089.

Knight, C. (2010). Field surveys of the effect of lamp spectrum on the perception of safety and comfort at night. *Lighting Research and Technology, 42,* 313–329.

Kramer, T., Buckhout, R., & Eugenio, P. (1990). Weapon focus, arousal, and eyewitness memory: Attention must be paid. *Law and Human Behavior, 14,* 167–184.

Krouse, F. (1981). Effects of pose, pose change, and delay on face recognition performance. *Journal of Applied Psychology, 66*(5), 651–654.

Lamberts, K., & Freeman, R. P. J. (1999). Building object representations from parts: Tests of a stochastic sampling model. *Journal of Experimental Psychology: Human Perception and Performance, 25,* 904–926.

Lampinen, J. M., Erickson, W. B., Moore, K. N., & Hittson, A. (2014). Effects of distance on face recognition: Implications for eyewitness identification. *Psychonomic Bulletin and Review.* doi:10.3758/s13423-014-0641-2

Lampinen, J. M., Neuschatz, J. S., & Cling, A. (2012). *The psychology of eyewitness identification*. New York, NY: Psychology Press.

Light, L. L., Kayra-Stuart, F., & Hollander, S. (1979). Recognition memory for typical and unusual faces. *Journal of Experimental Psychology: Human Learning and Memory, 5,* 212–228.

Lindsay, R. C. L., & Wells, G. L. (1985). Improving eyewitness identification from lineups: Simultaneous versus sequential lineup presentations. *Journal of Applied Psychology, 70,* 556–564.

Loftus, E. F., Loftus, G. R., & Messo, J. (1987). Some facts about "weapon focus." *Law and Human Behavior, 11,* 55–62.

Loftus, G. R., & Harley, E. M. (2005). Why is it easier to identify someone closer than far away? *Psychonomic Bulletin and Review, 12,* 43–65.

Luus, C. A. E., & Wells, G. L. (1991). Eyewitness identification and the selection of distracters for lineups. *Law and Human Behavior, 15*, 43–57.

Malpass, R. S., & Devine, P. G. (1981). Eyewitness identification: Lineup instructions and the absence of the offender. *Journal of Applied Psychology, 66*, 482–489.

Malpass, R. S., Tredoux, C. G., & McQuiston-Surrett, D. (2007). Lineup construction and lineup fairness. In R. Lindsay, D. Ross, J. D. Read, & M. P. Toglia (Eds.), *Handbook of eyewitness psychology*, Vol. 2. *Memory for people* (pp. 87–100). Mahwah, NJ: Lawrence Erlbaum Associates.

Mason, S. E. (1986). Age and gender as factors in facial recognition and identification. *Experimental Aging Research, 12*, 151–154.

Meissner, C. A., & Brigham, J. C. (2001). Thirty years of investigating the own-race bias in memory for faces: A meta-analytic review. *Psychology, Public Policy, and Law, 7*, 3–35.

Memon, A., Hope, L., & Bull, R. (2003). Exposure duration: Effects on eyewitness accuracy and confidence. *British Journal of Psychology, 94*, 339–354.

Meyers, A., & Hanseen, C. (2012). *Experimental psychology*. Belmont, CA: Wadsworth.

Michel, C., Rossion, B., Han, J., Chung, C.-S., & Caldara, R. (2006). Holistic processing is finely tuned for faces of our own race. *Psychological Science, 17*, 608–615.

Moody, H. R., & Sasser, J. R. (2014). *Aging: Concepts and controversies*. Thousand Oaks, CA: Sage.

Morgan, C. A., Hazlett, G., Doran, A., Garrett, S., Hoyt, G., Thomas, P., . . . Southwick, S. M. (2004). Accuracy of eyewitness memory for persons encountered during exposure to highly intense stress. *International Journal of Law and Psychiatry, 27*, 265–279.

New York State Justice Task Force. (2011). *Recommendations for improving eyewitness identifications*. Retrieved from www.nyjusticetaskforce .com/2011_02_01_Report_ID_Reform.pdf

Office of Attorney General, State of Wisconsin. (2010). *Model policy and procedure for eyewitness identification*. Retrieved from www.doj .state.wi.us/dles/tns/eyewitnesspublic.pdf

Office of the Attorney General, New Jersey. (2001). *Attorney general guidelines for preparing and conducting photo and live identification procedures*. Retrieved from www.state.nj.us/lps/dcj/agguide/ photoid.pdf

Phillips, M. R., McAuliff, B. D., Kovera, M. B., & Cutler, B. L. (1999). Double-blind photoarray administration as a safeguard against investigator bias. *Journal of Applied Psychology, 84*, 940–951.

Pickel, K. L. (2007). Remembering and identifying menacing perpetrators: Exposure to violence and the weapon focus effect. In R. C. L. Lindsay, D. F. Ross, & M. P. Toglia (Eds.), *The handbook of eyewitness psychology*, Vol. 2. *Memory for people* (pp. 339–360). Mahwah, NJ: Erlbaum.

Pigott, M. A., Brigham, J. C., & Bothwell, R. K. (1990). Field study of the relationship between quality of eyewitnesses' descriptions and identification accuracy. *Journal of Police Science and Administration, 17*, 84–88.

Platz, S., & Hosch, H. (1988). Cross-racial/ethnic eyewitness identification: A field study. *Journal of Applied Social Psychology, 18*, 972–984.

Pozzulo, J., & Lindsay, R. (1998). Identification accuracy of children versus adults: A meta-analysis. *Law and Human Behavior, 22*, 549–570.

Pozzulo, J., & Lindsay, R. (1999). Elimination lineups: An improved identification procedure for child eyewitnesses. *Journal of Applied Psychology, 84*, 167–176.

Raynham, P., & Saksvikronning, T. (2003). White light and facial recognition. *Lighting Journal, 68*, 29–33.

Rea, M. S., Bullough, J. D., & Akashi, Y. (2009). Several views of metal halide and high-pressure sodium lighting for outdoor applications. *Lighting Research Technology, 41*, 297–320.

Read, J. D. (1995). The availability heuristic in person identification: The sometimes misleading consequences of enhanced contextual information. *Applied Cognitive Psychology, 9*, 91–121.

Rosenthal, R. (1976). *Experimenter effects in behavioral research.* New York, NY: Irvington.

Rosenthal, R. (1994). Interpersonal expectancy effects: A 30-year perspective. *Current Directions in Psychological Science, 3*, 176–179.

Rosenthal, R., & Fode, K. L. (1961). The problem of experimenter outcome bias. In D. P. Ray (Ed.), *Series research in social psychology.* Washington, DC: National Institute of Social and Behavioral Research.

Scheck, B., Neufeld, P., & Dwyer, J. (2000). *Actual innocence.* New York, NY: Random House.

Searcy, J. H., Bartlett, J. C., & Memon, A. (1999). Age differences in accuracy and choosing in eyewitness identification and face recognition. *Memory & Cognition, 27*, 538–552.

Sheperd, J. W., Gibling, F., & Ellis, H. D. (1991). The effects of distinctiveness, presentation time, and delay on face recognition. *European Journal of Cognitive Psychology, 3*, 137–145.

Slater, A. (1994). *Identification parades: A scientific evaluation.* Police Research Award Scheme. London, UK: Police Research Group, Home Office.

Smith, A. D., & Winograd, E. (1978). Adult age differences in remembering faces. *Developmental Psychology, 14*, 443–444.

Steblay, N. M. (1997). Social influences in eyewitness recall: A meta-analytic review of lineup instruction effects. *Law and Human Behavior, 21*, 283–297.

Steblay, N. M., Dysart, J., Fulero, S., & Lindsay, R. C. L. (2001). Eyewitness accuracy rates in police showup and lineup presentations: A meta-analytic comparison. *Law and Human Behavior, 27*, 523–540.

Technical Working Group for Eyewitness Evidence. (1999). *Eyewitness evidence: A guide for law enforcement.* Washington, DC: U.S. Department of Justice.

Thompson-Cannino, J., Cotton, R., & Torneo, E. (2009). *Picking cotton: Our memoir of injustice and redemption.* New York, NY: St. Martin's Press.

Tooley, V., Brigham, J., Maass, A., & Bothwell, R. (1987). Facial recognition: Weapon effect and attentional focus. *Journal of Applied Social Psychology, 17*, 845–859.

Valentine, T. (1991). A unified account of the effects of distinctiveness, inversion, and race in face recognition. *Quarterly Journal of Experimental Psychology, 43A*, 161–204.

Valentine, T., & Bruce, V. (1986). Recognizing familiar faces: The role of distinctiveness and familiarity. *Canadian Journal of Psychology, 40*, 300–305.

Valentine, T., & Heaton, P. (1999). An evaluation of the fairness of police line-ups and video identifications. *Applied Cognitive Psychology, 13*, S59–S72.

Valentine, T., Pickering, A., & Darling, S. (2003). Characteristics of eyewitness identification that predict the outcome of real lineups. *Applied Cognitive Psychology, 17*, 969–993.

Verhaeghen, P., & Marcoen, A. (1993). Memory aging as a general phenomenon: Episodic recall of older adults is a function of episodic recall of young adults. *Psychology and Aging, 8*, 380–388.

Verhaeghen, P., Marcoen, A., & Goossens, L. (1993). Facts and fiction about memory aging: A quantitative integration of research findings. *Journal of Gerontology: Psychological Sciences, 48*, P157–P171.

Weiser, B. (2012). New Jersey court issues guidance for juries about reliability of eyewitnesses. *New York Times.* July 19, 2012. Retrieved from www.nytimes.com/2012/07/20/nyregion/judges-must-warn-new-jersey-jurors-about-eyewitnesses-reliability.html?_r=0

Wells, G. L. (1978). Applied eyewitness testimony research: System variables and estimator variables. *Journal of Personality and Social Psychology, 36*, 1546–1557.

Wells, G. L. (1984). The psychology of lineup identifications. *Journal of Applied Social Psychology, 14*, 89–103.

Wells, G. L. (n.d.). *Bad and good lineups.* Retrieved from www.psychology.iastate.edu/~glwells/badandgoodlineups.htm

Wells, G. L., Leippe, M. R., & Ostrom, T. M. (1979). Guidelines for empirically assessing the fairness of a lineup. *Law and Human Behavior, 3*, 285–293.

Wells, G. L., & Luus, C. A. E. (1990). Police lineups as experiments. *Personality and Social Psychology Bulletin, 16*, 106–117.

Wells, G. L., Small, M., Penrod, S. J., Malpass, R. S., Fulero, S. M., & Brimacombe, C. A. E. (1998). Eyewitness identification procedures: Recommendations for lineups and photospreads. *Law and Human Behavior, 22*, 603–647.

Wells, G. L., Steblay, N. K., & Dysart, J. E. (2011). *A test of simultaneous vs. sequential lineup methods.* Des Moines, IA: American Judicature Society.

Wickham, L. H. V., Morris, P. E., & Fritz, C. O. (2000). Facial distinctiveness: Its measurement, distribution and influence on immediate and delayed recognition. *British Journal of Psychology, 91*, 99–123.

Wilcock, R., & Bull, R. (2009). Novel lineup methods for improving the performance of older eyewitnesses. *Applied Cognitive Psychology, 24*, 718–736.

Winograd, E. (1981). Elaboration and distinctiveness in memory for faces. *Journal of Experimental Psychology: Human Learning and Memory, 7*, 181–190.

Wright, D. B., & McDaid, A. T. (1996). Comparing system and estimator variables using data from real line-ups. *Applied Cognitive Psychology, 10*, 75–84.

CHAPTER 4

Yerkes, R. M., & Dodson, J. D. (1908). The relation of strength of stimulus to rapidity of habit-formation. *Journal of Comparative Neurology and Psychology, 18,* 459–482.

Yurov, S. G. (1967). Photopic, mesopic, and scotopic vision. *Applied Optics, 6,* 1877–1883.

Remembering to Take the Cupcakes Out of the Oven: Prospective Memory

H ave you ever rented a movie, taken it home and watched it, and then forgot to return it the next day?[1] Have you ever purchased one of those reusable grocery bags so that you can do your part for the environment, and then when you get to the store, you realize you've left the bag at home? Have you ever gone to the store specifically to get one thing and returned home with a bag full of groceries only to realize that you forgot to pick up the very item you went to the store to get? Have you ever taken a bill, or birthday card, or other important correspondence with you, and forgotten to drop it in the mail, even though you passed several mailboxes during the day? Have you ever forgotten a meeting or an assignment that was due on a particular date? If you've had any of these types of experiences, you've experienced a failure in *prospective memory* (McDaniel & Einstein, 2007).

Prospective memory refers to memory for actions that you intend to engage in at some point in the future (Ellis, 1996). Prospective memory is typically contrasted with retrospective memory—memory for things in the past (Burgess & Shallice, 1997). Over the past century, psychologists have put a great deal of effort into understanding retrospective memory, but for most of the century, prospective memory has been given short shrift. This is odd. A huge number of the memory failures people report experiencing on a daily basis are errors of the type just described. Recently, however, this has been changing, and there is now a large and growing body of research trying to understand how prospective memory operates, the effect prospective memory has on our lives, and how prospective memory can be improved. Figure 5.1 shows the average annual number of

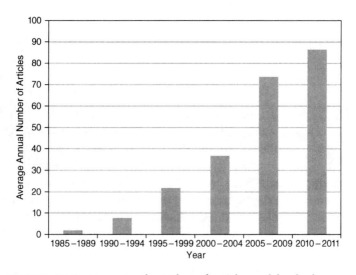

FIGURE 5.1 Average annual number of articles and book chapters dealing with the topic of prospective memory.

TABLE 5.1 **QUESTIONS FROM THE PROSPECTIVE AND RETROSPECTIVE MEMORY QUESTIONNAIRE (PRMQ)**

1	Do you decide to do something in a few minutes' time and then forget to do it?
2	Do you fail to recognize a place you have visited before?
3	Do you fail to do something you were supposed to do a few minutes later even though it's there in front of you, like take a pill or turn off the kettle?
4	Do you forget something that you were told a few minutes before?
5	Do you forget appointments if you are not prompted by someone else or by a reminder such as a calendar or diary?
6	Do you fail to recognize a character in a radio or television show from scene to scene?
7	Do you forget to buy something you planned to buy, like a birthday card, even when you see the shop?
8	Do you fail to recall things that have happened to you in the last few days?
9	Do you repeat the same story to the same person on different occasions?
10	Do you intend to take something with you, before leaving a room or going out, but minutes later leave it behind, even though it's there in front of you?
11	Do you mislay something that you have just put down, like a magazine or glasses?
12	Do you fail to mention or give something to a visitor that you were asked to pass on?
13	Do you look at something without realizing you have seen it moments before?
14	If you tried to contact a friend or relative who was out, would you forget to try again later?
15	Do you forget what you watched on television the previous day?
16	Do you forget to tell someone something you had meant to mention a few minutes ago?

Questions reprinted from Smith, Della Sala, Logie, and Maylor (2000). Copyright 2000, Taylor & Francis Ltd, www.tandfonline.com, reprinted by permission of the publisher.

publications dealing with prospective memory in 5-year intervals. We think you'll agree: Business is booming for researchers who study prospective memory.

To get a sense of your own prospective memory, have a look at the questionnaire shown in Table 5.1. These questions are from the Prospective and Retrospective Memory Questionnaire (PRMQ) (Crawford, Henry, Ward, & Blake, 2006; Crawford, Smith, Maylor, Della Sala, & Logie, 2003; Smith, Della Sala, Logie, & Maylor, 2000). The questionnaire lists different ways your memory might fail you and asks you to indicate how often you experience that kind of memory failure using a 5-point scale (1 = never; 5 = very often). Take a second to complete the questionnaire for yourself before turning back to the text. . . . Okay, done yet? Questions 1, 3, 5, 7, 10, 12, 14, and 16 refer to different types of prospective memory failures. If you add up your points on those eight items, you could get a prospective memory score of anything from 8 (you are the master of prospective memory) to 40 (you are the joker of prospective memory). So how did you do? The average person gets a score of around 20 (Crawford et al., 2003). More than 75% of people score somewhere between 14 and 26.

THE NATURE AND STRUCTURE OF PROSPECTIVE MEMORY

If you think about the prospective memory questions that are on the PRMQ, you'll notice that they refer to a range of slightly different kinds of situations. For instance, think about question 5. It asks whether you forget appointments if someone doesn't remind you or if you don't consult a calendar. This kind of prospective memory is known as *time-based prospective memory (TBPM)*. It involves remembering to do something at a particular time or after a certain amount of time has passed (Aberle & Kliegel, 2010; Cook, Marsh, & Hicks, 2005; Huang, Loft, & Humphreys, 2014; Kvavilashvili & Fisher, 2007; Mackinlay, Kliegel, & Mäntylä, 2009;

Mäntylä, Del Missier, & Nilsson, 2009). Question 7, on the other hand, says "Do you forget to buy something you planned to buy, like a birthday card, even when you see the shop?" This type of prospective memory is called *event-based prospective memory (EBPM)*. It occurs when people rely on some cue in the environment to remind them of the thing they were supposed to do (Guynn, McDaniel, & Einstein, 1998; Marsh, Hicks, Hancock, & Munsayac, 2002; Rendell & Craik, 2000). In the example, if you need to buy a birthday card, and you see a Hallmark store, then ideally seeing the store should remind you to buy the card. Time-based and event-based prospective memory are slightly different systems.

One of the most famous experiments on time-based prospective memory involved 10- and 14-year-old children who were asked to take cupcakes out of the oven half an hour after putting them in the oven (Ceci & Bronfenbrenner, 1985). There was a big clock on the wall so that children could check when the 30 minutes was up. However, 15 minutes before putting the cupcakes in the oven, children were given access to an engaging video game and were allowed to continue to play the video game during the entire course of the experiment. The video game and clock were in a different room entirely from the oven. Other children did an analogous task that involved removing battery cables from a motorcycle battery after it had charged for 30 minutes. Children of both ages spent a good deal of time looking at the clock during the first 10 minutes. The researchers concluded that this was a *calibration stage*, during which the children were getting a sense for how long the task was taking. This was followed by a period of around 10 to 15 minutes when clock checking dropped down to essentially nothing. Then, in the last 5 to 10 minutes, as the deadline approached, clock checking became increasingly common so that the children could complete the task right on time. The authors concluded that even 10-year-olds can engage in fairly sophisticated strategies for time-based prospective memory.

For an example of an event-based prospective memory experiment, consider an interesting study by Breneiser and McDaniel

(2006). Participants were asked to rate a group of words for how pleasant they were, how concrete they were, how familiar they were, and how meaningful they were. Participants were also told that if they saw two words (e.g., spaghetti and thread) that they should press a response key. There were a total of 52 words rated. The two prospective memory targets had only been seen once previously, when participants had gotten the instructions. The 50 nontarget words had been seen either twice previously (low discrepancy) or five times previously (high discrepancy). In the high-discrepancy condition, participants correctly identified more than three quarters of the prospective memory targets. In the low-discrepancy condition, only about half were identified. The authors reasoned that the prospective memory targets seemed more distinctive when all the nontarget words had been studied many, many times, and that made them stick out like a sore thumb. You can check out your own prospective memory if you want. If at any point while reading this chapter you encounter a type of breakfast cereal, you should clap your hands. Don't forget!

One important distinction between time-based and event-based prospective memory is that in time-based prospective memory, the reminding is self-generated (Craik, 1986). There is nothing in the environment to tell you to engage in the activity. In event-based prospective memory, on the other hand, there is a cue in the environment that can help you to remember what to do. Because of that, event-based prospective memory is typically easier than time-based prospective memory. This was demonstrated in an experiment by Khan, Sharma, and Dixit (2008). Participants answered multiple-choice, general-knowledge questions. The questions and answers appeared on the screen for 15 seconds, and participants answered the question by selecting a response on the right side of the screen. The general-knowledge test lasted 30 minutes, and for half that time, the participants' attention was divided by having them listen to a story while they were answering questions. Half the participants were to make a response on the left of the screen every 5 minutes (time-based prospective memory task), and half the participants were supposed to make a response on the left of the screen every time one of three words appeared in the question or answer (event-based task). These words occurred every 5 minutes, although participants were not aware of this. Dividing attention interfered with both types of prospective memory but had a bigger effect on time-based prospective memory.

Prospective memory is a complex, multifaceted skill. Most researchers agree that prospective memory involves both a prospective and a retrospective component (Einstein & McDaniel, 1990, 1996; Smith & Bayen, 2004; Zimmerman & Meier, 2010). To illustrate, imagine if I were to tell you that next time you hear the word "snorkel," you should dial a particular 10-digit number into your phone.[2] Imagine that 7 years, 3 months, and 2 days from now you hear somebody say "Snorkel!" and yet your phone stays in its holster. You have miserably failed this prospective memory task. But would this really be a failure in prospective memory per se? In a way, yes—you didn't engage in the delayed intention. But it is not really a failure in prospective memory in any meaningful way. Because you probably wouldn't even be able to tell us what the crucial word was if we asked you, nor could you probably tell us what the phone number was, nor even that you were supposed to make a phone call. Every prospective memory task involves a prospective component and a retrospective component. In a lot of experiments, the retrospective component is made easy so that researchers can focus their attention on the prospective component. But in real life, both components are important.

BASIC THEORIES OF EVENT-BASED PROSPECTIVE MEMORY

There has been an ongoing debate among researchers who study prospective memory about the mental processes involved. To understand that debate, it is necessary to understand the distinction between automatic and strategic processes (Hasher &

Zacks, 1979). Automatic and strategic processes have to do with the role of attention in performing a task. Strategic processes are those that require focused attention. They are effortful. They are demanding. They require your full attention, and you aren't able to do other things when you are doing them. Think, for instance, about doing long division. Most people, even people who are pretty darn good at math, can't do long division while having a conversation with someone about geopolitics. The long division requires your full attention. The geopolitics requires your full attention. You have to choose to concentrate on one or the other. Automatic processes, on the other hand, happen without intention, require little focused attention, and don't interfere with other tasks. You can walk and chew gum at the same time, because both walking and chewing gum require such little attention that they are unlikely to get in each other's way. Some theories of prospective memory assert that prospective memory is always automatic (Graf & Uttl, 2001). Some theories of prospective memory assert that performing a prospective memory task always requires focused attention (Smith, 2003). Other theories claim that under certain circumstances, prospective memory retrieval requires focused attention, and at other times, prospective memory retrieval can occur automatically, without focused attention (Einstein et al., 2005). Let's see who is right.

Preparatory Attention and Memory (PAM) Processes Model Versus Multiprocess Theory

Some researchers claim that prospective memory always occurs automatically (Graf & Uttl, 2001). To understand this claim, it's important to make a distinction between tasks that require vigilance and tasks that require prospective memory. Imagine, for instance, that you are working in airport security as an employee of the Transportation Safety Administration (TSA). You are working at a luggage x-ray machine keeping an eye out for bombs, guns, knives, and whatnot. Theorists typically argue that tasks like these are not prospective memory tasks, because in performing the tasks, you are constantly searching for the target items. In other words, there's nothing for you to retrieve from memory, because the things you are looking for are already in memory. The tasks are thus called *vigilance* tasks instead. According to this view, by definition, for something to be a prospective memory task, you have to be consciously attending to something else when the reminding occurs. So arguably, prospective memory never involves focused attention. Q.E.D.

Rebekah Smith (2003) proposed a model that claims that focused attention is always needed to successfully use prospective memory. The theory is called the preparatory attention and memory (PAM) processes model. According to the theory, successful prospective memory retrieval can only happen when preparatory attention and memory processes are used. One simple kind of preparatory attention and memory process might simply be checking. As each item is presented, you just ask yourself, "Is this one of the items?" Or you might engage in intermittent checking. In other words, you go about the ongoing task, but every now and then think, "Oh wait, I was supposed to be looking for something. Let's see, is this one of the items?" But preparatory attention and memory processes don't have to be as explicit as those examples imply. They may simply be an orientation toward retrieval that one maintains during the course of the task. An important assumption of the PAM theory is that these preparatory attention and memory processes take cognitive resources, making it harder for you to perform other tasks.

One prediction of the PAM theory is that it should be harder to do something else while also performing a prospective memory task than when you aren't also doing a prospective memory task. For instance, imagine you are at Penguin Ed's Barbeque having a conversation with your friend Denise about quantum mechanics over a plate of pulled pork. Denise asks you to flag down the server next time you see him, because she needs some more wet wipes. So while you are trying to make a lucid point about quantum indeterminacy, you are also keeping an eye out not just for any server, but for your particular server. You might imagine, under those circumstances, that your ability to hold your own in the conversation would be impaired.

A number of experiments have found that performing a prospective memory task impairs performance on the ongoing task. In one study, participants studied six words and were told to press the F1 key on their keyboard if they saw the words during the experiment (Smith, 2003). Other participants studied the same words but they did not have to make a response immediately upon seeing the words. Participants then performed a *lexical decision task*. They saw 126 strings of letters. Some of the letter strings formed words (e.g., life), but others did not (e.g., bife). Participants had to indicate as quickly as they could whether each letter string was a word. Participants were about a third of a second slower on the lexical decision task when they had to look for the prospective memory words than when they didn't, indicating that the prospective memory task was taking up cognitive resources. Smith and colleagues have found this to be the case even when looking for something as simple as one's own name (Smith, Hunt, McVay, & McConnell, 2007).

Still other theorists believe that prospective memory retrieval sometimes requires focused attention and sometimes does not (Einstein et al., 2005; McDaniel & Einstein, 2000). This, the multiprocess view, has been proposed by McDaniel and Einstein (no, not *that* Einstein). According to the multiprocess view, when the association between the prospective memory target and the intended action is very strong, then prospective memory retrieval may happen automatically. McDaniel and Einstein (2000) note that prospective memory retrieval is similar to cued recall (see Chapter 2) and that cued recall sometimes occurs automatically, unbidden. Think about it. Haven't you had the experience of walking down the street, seeing an old friend, and suddenly remembering a shared event, or that he or she owes you $5? Multiprocess theory appeals to the same kind of "reflexive associative memory system" (McDaniel, Guynn, Einstein, & Breneiser, 2004). We've all certainly had those kinds of spontaneous reminding of obligations, such as seeing a thesis student at the coffee shop and remembering that we've forgotten to reply to her or his e-mail with a thesis question—the cold stare makes that reminder all the more stark. That is an event-based prospective memory and phenomenologically appears to occur in a reflexive and automatic manner.

According to the theory (Einstein et al., 2005; McDaniel & Einstein, 2000), the following factors make it more likely that spontaneous prospective memories will occur: (1) The association between the prospective memory target and the intended action is strong, (2) the ongoing task and the prospective memory task overlap in terms of the type of information that they make use of, and (3) the prospective memory target is very salient. When those factors are present (bing!), you get a quick, spontaneous, low effect retrieval of the delayed intention.

An important determinant of whether prospective memory occurs automatically is whether the type of processing required by the ongoing task and the type of processing required by the prospective memory task overlap (Scullin, McDaniel, & Einstein, 2010). When they do, it is called a *focal* prospective memory task. When they don't, it is called a nonfocal task. For instance, in one experiment, participants engaged in an ongoing task that involved a lexical decision task. The prospective memory target was "tortoise" in the focal task, whereas it was simply the syllable "tor" in the nonfocal task. In the control condition, participants didn't have any prospective memory task at all. Response times for the ongoing task were slower when people were looking for the syllable "tor" but not when they were looking for the word "tortoise." According to the multiprocess view, this occurred because the focal cue led to the automatic retrieval of the prospective memory, but the nonfocal cue required constantly monitoring for the syllable, which slowed down responding on the ongoing task.

The jury is still out as to which of these views is correct. However, theorists have also proceeded in other directions in trying to explain prospective memory. Two of these theories are described in the paragraphs that follow.

Multinomial Model of Prospective Memory

One of these more formal theories of prospective memory is called the MPT model (Smith & Bayen, 2004). MPT stands for multinomial process tree model. To understand the theory, it is necessary to remind ourselves of some very simple ideas about how probabilities can be combined.

1. This *and* that: Let's say that I tell you that I will give you $15 if you flip a coin and it comes up heads and you roll a die and it lands on a 2. What are the odds that you'll be $15 richer? You can think about this by using a probability tree. The probability is 1/2 that you'll end up with a heads and 1/2 that you'll end up with a tails. If you get a tails, what happens with the die doesn't matter. But if you end up with heads, then the die has to land on 2 for you to win. The chance you'll get a 2 is 1/6 and the chance that you won't get a 2 is 5/6. So altogether your chance of winning the $15 is 1/6 of 1/2, or 1/12. The rule is: Probability of this and that = probability of this × probability of that (as long as this and that are independent of each other).

2. This *or* that: Let's say that I tell you that I'll give you $20 if you roll a 2 or a 4. The probability of rolling a 2 is 1/6. The probability of rolling a 4 is 1/6. So the probability of rolling a 2 or a 4 is 2/6. The rule is: The probability of this *or* that = probability of this + probability of that (as long as this and that are mutually exclusive).

3. *Not* this. Say that I give you $20 as long as you don't pick a diamond from a pack of cards. The probability of picking a diamond is 1/4. The probability of not picking a diamond is 3/4. The rule: The probability of *not* this = 1 − the probability of this.

An MPT model is one in which there is more than one way a particular outcome can occur (e.g., this can happen OR that can happen OR this other thing can happen) and each of those possibilities requires multiple things to happen (e.g., this has to happen AND this other thing has to happen AND this third thing has to happen).

To give you an idea of the MPT model, it's easiest to use an example of the task Smith and Bayen had students perform (2004). Like any event-based prospective memory experiment, there was both a prospective memory task and an ongoing task. The prospective memory task was to press the tilde ($\sim$) key on a keyboard if one of six specific words appeared. For the ongoing task, students were shown four colored squares, and then immediately afterward, they were shown a word that either was or was not in one of those four colors. They were supposed to say "yes" if the color matched and "no" if the color didn't match, but in any case to press the tilde key if the word was one of the prospective memory words.

The way this task was set up means that there were four types of trials: (1) prospective memory target present and the color matches, (2) prospective memory target present and the color doesn't match, (3) prospective memory target absent and the color matches, and (4) prospective memory target absent and the color doesn't match. Let's just consider one of these cases (prospective memory target present and color matches) and see how Smith and Bayen (2004) analyzed the possible ways to get successful prospective memory. Their tree diagram is shown in Figure 5.2. There are basically four ways that you could make the prospective memory response (press the tilde key) when the prospective memory target is present and the color matches.

1. Route 1: You notice that the color matches with a probability of C1 *and* you devote some attention to looking for the prospective memory target with a probability P ("P" stands for preparatory attention) *and* you retrieve the prospective memory target from memory with a probability of M. So route 1 happens with a probability of C1 $\times$ P $\times$ M.
2. Route 2: You notice that the color matches with a probability of C1 *and* you devote some attention to looking for the

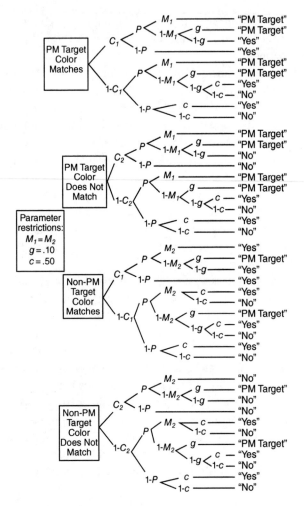

FIGURE 5.2 Multinomial processing tree (MPT) model.
Reprinted from Smith and Bayen (2004). Copyright 2004, American Psychological Association. Reprinted with permission.

prospective memory target with a probability P ("P" stands for preparatory attention) *and* you fail to retrieve the prospective memory target from memory with a probability of $(1 - M)$ *but* you just happen to guess that the prospective memory target is present with a probability of g. So route 2 happens with a probability of C1 $\times$ P $\times$ (1 – M) $\times$ g.

3. Route 3: You don't notice that the color matches with a probability of (1 – C1), *but* you devote some attention to looking for the prospective memory target with a probability of P *and* you retrieve the prospective memory target from memory with a probability of M. So route 3 happens with a probability of (1 – C1) $\times$ P $\times$ M.

4. Route 4: You don't notice that the color matches with a probability of (1 – C1), *but* you devote some attention to looking for the prospective memory target with a probability P ("P" stands for preparatory attention) *and* you fail to retrieve the prospective memory target from memory with a probability of (1 – M) *but* you just happen to guess that the prospective memory target is present with a probability of g. So route 2 happens with a probability of (1 – C1) $\times$ P $\times$ (1 – M) $\times$ g.

To get the total probability, it is a matter of route 1 or route 2 or route 3 or route 4 happening. Taking our rules, that means you add up the aforementioned four probabilities. What's neat about a theory like this is that it shows you explicitly all the different ways that you can get to a prospective memory response. It also gives you a way to estimate the various values of C1 and P and M and g and so on if you know the outcome of the experiment.

Prospective Memory Diffusion Race (PMDR) Model

McDaniel College professor Jack Arnal came up with another way of describing why event-based prospective memory can be so hard by his race model of prospective memory (Arnal & Lampinen, 2009). Arnal's theory is based on the *diffusion model* of recognition (Ratcliff, 1978; Ratcliff, Gomez, & McKoon, 2004; Ratcliff & Rouder, 2000). Here's how diffusion models work: Imagine that you are standing on the 50-yard line of a football field. There are red and green marbles in a football helmet. You randomly pick a marble from the helmet. If it's green, you walk 10 yards toward the green end zone. If it's red, you walk 10 yards toward the red end zone. Because there are both red and green marbles in the helmet, you'll zigzag back and forth on the field. Sometimes though, even if the number of red and green marbles is even, you'll get a run of a bunch of red in a row or a run of a bunch of green in a row. Given enough time, and enough marbles, eventually you'll cross one of the goal lines and end up in either the north or south end zone—touchdown!

One thing that can influence which end zone you end up in, and how fast you get there, is how many red versus green marbles there are. If there are 11 green marbles for every 10 red marbles, then you're more likely to end up in the green end zone, but sometimes you'll end up in the red end zone because, just by chance, you pick a bunch of red ones in a row. If there are 12 green for every 10 red, the odds of ending up in the green end zone goes up. If there are 15 green for every 10 red, the odds go up even more. Not only do the odds of ending up in the red or green end zone depend on the relative number of red versus green marbles, but they also influence how quickly you end up there. The more uneven the number of marbles, the faster you'll end up in one end zone versus another. In the diffusion model, this is called the *drift rate*.

Another thing that can influence which end zone you end up in, and how quickly you get there, is where you start out. That is, instead of starting at the 50-yard line, you might start at the 40-yard line, closer to the red end zone than the green end zone. Everything else being equal, if you start closer to the red end zone, you're more likely to end up in the red end zone, and you'll get there more quickly than the times you end up in the green end zone. In the diffusion model, where you start out on the field is called the *bias*.

The diffusion model is a theory of recognition that works in a way analogous to the aforementioned example. Imagine that, taking a test, you are asked "Is Joplin the capital of Missouri?" According to the diffusion model, to answer that question, you sample information from memory. You sample one bit of information from memory, and that piece of information either makes you more likely or less likely to believe that Joplin is the capital of Missouri. If the information seems to support the idea of Joplin's being the Show Me State's capital, then you take a step toward a "yes" response. If the information seems to contradict the idea of Joplin's being the capital of the Show Me State, then you take a step toward a "no" response. Across time, you sample piece of information after piece of information, each time taking a step toward either yes or no. Eventually, you cross a threshold that causes you to answer the question one way or the other.

Typically, if the answer to the question is "yes," and if you have previously studied the information carefully, there will be a lot more information in memory consistent with yes than with no. The drift rate will be high, and you should respond quickly and accurately most of the time. If you don't know much about the subject, the drift rate will be around 50%. So you'll get the answer wrong more often, and you'll be slower in responding. There'll be lots of zigging and zagging. And just as in the football field example, your speed and accuracy can also be influenced by your bias. For instance, if you have a predilection to respond "yes" to questions (i.e., you are a yeasayer!), then you might start closer to the "yes" boundary than the "no" question. Thus, you'll be more likely to say yes, and you'll say yes faster than you'll say no. A nice feature of the diffusion model (Figure 5.3) is that it not only does a good job of accounting for how accurate people are, but it also can account for the overall shape of reaction time distributions.

Jack Arnal applied this model to the problem of event-based prospective memory (Arnal & Lampinen, 2009). Participants completed a lexical decision task as their ongoing task. At the same time, participants were supposed to be looking for six prospective memory targets (e.g., KNOB) and to hit the "Q" key on their keyboard if they saw one of the target words. Arnal argued that essentially there were two diffusion processes going on at the same time. The first diffusion process concerned the lexical

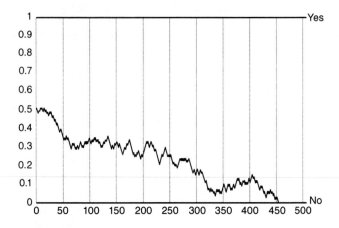

FIGURE 5.3 Illustration of the diffusion model.
Note: This shows a single run of the diffusion model. At each time unit, the model takes a step toward the YES boundary with a probability of .45 and a step toward the NO boundary with a probability of .55. In this example, the model crossed the NO boundary in about 450 time steps.

decision task. People were sampling information from the letter string. With each piece of information, they were determining whether it supported the item being a word or if it disconfirmed the item being a word. Based on that, they took a step toward either the yes or the no boundary for the lexical decision task. Simultaneously, participants were sampling information from the letter string and comparing it to information stored in memory to see if it was one of the prospective memory targets. If the information was consistent with its being one of the targets, they took a step toward making the prospective memory response; otherwise, they took a step away from the prospective memory response. Because two diffusion processes were going on at the same time, Arnal concluded that failure to make the prospective memory response sometimes occurs because the lexical decision diffusion process terminates before the prospective memory process terminates. What's nice about this is that it gives a natural way of thinking about how the ongoing task and the prospective memory task interfere with each other. We jump the gun and complete the ongoing task before we even realize that an opportunity exists to respond to the prospective memory target.

WHY SHOULD YOU CARE ABOUT PROSPECTIVE MEMORY?

In this chapter, we described some research and theories dealing with prospective memory, but you may be asking yourself, "Why should I care about this stuff?" The answer is really simple. Everybody has goals in life, things they are trying to accomplish, things that they want to do, or need to do, things they'll get in trouble for if they don't do. Sometimes it's possible to act on a goal right away, but sometimes what you need to accomplish a goal (i.e., the enabling conditions) isn't available, or the thing you want to do can only be accomplished at a certain time, and that time isn't now. Because you can't always act on your intentions right away, sometimes you need to put those intentions on the back burner to act on them when the time is right. But of course that requires you to remember them—and, not only that, to remember those intentions at exactly the right time and place. There are a number of situations in which failure to remember delayed intentions can be inconvenient, or expensive (like forgetting to return your Redbox movie), or socially awkward (like forgetting a planned outing with a friend), or detrimental to a relationship (like forgetting a spouse's birthday). But prospective memory failure can have larger, more dire consequences as well. Here are some examples.

Medication Adherence

With the baby boom generation getting older, chronic medical conditions such as heart disease, diabetes, and HIV infection are affecting a larger and larger percentage of the population (World Health Organization, 2005). These conditions often require complicated treatment regimens, with patients taking multiple doses of multiple drugs at specific times of day. Full compliance with these treatment plans hovers at around 50% (Dunbar-Jacob et al., 2000). Part of the problem is poor prospective memory. Patients will sometimes fail to take their medication at the right time because they get involved in some other task and the medication simply slips their minds. At other times, a patient may forget having taken a drug and later take a dose when he or she is not supposed to. Studies have shown that laboratory-based prospective memory tasks reliably predict which patients will have the greatest difficulty adhering to their prescribed treatment plan (Zogg et al., 2012).

Air Traffic Control

In 1991, a fatal accident occurred in Los Angeles when a plane landed on a runway already occupied by another plane (Loft & Remington, 2010). The plane should have been cleared for take-off before allowing the other plane to land, but the air traffic controller forgot to do so, and 34 people were killed in the crash. In a review of 3 years of data from UK air traffic controllers, Shorrock (2005) concluded that these sorts of memory errors are a major impediment to the effectiveness of air traffic controllers. Loft and Remington (2010) point out that prospective memory is constantly being used by air traffic controllers, because they commonly get requests for actions that cannot be performed until the plane gets in a certain sector of airspace.

One way errors occur is "habit capture" (Loft & Remington, 2010). The air traffic controller gets used to doing things one way and has difficulty overcoming that habit. To demonstrate this problem, Loft and Remington had participants perform a simulated air traffic control task. Participants monitored an air traffic control display with 10 aircraft displayed at the start and more aircraft coming into the display. The participants had to accept aircraft into the airspace and resolve conflicts to prevent midair collisions. Some participants mostly dealt with aircraft speed, whereas other participants mostly with aircraft altitude.

Thus participants developed a habit of looking mostly for one type of issue. The researchers were interested in whether this habit capture would make it harder for them to notice the other type of problem. Results confirmed this hypothesis.

Prospective Person Memory

When police are looking for someone—a wanted fugitive, a missing kid—they will sometimes release the person's picture to the general public in hopes that someone will recognize the person and contact authorities. Recently researchers have noted that these situations rely on a type of memory called prospective person memory (Lampinen, Arnal, & Hicks, 2009). Imagine you are home watching the television and a breaking news alert interrupts your favorite reality TV show. The alert shows you a picture of a man who just recently escaped from a maximum security prison. You're told to be on the lookout for the criminal—if you see him, you should call the authorities. Clearly, this is a prospective memory task. The guy isn't right there in the room with you (hopefully). Rather, you have to store away in memory an intention that you can't immediately act upon, and if at some point in the future you encounter the person, you have to retrieve that intention from memory to act upon it. How do you think you would do if you were in that situation—that is, you saw a news alert about someone wanted by authorities and then the next day you actually encountered that person? Research indicates that most people are pretty bad at this. In one recent study, researchers showed intact classes professional-quality mock missing-persons alerts showing two individuals (Lampinen, Erickson, Peters, Sweeney, & Culbertson-Faegre, 2012). Students were told that if they saw either of the individuals, they could win up to $200. Half the classes saw a video each week for 6 weeks (each week with different missing people). The other half of the classes saw a single video during the sixth week of the study. After the video presentation on the sixth week of classes, the people shown in the video were staged so that they were standing at the building exits—students had to walk right past one of them to leave the building. In the single-video condition, right around 10% of students made identifications. In the six-video condition, it was even worse: Only 1.35% of students made identifications.

Programs that display missing child posters often display a large number of posters in the hopes that members of the general public will encounter one of the missing children and contact authorities. However, increasing the number of children to be looked for may decrease the odds of noticing any particular child. Lampinen, Peters, and Gier (2012) had participants look at missing child posters displayed on a bulletin board for as long as they wanted. For some participants, the bulletin board had four missing child posters. For other participants, the bulletin board had 12 missing child posters. Participants then engaged in a laboratory-based prospective person memory task. Participants were asked to imagine that they were camp counselors and that they were to create two teams—a P team and a Q team. They were presented with pictures of a large number of children and were to assign them to these two teams, keeping the number of boys and girls equal on the two teams. Participants were told that if they saw one of the "missing" children that they should press "H" to "alert authorities." Overall prospective person memory accuracy was higher in the four-poster condition, although this primarily occurred because of an increase in false alarms in the 12-poster condition.

Another factor that may influence prospective person memory is whether one is able to develop a viewpoint-independent representation of the target person's face. Most of the prospective memory tasks we have reviewed in this chapter involve prospective memory targets that are clear and unambiguous. If you are told to make a response if you see the word "platypus," then something simply is or is not the word "platypus." But faces are different. They are not the same from day to day, even from moment to moment. Considering this, Sweeney and Lampinen (2012) reasoned that there might be benefit to providing multiple pictures of the sought-after individual on missing-persons posters. Participants studied four missing-persons posters. For half of the posters, three different pictures of the missing individual were shown. For the other half of the participants, only a single picture was shown. Prospective person memory was about twice as high in the multiple-picture condition, suggesting a large advantage to providing multiple pictures.

CONCLUSIONS

Research on prospective memory was once a neglected topic among memory researchers, but boy, have times changed. Scientists have begun to appreciate how important prospective memory is to everyday cognitive functioning and how interesting the underlying processes are that are involved in successful prospective memory. Although debate continues between advocates of PAM and advocates of the multiprocess view, work continues to advance on applied topics related to prospective memory. But, you might be asking, how can I make my prospective memory better? Luckily, researchers have addressed this, too.

The first key to improving your prospective memory is to create a strong mental association between the prospective memory cue and the intended action. There are different ways of doing this. One method is to use an approach called "implementation intentions" (Gollwitzer, 1999). This involves mentally rehearsing the association between the cue and the intended action. For instance, if you need to remember to make your car payment in the morning, mentally rehearse something that will happen in the morning and an intended action. "When I pour my Cap'n Crunch, I will log in and make my car payment online; when I pour my Cap'n Crunch, I will log in and make my car payment online; when I pour my Cap'n Crunch, I will log in and make my car payment online." Studies have shown that this simple process can greatly increase prospective memory performance (Chasteen, Park, & Schwarz, 2001).

A second important strategy is to use external memory aids, like notes and calendars (Intons-Peterson & Newsome, 1992). For instance, in addition to mentally rehearsing making one's car payment, you can tape the bill to your coffee mug. Keep in mind that not all memory aids are equally effective. For instance, you have to actually look at the memory aid in order for it to work. It doesn't help to have a planning calendar if you don't look at the planning calendar.

A third strategy is to try to keep your to-do list short and sweet. Remember, that both the multiprocess theory and the PAM theory indicate that maintaining delayed intentions can sometimes require cognitive resources. So try to keep things simple and organized. Prospective memory is a very important skill, because it is central to accomplishing your goals. But by thinking about how prospective memory works, you might be able to improve your prospective memory and accomplish more of your goals. By the way, did you clap your hands? Cap'n Crunch is, after all, a kind of breakfast cereal. By the way, so is Life, which appeared multiple times in this chapter.

NOTES

1. One time I forgot to return a movie for 13 days straight. The late fees cost as much as it would have cost to purchase the movie. It wasn't even a good movie!
2. I'm not actually going to list a phone number, because invariably some yahoo would dial that number, and then whoever owned the number would get mad and call our university and yell at us.

REFERENCES

Aberle, I., & Kliegel, M. (2010). Time-based prospective memory performance in young children. *European Journal of Developmental Psychology, 7*(4), 419–431.

Arnal, J. D., & Lampinen, J. M. (2009). A stochastic model of prospective memory. In E. B. Hartonek (Ed.) *Experimental psychology research trends*. Hauppauge, NY: Nova.

Breneiser, J. E., & McDaniel, M. A. (2006). Discrepancy processes in prospective memory retrieval. *Psychonomic Bulletin and Review, 13*, 837–841.

Burgess, P. W., & Shallice, T. (1997). The relationship between prospective and retrospective memory: Neuropsychological evidence. In M. A. Conway (Ed.), *Cognitive models of memory* (pp. 247–272). Cambridge, MA: The MIT Press.

Ceci, S. J., & Bronfenbrenner, U. (1985). "Don't forget to take the cupcakes out of the oven": Prospective memory, strategic time-monitoring, and context. *Child Development, 56*, 152–164.

Chasteen, A. L., Park, D. C., & Schwarz, N. (2001). Implementation intentions and facilitation of prospective memory. *Psychological Science, 12*, 457–461.

Cook, G. I., Marsh, R. L., & Hicks, J. L. (2005). Associating a time-based prospective memory task with an expected context can improve or impair intention completion. *Applied Cognitive Psychology, 19*(3), 345–360.

Craik, F. I. M. (1986). A functional account of age differences in memory. In F. Klix & H. Hagendorf (Eds.), *Human memory and cognitive capabilities: Mechanisms and performances* (Pt. A, pp. 409–422). Amsterdam, The Netherlands: Elsevier Science.

Crawford, J. R., Henry, J. D., Ward, A. L., & Blake, J. (2006). The Prospective and Retrospective Memory Questionnaire (PRMQ): Latent structure, normative data and discrepancy analysis for proxy-ratings. *British Journal of Clinical Psychology, 45*, 83–104.

Crawford, J. R., Smith, G., Maylor, E. A., Della Sala, S., & Logie, R. H. (2003). The Prospective and Retrospective Memory Questionnaire (PRMQ): Normative data and latent structure in a large non-clinical sample. *Memory, 11*, 261–275.

Dunbar-Jacob, J., Erlen, J. A., Schlenk, E. A., Ryan, C. M., Sereika, S. M., & Doswell, W. M. (2000). Adherence in chronic disease. *Annual Review of Nursing, 18*, 48–90.

Einstein, G. O., & McDaniel, M. A. (1990). Normal aging and prospective memory. *Journal of Experimental Psychology: Learning, Memory and Cognition, 16*, 717–726.

Einstein, G. O., & McDaniel, M. A. (1996). Retrieval processes in prospective memory: Theoretical approaches and some new empirical findings. In M. Brandimote, G. O. Einstein, & M. A. McDaniel (Eds.), *Prospective memory: Theory and applications* (pp. 115–142). Mahwah, NJ: Erlbaum.

Einstein, G. O., McDaniel, M. A., Thomas, R., Mayfield, S., Shank, H., Morrisette, N., & Breneiser, J. (2005). Multiple processes in prospective memory retrieval: Factors determining monitoring versus spontaneous retrieval. *Journal of Experimental Psychology: General, 134*, 327–342.

Ellis, J. (1996). Prospective memory or the realization of delayed intentions: A conceptual framework for research. In M. Brandimonte, G. O. Einstein, & M. A. McDaniel (Eds.), *Prospective memory: Theory and applications* (pp. 1–22). Mahwah, NJ: Lawrence Erlbaum Associates.

Gollwitzer, P. M. (1999). Implementation intentions: Strong effects of simple plans. *American Psychologist, 54*, 493–503.

Graf, P., & Uttl, B. (2001). Prospective memory: A new focus for research. *Consciousness and Cognition, 10*, 437–450.

Guynn, M. J., McDaniel, M. A., & Einstein, G. O. (1998). Prospective memory: When reminders fail. *Memory and Cognition, 26*, 287–298.

Hasher, L., & Zacks, R. T. (1979). Automatic and effortful processes in memory. *Journal of Experimental Psychology: General, 108*, 356–388.

Huang, T., Loft, S., & Humphreys, M. S. (2014). Internalizing versus externalizing control: Different ways to perform a time-based prospective memory task. *Journal of Experimental Psychology: Learning, Memory, and Cognition, 40*, 1064–1071. doi:10.1037/a0035786

Intons-Peterson, M., & Newsome, G. L. (1992). External memory aids: Effects and effectiveness. In D. J. Hermann, H. Weingartner, A. Searleman, & C. McEvoy (Eds.), *Memory improvement: Implications for memory theory* (pp. 101–121). New York, NY: Springer-Verlag.

Khan, A., Sharma, N. K., & Dixit, S. (2008). Cognitive load and task condition in event and time based prospective memory: An experimental investigation. *Journal of Psychology, 142*, 517–531.

Kvavilashvili, L., & Fisher, L. (2007). Is time-based prospective remembering mediated by self-initiated rehearsals? Role of incidental cues, ongoing activity, age, and motivation. *Journal of Experimental Psychology: General, 136*(1), 112–132.

Lampinen, J. M., Arnal, J. D., & Hicks, J. L. (2009). Prospective person memory. In M. Kelley (Ed.), *Applied memory* (pp. 167–184). Hauppauge, NY: Nova.

Lampinen, J. M., Erickson, W. B., Peters, C. S., Sweeney, L. N., & Culbertson-Faegre, A. J. (2012). *Car alarms and AMBER alerts: Do repeated alerts impair prospective person memory?* Paper presented at the annual meeting of the American Psychology Law Society Conference, Caribe Hilton, San Juan, Puerto Rico.

Lampinen, J. M., Peters, C. S., & Gier, V. S. (2012). Power in numbers: The effect of target set size on prospective person memory in an analog missing child scenario. *Applied Cognitive Psychology, 26,* 702–708.

Loft, S., & Remington, R. W. (2010). Prospective memory and task interference in a continuous monitoring dynamic display task. *Journal of Experimental Psychology: Applied, 16,* 145–167.

Mackinlay, R. J., Kliegel, M., & Mäntylä, T. (2009). Predictors of time-based prospective memory in children. *Journal of Experimental Child Psychology, 102*(3), 251–264.

Mäntylä, T., Del Missier, F., & Nilsson, L. (2009). Age differences in multiple outcome measures of time-based prospective memory. *Aging, Neuropsychology, and Cognition, 16*(6), 708–720.

Marsh, R. L., Hicks, J. L., Hancock, T. W., & Munsayac, K. (2002). Investigating the output monitoring component of event-based prospective memory performance. *Memory and Cognition, 30,* 302–311.

McDaniel, M. A., & Einstein, G. O. (2000). Strategic and automatic processes in prospective memory retrieval: A multiprocess framework. *Applied Cognitive Psychology, 14,* S127–S144.

McDaniel, M. A., & Einstein, G. O. (2007). *Prospective memory: An overview and synthesis of an emerging field.* Thousand Oaks, CA: Sage.

McDaniel, M. A., Guynn, M. J., Einstein, G. O., & Breneiser, J. (2004). Cue-focused and reflexive associative processes in prospective memory retrieval. *Journal of Experimental Psychology: Learning, Memory, and Cognition, 30,* 605–614.

Ratcliff, R. (1978). A theory of memory retrieval. *Psychological Review, 85,* 59–108.

Ratcliff, R., Gomez, P., & McKoon, G. (2004). A diffusion model account of the lexical decision task. *Psychological Review, 111,* 159–182.

Ratcliff, R., & Rouder, J. N. (2000). A diffusion model account of masking in two-choice letter identification. *Journal of Experimental Psychology: Human Perception and Performance, 26,* 127–140.

Rendell, P. G., & Craik, F. I. M. (2000). Virtual week and actual week: Age-related differences in prospective memory. *Applied Cognitive Psychology, 14,* S43–S62.

Scullin, M. K., McDaniel, M. A., & Einstein, G. O. (2010). Control of cost in prospective memory: Evidence for spontaneous retrieval processes. *Journal of Experimental Psychology: Learning, Memory and Cognition, 36,* 190–203.

Shorrock, S. T. (2005). Errors of memory in air traffic control. *Safety Science, 43,* 571–588.

Smith, G., Della Sala, S., Logie, R. H., & Maylor, E. A. (2000). Prospective and retrospective memory in normal aging and dementia: A questionnaire study. *Memory, 8,* 311–321.

Smith, R. E. (2003). The cost of remembering to remember in event-based prospective memory: Investigating the capacity demands of delayed intention performance. *Journal of Experimental Psychology: Learning, Memory, and Cognition, 29,* 347–361.

Smith, R. E., & Bayen, U. J. (2004). A multinomial model of event-based prospective memory. *Journal of Experimental Psychology: Learning, Memory, and Cognition, 30,* 756–777.

Smith, R. E., Hunt, R. R., McVay, J. C., & McConnell, M. D. (2007). The cost of event-based prospective memory: Salient target events. *Journal of Experimental Psychology: Learning, Memory, and Cognition, 33,* 734–746.

Sweeney, L. N., & Lampinen, J. M. (2012). The effect of presenting multiple images on prospective and retrospective person memory for missing children. *Journal of Applied Research in Memory and Cognition, 1,* 235–241.

World Health Organization. (2005). *Preventing chronic diseases: A vital investment.* Geneva, Switzerland: Author.

Zimmerman, T. D., & Meier, B. (2010). The effect of implementation instructions on prospective memory performance across the lifespan. *Applied Cognitive Psychology, 24,* 645–658.

Zogg, J. B., Woods, S. P., Sauceda, J. A., Wiebe, J. S., & Simoni, J. M. (2012). The role of prospective memory in medication adherence: A review of an emerging literature. *Journal of Behavioral Medicine, 35,* 47–62.

6

That's the Story of My Life: The Autobiographical Memory System

hat is your earliest memory? What is the worst movie you've ever seen? How did you decide you wanted to take this class or read this book? To answer these questions, you need to use a special type of memory known as autobiographical memory, or memory for your own life experiences. We rely on autobiographical memory unquestioningly, hold it tightly to our hearts, and even get lost in it from time to time.

As a vivid literary example of the ability of autobiographical memory to transport, consider the experience of Proust's fictional character upon sampling a cake soaked in tea. As he tastes the spoonful of cake and tea, he is struck by a vivid memory of having eaten such a concoction in the long-ago past. He is deeply moved by how that unbidden memory takes him out of the here and now: "And at once the vicissitudes of life had become indifferent to me, its disasters innocuous, its brevity illusory—this new sensation having had on me the effect which love has of filling me with a precious essence . . . . I had ceased now to feel mediocre, contingent, mortal" (Proust, 1913, translated by Moncrieff, 1922, p. 51). A form of memory imbued with the powers of love and capable of causing one to feel immortal? This is powerful stuff, so we had better explore it in detail.

Autobiographical memory overlaps to some degree with the types of memory we discussed in Chapters 2 and 3 (semantic, episodic, and procedural; implicit and explicit) but has unique properties of its own. Semantic memory refers to memory for facts or knowledge in general; autobiographical memory refers to memory for personally experienced events only. Episodic memory refers to memory for having learned particular information in a particular context; autobiographical memory refers to memory for events, which stretch across longer periods of time. Procedural memory refers to memory for how to do a task; autobiographical memory is declarative knowledge rather than being behaviorally based. Explicit memory refers to any memory that we can consciously recollect; autobiographical memory is conscious recollection of one's own life experiences specifically (i.e., not facts or lists or other people's stories). This personal form of memory is so interwoven in our everyday thoughts that it often doesn't feel like memory at all. It sometimes feels like reliving the past, taking a small sample from that seemingly coherent set of happenings collectively called *my life*. But the notion of a seamless, unchanging documentary of one's life in one's head is pure illusion. The reality of autobiographical memory is much more complicated and interesting!

Despite the ubiquity of autobiographical memories in our mental worlds, memory researchers avoided for many years putting them under their metaphorical microscopes. The reason why is simple: Control. Imagine you are accustomed to creating balanced lists of word pairs that can be perfectly matched and randomized, to choosing the presentation time and conditions, the length of time to retain the material and the activity that might fill that time, and the situation under which the material is retrieved from memory. In most laboratory memory research, the retention interval is on the order of minutes or, at most, days. Now compare that to studying people's highly varied, personal, and deeply meaningful and messy life experiences, with retention intervals of decades. It can be challenging and perhaps slightly distasteful to dive into all of that disorder. Yet even without complete experimental control over all variables, autobiographical memory can be studied rigorously. Researchers use a combination of methods to hone in on answers to their questions about autobiographical memory (Rubin, 2005; Rubin & Wenzel, 2005). For example, one may use surveys or questionnaires to ask people about the characteristics of their memories, provide words as cues for memories, ask people to tell their life narratives, have participants record everyday life experiences as they happen via diary or camera (e.g., Cabeza et al., 2004), or create novel experiences to be remembered later (e.g., St. Jacques & Schacter, 2013).

ACCURACY OF AUTOBIOGRAPHICAL MEMORIES

One of the first questions we can answer with careful methodologies is whether our life event memories are accurate. By and large, people see memory as the repository of truth. We judge what did and did not happen to us in our lives based on whether we remember it (Scoboria et al., 2014). As we mentioned in Chapter 3, in a 2011 survey, the majority (63%) of nonpsychologist respondents in an opinion poll agreed that memory works like a video camera that records events accurately for later (Simons & Chabris, 2011).

However, in the same 2011 survey, none (0%) of a sample of memory experts agreed that memory records accurately like a camera. Even a cursory examination of the research reveals inaccuracies, distortion, and forgetting in autobiographical memory just like other kinds of memories. For one thing, there is simple forgetting: We do not retain a memory of everything that happens to us. For another (and this can be mightily weird), there are mistakes: Not everything that we do remember is actually the truth. Weirder still: We are *aware* that some events we remember didn't really happen (Scoboria et al., 2014).

How much of what happens to us do we remember? This question is best addressed by diary studies. The results of one early study were published in 1986 by William Wagenaar, in a paper entitled "My Memory." In the great tradition of scientists whose first experimental subjects were themselves, Wagenaar recorded several life experiences a day over a 6-year period, then tested his own memory for those experiences by having his (uncredited) secretary choose a detail from each memory to serve as a retrieval cue and to see whether he could produce the remaining details. By this criterion, Wagenaar recalled 80% of his experiences, but when given the entire record, he recognized virtually *all* of them (although in a few cases he had to seek out people who were present at the time of the event to provide him with additional cues to remember the exact experience). In a similar diary study with undergraduate students, participants were able to accurately recall the location and who they were with for about 90% of their life experiences 3 months later (Thompson, Skowronski, Larsen, & Betz, 1996).

The skeptical among you may wish to write in and ask us this: Couldn't it be the act of writing down these several events every day that serves as the elaborative rehearsal preserving them so clearly? It's a reasonable question, but the answer is no. When roommates unobtrusively recorded events, the unknowing target still recognized the events at the same rate 3 months later (Thompson, 1982). So it must be in part the repeated internal rehearsals of life events rather than writing them or talking about them that preserve them so well in memory.

Our memory for life events is pretty impressive, especially since life experiences keep coming and coming, leaving us little chance to memorize them. But without a comparison, it's hard to evaluate just how impressed we should be. So here's a comparison: People are far better at remembering their own life events than they are at remembering news events that happened on the same day (Larsen & Plunkett, 1987; Larsen & Thompson, 1995). That may not seem surprising until you think about the fact that we discuss news events with many people and hear about them over and over, whereas most daily life events are never discussed at all. News events are also arguably more significant than what you bought at the grocery store or the sock your dog chewed up, but we remember these insignificant daily events better anyway.

But hold on there—don't pat yourself on the back too much for your wondrous ability to retain memory for everything that happens to you. There's much more to this story about the accuracy of autobiographical memory. First, let us quickly dismiss the idea of autobiographical memories being actually stored in the brain in any kind of chronological order. The evidence is damning for this view. The time at which a remembered event occurred, and even to some extent the order in which two or more events occurred, is inferred or reconstructed rather than being stored as part of the memory trace. Part of the evidence for reconstruction is that time cues are the poorest type of cue—compared to person, location, or activity—in diary studies (e.g., Wagenaar, 1986). Take a moment to try this: What happened to you on June 12, 2007? Pretty tough to answer, likely because nothing comes to mind at all (unless that date happens to be your birthday or wedding date). But try this instead: Choose any particular day that you went to the beach (the gym, the pub, etc.). If that is tough, it's for a different reason: Rather than nothing coming to mind, you likely have so many memories that involve the beach or gym or pub that it is impossible to settle on just one without more information to help you locate a specific memory.

Moreover, events that happened close in time don't activate one another in memory (Wagenaar, 1986). Instead, two events are only remembered to have occurred close in time to the extent that they are similar in content (Friedman & Janssen, 2010). Dates are remembered better when an event happens close to a landmark for which the date is known (e.g., a birthday or major news event; Shum, 1998). All of this evidence suggests that we rarely store the exact date of an event in memory. Instead, we estimate it based on clues such as how vividly we remember it, other events we can date that happened near it in time, and whether it reminds us of other events (Friedman, 2004). So we remember what happened to us quite well, although we don't remember very well when it happened.

Second, keep in mind (as we discussed in Chapter 2) that it's important not just to remember what happened, but also to *not* remember what *didn't* happen. We may be great at the former, but we're not so great at the latter. We forget some of the things that happen to us, to be sure, but we also misremember things so that we end up believing things happened that really didn't.

The primary way we end up with inaccurate memories is that the mind mixes together details from different experiences. To see what mixing of details looks like, let's eavesdrop on the thought process of Steven Hyden, a music reviewer for the AVClub website (Hyden, 2011). He shares a personal memory about the band Oasis that he knows for a fact to be wrong. Hyden goes on to describe hearing for the first time a song on the album *Definitely Maybe*, which was released in August of 1994. His memory is of listening to the song while driving his mother's car after having just gotten his driver's license in September of 1993. He realizes this can't be. In his own words: "Here's the part where I have to call bullshit on myself. [The release date] is a fact, and yet my memory of hearing it a year earlier still seems right to me . . . *Definitely Maybe* fits with my first drive because I associate both things with my life starting to not completely suck." Hyden has mixed together the detail of driving for the first time from one life experience, with the memory of hearing Oasis for the first time from an entirely different experience. This mixing of details is sometimes referred to as content borrowing, but we'll call these *mashup memories*.

Here's another real-life example of a mashup memory, reported by a historian whose friend Dean Acheson was writing his memoirs. Acheson reported with considerable distress: "I have the most vivid memory of the meeting in President Roosevelt's office. The President was sitting at his desk; Cordell Hull (the Secretary of State) was sitting opposite him. I was in a chair by the Secretary's side. I can close my eyes and see the scene" (Schlesinger, 2002, p. xiv). However, the minutes from the meeting revealed that Hull was ill that day and not present. Acheson was dumbstruck by the conflict between reality and his memory. Even when we realize that our memories must be inaccurate mashups, we nonetheless refuse to let go of them.

Mashup memories have even been produced in the laboratory. In one study, Barclay and Wellman (1986) rewrote participants' diary entries to alter one detail. In some cases, they altered a central detail (such as replacing a description of the menu in a restaurant with a description of the waiter). In other cases, they altered a more trivial detail (such as replacing the evaluation of the menu as good versus acceptable). As in previous studies, participants were able to recognize their own original event descriptions quite accurately at about 95%. They also were able to reject the rewritten event descriptions reasonably well at about 37%.

But here's where it gets interesting: As time went on, the hit rate for actual event descriptions stayed about the same, whereas the false alarm rate (saying "yes" to rewritten descriptions) went up. And even more tellingly, the confidence ratings stayed the same (Barclay & Wellman, 1986). In other words, more and more event descriptions were judged to be actual memories over time, and these false memories felt just as true as the real ones. In another diary study, after only a few weeks, participants accepted 20% to 40% of the details falsely imported from another event in the participant's own diary as having occurred during the event. More interestingly, participants overwhelmingly said that they *remembered* the event detail as happening during this event, rather than just knowing or guessing that it had happened (Odegard & Lampinen, 2004). In yet a third diary study, after 13 years, almost two thirds (62%) of false event descriptions created from details from other events were accepted as true, and 20% of these accepted false events were described as remembered (Burt, Kemp, & Conway, 2004).

You see, autobiographical memories are constructed in the brain just like all memories are, as we discussed in Chapter 3. The difference is that autobiographical memories provide a sense of reliving, of traveling back in time, that comes with a ring of truth. If an autobiographical memory is filled with perceptual and visual details, it transports us into a memory world that feels like it is being re-experienced, whether that memory is accurate or not (Daselaar et al., 2008). So any details our brain happens to latch onto at a given moment might become part of the memory. Sometimes merely hearing about details will be sufficient to import them into a memory, which explains why people (particularly twins) "steal" each other's memories sometimes (Ikier, Tekcan, Gülgöz, & Küntay, 2003; Sheen, Kemp, & Rubin, 2006). Let's examine the construction process to get a sense of how mashup memories come about.

AUTOBIOGRAPHICAL MEMORY IN THE BRAIN

In theory, the construction of an autobiographical memory begins with a retrieval model being generated in the brain. This retrieval model activates general knowledge about the self, which is used to retrieve episodic memory details consistent with the desired memory (Conway, Pleydell-Pearce, & White-cross, 2001). Two aspects of the self, *lifetime periods* and *general event memories*, are consulted to help us search for episodic details. Lifetime periods are something like chapters in the book of your life; they divide the story into segments. Also like book chapters, lifetime periods may overlap in time (e.g., "summers I worked at Disneyland" may overlap with "college years"). General memories are summaries of the types of repeated experiences you had during these lifetime periods (e.g., "posing for photos with kids while dressed as Goofy" or "eating ramen noodles for dinner"). The process of autobiographical memory construction proceeds from lifetime periods to general events, and finally to the construction of an autobiographical memory of one particular experience that occurred at a specific place and time (Conway, 2005).

It's complicated, but you can deconstruct the retrieval process one step at a time to get a glimpse into it. Haque and Conway (2001) provided participants with cues and asked them to produce a specific autobiographical memory for each. They allowed 2, 5, or 30 seconds after each cue. Participants were asked to report what they were thinking even if they had not yet retrieved (constructed) a specific memory yet. After a short 2 seconds, most participants were thinking of general knowledge about periods in their lives that they thought would help them find a suitable memory. After 5 seconds, most participants were thinking about a general memory, a category of memories of the type they were seeking. After 30 seconds, most had constructed a specific autobiographical memory. The process of constructing a memory therefore proceeds from finding a time period in which to search, then a category of events, then to details. Once the episodic details of the desired specific event are found in memory, they are bound together temporarily with the general self-information (lifetime period and general memory) by the hippocampus. This temporarily coactive neural pattern is experienced as a recollection of a specific experience and yields a sense of mental time travel back to the event (Daselaar et al., 2008).

Now we can explain why mashup memories made up of some proper and some false details occur. As we reviewed in Chapter 3, memories are constructed each time they are brought to mind. Over a period of time, the memory will consolidate neurally into what is best described as a semipermanent state: resistant to brain injury, but still malleable under the right circumstances. When a consolidated memory is retrieved, it becomes temporarily labile so that details extraneous to the original experience but present during the retrieval context might be added and then reconsolidated into the memory (thus being more likely to be brought up the next time).

In an intriguing example of this reactivation and reconsolidation process, St. Jacques and Schacter (2013) had participants tour a museum wearing a camera that took pictures of their museum experience every 15 seconds. Then, 2 days later, the participants returned to view some sets of pictures their own camera had recorded in correct temporal order to reactivate the memory, or some sets of those pictures in incorrect order, to less successfully reactivate the memory. Then they were shown pictures of museum sites they had not in fact seen. Those whose memories had been more successfully reactivated by seeing pictures identical to their original experience were more susceptible to updating this memory by including the misinformation. That is, when the current environment helps us reactivate a memory, the memory becomes labile and may start to include new information that wasn't actually encountered during the original event. In this way autobiographical memories change over time as we recall them, with details from other experiences (or even television shows or novels) getting bound up with the other details into a memory that feels entirely like re-experiencing.

Autobiographical memory is a complicated skill that results from the union of episodic memory and an abstract concept of self laid out over time. But episodic memories are fleeting, so autobiographical memory can only preserve so much and memories must be remade each time they are brought to mind (Conway, 2009). This transformation of episodic into autobiographical memories results in forgetting of some incidents, and mashups of details from two or more separate incidents into a single memory that feels like it happened to the self at a particular point in time.

AUTOBIOGRAPHICAL MEMORY ACROSS THE LIFESPAN

So far, the way we have discussed autobiographical memory makes it seem like you remember almost everything that happens to you, with just a few incidents missing or distorted here or there. But that notion of a whole cloth of autobiographical memories is only true if you take the (relatively) short view of months or a few years. Looking at memory for experiences over a lifetime reveals emptier and fuller places in the story. To return to the analogy of autobiographical memory as a documentary in the head, it is not a seamless list of experiences laid out over the course of one's life, but rather a story with some significant gaps, which appear in predictable places.

For most people age 40 and over, the shape of the retention curve (see Chapter 2) over a lifetime is not a smooth or regular pattern. Across people and cultures, the general shape is as follows: The curve is at zero and flat for the first few years of life (no memories at all from this period). Then the curve takes an upward turn for a few years, peaking at around age 20, followed by a downward turn (but not all the way to zero) at about age 30. The curve stays low until a sudden sharp upturn at its very end, the most recent year of life (Rubin & Schulkind, 1997).

Childhood Amnesia

That first part of the curve is referred to as childhood amnesia. Adults cannot recall memories from the first few years of their lives. Why does that happen? One explanation we can rule out right away is that *children* have no memories for the first few years of life. Children and even newborns can remember new information, for hours, weeks, and months afterward (Bauer, 1996). Yet this information will not be remembered as an adult. Oddly, this means that young children can remember for weeks or months things that happen to them at age 3, that they will (rather suddenly—Peterson, Warren, & Short, 2011) lose access to a few months later. One of us once gave a talk in which childhood amnesia was discussed, which had the unintended side effect of mildly upsetting some nonpsychologist colleagues in attendance. They were dejected to discover that the once-in-a-lifetime trip to Europe they had just taken with their 2-year-old, who was currently able to discuss a few of the experiences there, was not likely to stay in her autobiographical memory. Save your money for exotic family travels until your children are 4 or 5!

So the childhood amnesia portion of the lifetime retention curve reveals a bright line around age 3 or 4 between no lasting memories and lasting memories. As is the case with most developmental changes, there's not a single or simple reason why this shift occurs. Instead, it appears that several different abilities come online and converge to support autobiographical memory. First and foremost, children need to learn language in which to record their life experiences, and an organized conceptual understanding of what words refer to in the world (Fivush & Nelson, 2004; Morrison & Conway, 2010). Second, they need to have a sophisticated concept of the self to use as a memory-supporting structure (Howe, 2003). Third, they need to learn from caregivers the format and rules of storytelling to translate their life experiences from random patterns into memorable narratives (Fivush & Nelson, 2004). Finally, they need to understand that they have knowledge not shared by others, that their experiences are unique and special and therefore worthy of remembering (Spreng & Grady, 2010). All of these abilities are necessary for sophisticated adultlike remembering of life experiences—the stories that make up one's life.

Reminiscence Bump

The second important portion of the lifetime retention curve is called the reminiscence bump. Why so many well-recalled memories from this period of life? One explanation is that the actual life experiences that tend to occur in one's teens and 20s are vivid, first-time events, and therefore stand out in memory as distinctive. However, memories from the reminiscence bump are not particularly vivid. That is, events occurring in one's teens and 20s are no more likely to be experienced as vividly relived upon recall than events occurring at any other time (Janssen, Rubin, & St. Jacques, 2011). A second explanation has to do with the formation of self-concepts, which in an Eriksonian sense is most likely to occur during this time period. One's developmental task in the teens and 20s is to create a strong and stable sense of identity. In the process, life experiences that support this identity are rehearsed and elevated in importance such that they stick in the mind. Consistent with this identity development idea, in one study people were asked to complete the sentence "I am" with a number of different endings, to elicit self-concepts. Then they were asked to come up with autobiographical memories relevant to each self-concept, and to give the year of self-concept formation and the year in which each relevant memory occurred. The results showed a bell-shaped curve of time around the formation of the self-concept, suggesting that experiences occurring around the time of self-concept formation get a memory advantage (Rathbone, Moulin, & Conway, 2008).

A third explanation of the reminiscence bump is based on the life story or so-called cultural life scripts, which organize autobiographical memory and direct the search toward particular time periods. People in the same culture tend to have the same notion of what a "life" looks like, what major events make it up. North Americans, for example, think of a life as consisting of a lengthy early period of formal schooling, punctuated by a few graduation ceremonies, followed by the beginning of a career, marriage, childbirth, a long period of not many milestones, then retirement. The milestones most people mention just happen to occur mainly during the teens and 20s (graduation, first job, marriage, childbirth). Because these milestones are considered particularly important in our culture, they become frequently rehearsed landmarks in autobiographical memory that we turn to to organize our memories of the other events that fill the gaps between (Berntsen & Rubin, 2004). These cultural life scripts are learned quite early and serve as a framework upon which to hang our experiences for later remembering. Children as young as 10 years old imagine a greater number of future life events happening during the reminiscence bump period of their lives than during other periods in their lives (Bohn & Berntsen, 2011). Mental attentions are routinely directed toward the events experienced in the teens and 20s before, during, and after the living of them. Memory follows suit.

Recency

The final interesting portion of the lifetime retention curve is called the recency portion. Why are memories from the past year well remembered? As we discussed in Chapter 2, memory is almost always biased toward the recent. Information in the brain fades over time as unexercised neural connections weaken. If you don't think and talk frequently about what you had for lunch last Tuesday, it won't be very long until you don't remember that incident much at all. Over short time frames, autobiographical memory shows a classic retention function that is steeply negatively accelerated (Kristo, Janssen, & Murre, 2009)—which simply means we forget a lot very quickly and then continue to forget slowly. We need to form all of those tiny details about who was there, what happened, what everyone was wearing, what it all looked and smelled and sounded like, into a nice orderly story in order for it to be remembered. That is, we need to form small time slices of episodic memory into true autobiographical memories (Conway, 2009).

What are the implications of the reminiscence bump that pops up in the early–middle portion of the lifetime retention curve? (By the way, the older you get, the more prominent the bump becomes.) Because we bring to mind many memories from the reminiscence bump compared to other time periods, time, in retrospect, seems to have passed more slowly in one's young adult than in one's middle and older adult years. The more events that happen in a given time interval, the longer the time interval feels subjectively (Zauberman, Levav, Diehl, & Bhargave, 2010). In short, time speeds up as we get older because fewer events seem important enough to bother remembering (Draaisma, 2004). There's a bit of a possible upside to time speeding up, though: People feel increasingly younger than they are throughout their lifespan. One's cognitive age is 20% or so lower than actual age (Rubin & Berntsen, 2006). If you really are as young as you feel, then look forward to being progressively younger than your actual age every year!

A second implication of the reminiscence bump is that we have a broadly shared notion of what a life looks like: You are a child and not much happens. Then you are a teenager and you begin to become a person—you complete high school, you go to college. You become a young adult, and your personhood reaches its apex—you graduate college, you begin your career, you meet and settle down with a significant other, you start a family. Then you reach middle adulthood, and once again not much happens, except for whatever has been going on in the last year. As people of a certain age, the authors are disconcerted by the suggestion that nothing important happens to you after age 30. However, we assure our younger readers that much of importance happens in middle and later adulthood; it's just that these happenings are idiosyncratic in their nature and therefore in their timing (e.g., getting tenure, winning a major award) or are private and therefore not usually rehearsed in discussion with others (e.g., conquering a personal fear). Thus, the important events of middle and later adulthood simply fail to conform to the cultural life script and therefore cannot benefit from the schema-driven memory benefits that it provides.

If you are a college student, and like most college students are currently living in the time period that will later appear as the reminiscence bump, we have some advice for you: *Enjoy these years!* You will look back on the experiences that took place during these particular years over and over again throughout the rest of your life. Fill them with positive experiences that will form the foundation for your adult identity.

If you are beyond the time period of the reminiscence bump, we have advice for you, too: *Enjoy these years!* New aspects of the self can form at any point in life, and the memories associated with the birth of these self-aspects will come to mind over and over throughout the rest of your life. Add a positive new aspect to your self-concept, and let the memories that support it become a part of your frequently visited memory repertoire. Another way to put this: *Forget the reminiscence bump!* The story of your life need not conform to the culturally mandated shape that leads us to return to the same store of memories over and over. *You* decide what the important milestones are in your life. Why not choose something that has happened recently as a milestone, or better yet, plan a new experience or challenge for yourself in the future to act as a milestone?

Think, too, of the implications of the recency portion of the lifetime retention curve. Life recedes quickly when seen in the rearview mirror, particularly for unpleasant events. Life's little (and big) ups and downs certainly affect us emotionally; people's overall happiness is buoyed and sunk by good and bad life events, respectively. But studies in which people record their daily happenings and their daily sense of well-being reveal that the emotional effects of a single life event are undetectable after a few weeks (Suh, Diener, & Fujita, 1996). In fact, the effect of life events on happiness is generally far less severe and less lasting than people think it will be (Gilbert, Pinel, Wilson, Blumberg, & Wheatley, 1998)—a concept to which we return in Chapter 7. Take some comfort in this fact when you experience setbacks, embarrassments, and hurts. Unless you make them central to your life story by making them into milestones, autobiographical memory will bleach out the vivid colors of these experiences and fade them to a more tolerable gray.

FUNCTIONS OF AUTOBIOGRAPHICAL MEMORY

Autobiographical memory is said to serve at least three important functions: identity, directive, and social. We discuss each in turn.

Identity

The life story with its reminiscence bump is composed of many autobiographical memories. During adolescence people first create a life narrative with key scenes, turning points, and self-defining memories that encapsulate the sense of self. It has been argued that our autobiographical memory in the form of the life story is actually our personality (McAdams, 1995, 2001). The story we tell about the self is who we think we are. People whose life stories contain many examples of redemption (things at first looked bleak but improved) have upbeat personalities and are productive and well adjusted. People whose life stories contain many examples of contamination (things that appeared golden turned to dust) experience low well-being. How many positive or negative events are reported in the life story matters some, but the way these events are told as part of that life story matters, too. When life gives you lemons, you can construct a healthy, happy identity by creating a story of how life's lemons turned into lemonade. In this way, our memories shape the concept of the self (McAdams, Reynolds, Lewis, Patten, & Bowman, 2001).

In addition, the self shapes memories. If you are motivated to believe that you have a particular quality, memories that exemplify that quality come to mind more readily than usual (Sanitioso, Kunda, & Fong, 1990). For example, if you are told that being punctual is the best predictor of success in college, memories of times you were punctual will spring to mind. But if you are told that punctual people perform poorly in college because they are not independent thinkers, memories of times you ran late will spring to mind. The autobiographical memory system is adjusting itself temporarily to allow us to access information that will support desired conclusions about the self. Not only can you pick out particular memories that allow you to conclude what you wish to about yourself, but also the past may be altered in memory to support such conclusions. For example, students who completed a (worthless) study skills program afterward rated their initial study skills as terrible, in contrast to how they had assessed their study skills before they started the program (Conway & Ross, 1984). They wanted to think of themselves as improved, so they took their current skills as a starting point and then adjusted their memories of their prior study skills to support their belief that they were now better at studying.

Indeed the whole of autobiographical memory is biased in a positive direction. Because most people like to maintain the most positive view of themselves and their lives as they can, memory for unflattering behaviors and poor performances is worse than memory for moments of happiness and well-deserved pride. People remember getting higher grades than they actually did, and forget the slights they inflicted upon others (Bahrick, Hall, & Da Costa, 2008; Sheen et al., 2006). Also people feel less intense negative emotion over time when recalling unpleasant events, but not less intense positive emotion (Walker, Vogl, & Thompson, 1997). Remembering a relationship breakup produces less sadness than the initial experience did, and the intensity of that sadness continues to decrease each time the experience is remembered. Remembering winning a swim meet produces only slightly less joy than the initial experience did, and the intensity of that joy persists each time the experience is remembered. In this way life as seen through memory seems better with every passing day.

The distortion of the past cannot be too profound, of course, because we do need to know what has happened to us with some degree of accuracy. Instead, the autobiographical memory system maintains a delicate balance between accurately recording the past on the one hand, and biasing our recollections to suit the desires of the self at the moment on the other (Conway, Singer, & Tagini, 2004). Therefore, it's not just what we remember but the *experience* of recalling those memories that informs conclusions about the self. Try this: Think of six autobiographical memories of specific times that you were helpful to others. Now imagine instead you had been asked this: Think of 12 autobiographical memories of specific times that you were helpful to others. (Most people can think of 12 memories for most traits, by the way.) If you had to guess, which question do you think leads people to believe they are more helpful people? The answer is counterintuitive. Logically, it would seem that having a longer list of times you were helpful convinces you that you are indeed a more helpful person. But thinking of a large number of times you were helpful is actually much more difficult than thinking of a small number of such instances. You start to say to yourself, "It's pretty hard to think of any more examples of being helpful. I guess it's not something I do a lot. So I must not be a very helpful person" (Schwarz et al., 1991).

Bringing to mind a specific memory may or may not affect one's sense of self, depending upon a whole laundry list of additional factors: Is the memory recent, or distant? Is it seen as closed and behind oneself, or open and unfinished? Is it seen from a first-person or a third-person perspective in memory? (See Beike, 2013, for a review.) Rather than our memories shaping our sense of self, it is more accurate to say that we allow certain memories to shape our sense of self and prevent other memories from doing so. For example, imagine an experience such as driving and having a fender bender. One person may recall this instance and make an inference about the self: "I am a bad driver." Yet another may recall this instance equally vividly but refrain from seeing it as relevant for the self. He may think, "People in this town are terrible drivers," or "That was a dangerous intersection," or nothing at all . . . just, "Oh, yeah, that happened one time." We can be biased about what autobiographical memories *mean* for the self, without always having biased autobiographical memories.

Directive

Autobiographical memories also serve as guides for future behavior. When you remember an experience, you might say to yourself, "I'll never do *that* again!" Or in determining how to approach a problem, you might wonder, "Now, how did I do this last time?" Both of these thought processes involve the application of a specific memory to the choice of behavior in a current situation, the directive function of autobiographical memory.

Laboratory evidence for the directive function of autobiographical memory is beginning to accumulate. In a study of recent college graduates, those who were asked to describe either a pleasant or an unpleasant memory of their college years were more likely to choose to have money donated to the college than to another organization compared to graduates not asked to describe a memory (Kuwabara & Pillemer, 2010). Participants in a study about charitable actions who described a time they passed up an opportunity to donate to a charity clicked a button to add money to a charitable donation twice as many times than those not asked to describe such a memory—but only if they wrote about how the memory was still open and unfinished for them psychologically (Beike, Adams, & Naufel, 2010). Perhaps most convincing is the study showing that after reporting autobiographical memories about positive public-speaking experiences participants gave better public-speaking performances and even evinced less physiological stress (Pezdek & Salim, 2011).

Autobiographical memory and behavior might be linked because they activate the same parts of the brain. Amnesic patients, who cannot remember specific past experiences, cannot imagine specific future scenarios either (Klein, Loftus, & Kihlstrom, 2002). Neuroimaging studies reveal that remembering a past experience and imagining a future experience both engage the left hippocampus, a structure that would be damaged in amnesic patients. In addition, thinking about the past and the future both engage areas known to be important for the construction of autobiographical memories, including the left medial prefrontal cortex, which is often activated during tasks that require thinking about the self. Areas further back in the brain that enable imagery were also active in both types of thinking (Addis, Wong, & Schacter, 2007). Autobiographical remembering therefore allows thoughts about the future to be filled in with concrete details. These thoughts about the future then become the basis of plans and actions. The mental past becomes the actual future.

Social

A third function of autobiographical memory is to create and strengthen bonds between people. Autobiographical memory is inherently social. Children need to learn how to tell stories that will inform a listener before they are able to form adultlike memories. Children also learn life story schemas from adults and from fictional stories they are told about people's lives, and this schema organizes their own autobiographical memories as they go through life. Adults spend a good portion of their time discussing autobiographical memories; one study found that 14% of adult conversations involved both people sharing autobiographical memories (Pasupathi & Carstensen, 2003). In fact, the true percentage is higher, as we need to include the percentage of conversations that involved only one person talking about a memory, which the researchers did not report.

Adults who kept track of the autobiographical memories they told to others over a 4-week period demonstrated what the social function looks like in action. They tended to discuss autobiographical memories with friends and significant others more than with anyone else, and their reasons for discussing these memories were most frequently to convey facts, to amuse, and to garner sympathy from the listener (Marsh & Tversky, 2004). So generally we discuss our autobiographical memories with close others, and we share them as a sort of social glue, to bring people closer to us via entertainment or arousal of tender emotions. Indeed, couples who recounted an autobiographical memory about their relationship with an experimenter felt closer to their partner than those who recounted an impersonal narrative (Alea & Bluck, 2007). And when people share their everyday positive experiences with important others, they feel better, and their trust for the other person deepens (Reis et al., 2010).

When other people aren't around to reminisce with, we can engage in solo reminiscence that provides similar benefits. People who feel sad or lonely often experience the emotion of nostalgia. They have an intense longing for the past—the "good old days." It's a mixed emotion, sad but sweet. People who recollected a nostalgic event felt better about themselves and more connected to other people afterward, even though they remembered this event with no one else around to tell it to. Nostalgia is an example of the social nature of autobiographical memory even when it is divorced from its social context—mere remembering makes us feel more tied into a social network (Wildschut, Sedikides, Arndt, & Routledge, 2006).

Perhaps the best evidence for the social function of autobiographical memory can be found by examining your own reactions to everyday events. When something noteworthy happens to you, don't you find yourself going back through the event to decide how you're going to tell the story to someone else—your significant other, your roommate, your mother, someone important to you? You are forming a narrative with the goal of communicating it to another person, thereby preserving the memory in an easy-to-recollect story form and also possibly situating it in your life story. You are making a story of a collection of facts, not primarily as a mnemonic device for yourself, but rather as a way of maintaining and enhancing social bonds. Your friends and family will want to hear about your experiences; you will want to entertain them or seek emotional support from them, depending upon whether the experience in question is positive or negative. The autobiographical memories you form will help you to achieve these ends.

For the next few days, pay attention to your conversations with others, and notice how much of the conversation entails telling autobiographical memories. Imagine how impoverished your interactions with others would be if you could not talk about remembered life experiences with them. What would be left to discuss? Unless you can sprinkle memories of relevant life experiences throughout, conversations about your beliefs, your goals, and your hopes and dreams will be too abstract to draw your listener in.

In summary, autobiographical memory is a complex, uniquely human skill that allows us to merge episodic slices, before they completely evaporate, into a meaningful unit of the event that persists over time in a way that feels alive and that is easily shared with others. It therefore provides a sense of continuity over time and connection with other people. It also provides a catalog of details with which to fill in our simulations of future events to help us plan. It is a valuable tool and a crucial aspect of what makes us human. Without it, you might be less *you* . . . or a different you. We delve further into the relationships among memory, the self, and social connections in Chapter 8 when we discuss life with impaired memory.

REFERENCES

Addis, D., Wong, A. T., & Schacter, D. L. (2007). Remembering the past and imagining the future: Common and distinct neural substrates during event construction and elaboration. *Neuropsychologia, 45*(7), 1363–1377. doi:10.1016/j.neuropsychologia.2006.10.016

Alea, N., & Bluck, S. (2007). I'll keep you in mind: The intimacy function of autobiographical memory. *Applied Cognitive Psychology, 21*(8), 1091–1111. doi:10.1002/acp.1316

Bahrick, H. P., Hall, L. K., & Da Costa, L. A. (2008). Fifty years of memory of college grades: Accuracy and distortions. *Emotion, 8*(1), 13–22. doi:10.1037/1528-3542.8.1.13

Barclay, C. R., & Wellman, H. M. (1986). Accuracies and inaccuracies in autobiographical memories. *Journal of Memory and Language, 25*(1), 93–103. doi:10.1016/0749-596X(86)90023-9

Bauer, P. J. (1996). What do infants recall of their lives? Memory for specific events by one- to two-year-olds. *American Psychologist, 51*(1), 29–41. doi:10.1037/0003-066X.51.1.29

Beike, D. R. (2013). Cherished memories: Autobiographical memory and the self. In D. Carslton (Ed.), *The Oxford handbook of social cognition* (pp. 517–533). New York, NY: Oxford University Press.

Beike, D. R., Adams, L. P., & Naufel, K. Z. (2010). Closure of autobiographical memories moderates their directive effect on behaviour. *Memory, 18*(1), 40–48. doi:10.1080/09658210903405729

Berntsen, D., & Rubin, D. C. (2004). Cultural life scripts structure recall from autobiographical memory. *Memory and Cognition, 32*(3), 427–442. doi:10.3758/BF03195836

Bohn, A., & Berntsen, D. (2011). The reminiscence bump reconsidered: Children's prospective life stories show a bump in young adulthood. *Psychological Science, 22*(2), 197–202. doi:10.1177/0956797610395394

Burt, C. B., Kemp, S., & Conway, M. (2004). Memory for true and false autobiographical event descriptions. *Memory, 12*(5), 545–552. doi:10.1080/09658210344000071

Cabeza, R., Prince, S. E., Daselaar, S. M., Greenberg, D. L., Budde, M., Dolcos, F., . . . Rubin, D. C. (2004). Brain activity during episodic retrieval of autobiographical and laboratory events: An fMRI study using a novel photo paradigm. *Journal of Cognitive Neuroscience, 16*(9), 1583–1594. doi:10.1162/0898929042568578

Conway, M. A. (2005). Memory and the self. *Journal of Memory and Language, 53*(4), 594–628. doi:10.1016/j.jml.2005.08.005

Conway, M. A. (2009). Episodic memories. *Neuropsychologia, 47*(11), 2305–2313. doi:10.1016/j.neuropsychologia.2009.02.003

Conway, M. A., Pleydell-Pearce, C. W., & Whitecross, S. E. (2001). The neuroanatomy of autobiographical memory: A slow cortical potential study of autobiographical memory retrieval. *Journal of Memory and Language, 45*(3), 493–524. doi:10.1006/jmla.2001.2781

Conway, M., & Ross, M. (1984). Getting what you want by revising what you had. *Journal of Personality and Social Psychology, 47*(4), 738–748. doi:10.1037/0022-3514.47.4.738

Conway, M. A., Singer, J. A., & Tagini, A. (2004). The self and autobiographical memory: Correspondence and coherence. *Social Cognition, 22*(5), 491–529. doi:10.1521/soco.22.5.491.50768

Daselaar, S. M., Rice, H. J., Greenberg, D. L., Cabeza, R., LaBar, K. S., & Rubin, D. C. (2008). The spatiotemporal dynamics of autobiographical memory: Neural correlates of recall, emotional intensity, and reliving. *Cerebral Cortex, 18*(1), 217–229. doi:10.1093/cercor/bhm048

Draaisma, D. (2004). *Why life speeds up as you get older: How memory shapes our past.* New York, NY: Cambridge University Press. doi:10.1017/CBO9780511489945

Fivush, R., & Nelson, K. (2004). Culture and language in the emergence of autobiographical memory. *Psychological Science, 15*(9), 573–577. doi:10.1111/j.0956-7976.2004.00722.x

Friedman, W. J. (2004). Time in autobiographical memory. *Social Cognition, 22*(5), 591–605. doi:10.1521/soco.22.5.591.50766

Friedman, W. J., & Janssen, S. J. (2010). Do people remember the temporal proximity of unrelated events? *Memory and Cognition, 38*(8), 1122–1136. doi:10.3758/MC.38.8.1122

Gilbert, D. T., Pinel, E. C., Wilson, T. D., Blumberg, S. J., & Wheatley, T. P. (1998). Immune neglect: A source of durability bias in affective forecasting. *Journal of Personality and Social Psychology, 75*(3), 617–638. doi:10.1037/0022-3514.75.3.617

Haque, S., & Conway, M. A. (2001). Sampling the process of autobiographical memory construction. *European Journal of Cognitive Psychology, 13*(4), 529–547. doi:10.1080/09541440042000160

Howe, M. L. (2003). Memories from the cradle. *Current Directions in Psychological Science, 12*(2), 62–65. doi:10.1111/1467-8721.01227

Hyden, S. (2011, January 25). *Part 8: 1997: The ballad of Oasis and Radiohead* [Blog message]. Retrieved from www.avclub.com/articles/part-8-1997-the-ballad-of-oasis-and-radiohead,50557

Ikier, S., Tekcan, A. I., Gülgöz, S., & Küntay, A. (2003). Whose life is it anyway? Adoption of each other's autobiographical memories by twins. *Applied Cognitive Psychology, 17*(2), 237–247. doi:10.1002/acp.869

Janssen, S. J., Rubin, D. C., & St. Jacques, P. L. (2011). The temporal distribution of autobiographical memory: Changes in reliving and vividness over the life span do not explain the reminiscence bump. *Memory and Cognition, 39*(1), 1–11. doi:10.3758/s13421-010-0003-x

Klein, S. B., Loftus, J., & Kihlstrom, J. F. (2002). Memory and temporal experience: The effects of episodic memory loss on an amnesic patient's ability to remember the past and imagine the future. *Social Cognition, 20*(5), 353–379. doi:10.1521/soco.20.5.353.21125

Kristo, G., Janssen, S. J., & Murre, J. J. (2009). Retention of autobiographical memories: An Internet-based diary study. *Memory, 17*(8), 816–829. doi:10.1080/09658210903143841

Kuwabara, K. J., & Pillemer, D. B. (2010). Memories of past episodes shape current intentions and decisions. *Memory, 18*(4), 365–374. doi:10.1080/09658211003670857

Larsen, S. F., & Plunkett, K. (1987). Remembering experienced and reported events. *Applied Cognitive Psychology, 1*(1), 15–26. doi:10.1002/acp.2350010104

Larsen, S. F., & Thompson, C. P. (1995). Reconstructive memory in the dating of personal and public news events. *Memory and Cognition, 23*(6), 780–790. doi:10.3758/BF03200929

Marsh, E. J., & Tversky, B. (2004). Spinning the stories of our lives. *Applied Cognitive Psychology, 18*(5), 491–503. doi:10.1002/acp.1001

McAdams, D. P. (1995). What do we know when we know a person? *Journal of Personality, 63*(3), 365–396. doi:10.1111/j.1467-6494.1995.tb00500.x

McAdams, D. P. (2001). The psychology of life stories. *Review of General Psychology, 5*(2), 100–122. doi:10.1037/1089-2680.5.2.100

McAdams, D. P., Reynolds, J., Lewis, M., Patten, A. H., & Bowman, P. J. (2001). When bad things turn good and good things turn bad: Sequences of redemption and contamination in life narrative and their relation to psychosocial adaptation in midlife adults and in students. *Personality and Social Psychology Bulletin, 27*(4), 474–485. doi:10.1177/0146167201274008

Morrison, C. M., & Conway, M. A. (2010). First words and first memories. *Cognition, 116*(1), 23–32. doi:10.1016/j.cognition.2010.03.011

Odegard, T. N., & Lampinen, J. M. (2004). Memory conjunction errors for autobiographical events: More than just familiarity. *Memory, 12*(3), 288–300. doi:10.1080/09658210244000621

Pasupathi, M., & Carstensen, L. L. (2003). Age and emotional experience during mutual reminiscing. *Psychology and Aging, 18*(3), 430–442. doi:10.1037/0882-7974.18.3.430

Peterson, C., Warren, K. L., & Short, M. M. (2011). Infantile amnesia across the years: A 2-year follow-up of children's earliest memories. *Child Development, 82*(4), 1092–1105. doi:10.1111/j.1467-8624.2011.01597.x

Pezdek, K., & Salim, R. (2011). Physiological, psychological and behavioral consequences of activating autobiographical memories. *Journal of Experimental Social Psychology, 47*(6), 1214–1218. doi:10.1016/j.jesp.2011.05.004

Proust, M. (1913). *Swann's way: Remembrance of things past*, Vol. 1. Translated by C. K. S. Moncrieff (1922). New York, NY: Henry Holt. Retrieved from www.gutenberg.org/files/7178/7178-h/7178-h.htm

Rathbone, C. J., Moulin, C. A., & Conway, M. A. (2008). Self-centered memories: The reminiscence bump and the self. *Memory and Cognition, 36*(8), 1403–1414. doi:10.3758/MC.36.8.140

Reis, H. T., Smith, S. M., Carmichael, C. L., Caprariello, P. A., Tsai, F., Rodrigues, A., & Maniaci, M. R. (2010). Are you happy for me? How sharing positive events with others provides personal and interpersonal benefits. *Journal of Personality and Social Psychology, 99*(2), 311–329. doi:10.1037/a0018344

Rubin, D. C. (2005). Autobiographical memory tasks in cognitive research. In A. Wenzel & D. C. Rubin (Eds.), *Cognitive methods and their application to clinical research* (pp. 219–241). Washington, DC: American Psychological Association. doi:10.1037/10870-014

Rubin, D. C., & Berntsen, D. (2006). People over forty feel 20% younger than their age: Subjective age across the lifespan. *Psychonomic Bulletin and Review, 13*(5), 776–780. doi:10.3758/BF03193996

Rubin, D. C., & Schulkind, M. D. (1997). The distribution of autobiographical memories across the lifespan. *Memory and Cognition, 25*(6), 859–866. doi:10.3758/BF03211330

Rubin, D. C., & Wenzel, A. (2005). Autobiographical memory tasks: Six common methods. In A. Wenzel & D. C. Rubin (Eds.), *Cognitive methods and their application to clinical research* (pp. 215–217). Washington, DC: American Psychological Association. doi:10.1037/10870-013

Sanitioso, R., Kunda, Z., & Fong, G. T. (1990). Motivated recruitment of autobiographical memories. *Journal of Personality and Social Psychology, 59*(2), 229–241. doi:10.1037/0022-3514.59.2.229

Schlesinger, A. M., Jr. (2002). *A life in the 20th century: Innocent beginnings, 1917–1950.* New York, NY: Houghton Mifflin.

Schwarz, N., Bless, H., Strack, F., Klumpp, G., Rittenauer-Schatka, H., & Simons, A. (1991). Ease of retrieval as information: Another look at the availability heuristic. *Journal of Personality and Social Psychology, 61*(2), 195–202. doi:10.1037/0022-3514.61.2.195

Scoboria, A., Jackson, D. L., Talarico, J., Hanczakowski, M., Wysman, L., & Mazzoni, G. (2014). The role of belief in occurrence within autobiographical memory. *Journal of Experimental Psychology: General, 143*(3), 1242–1258. doi:10.1037/a0034110

Sheen, M. M., Kemp, S. S., & Rubin, D. C. (2006). Disputes over memory ownership: What memories are disputed? *Genes, Brain and Behavior, 5*(Suppl. 1), 9–13. doi:10.1111/j.1601-183X.2006.00189.x

Shum, M. S. (1998). The role of temporal landmarks in autobiographical memory processes. *Psychological Bulletin, 124*(3), 423–442. doi:10.1037/0033-2909.124.3.423

Simons, D. J., & Chabris, C. F. (2011). What people believe about how memory works: A representative survey of the U.S. population. *PLoS ONE, 6*(8), e22757. doi:10.1371/journal.pone.0022757

Spreng, R., & Grady, C. L. (2010). Patterns of brain activity supporting autobiographical memory, prospection, and theory of mind, and their relationship to the default mode network. *Journal of Cognitive Neuroscience, 22*(6), 1112–1123. doi:10.1162/jocn.2009.21282

St. Jacques, P. L., & Schacter, D. L. (2013). Modifying memory: Selectively enhancing and updating personal memories for a museum tour by reactivating them. *Psychological Science, 24*(4), 537–543. doi:10.1177/0956797612457377

Suh, E., Diener, E., & Fujita, F. (1996). Events and subjective well-being: Only recent events matter. *Journal of Personality and Social Psychology, 70*(5), 1091–1102. doi:10.1037/0022-3514.70.5.1091

Thompson, C. P. (1982). Memory for unique personal events: The roommate study. *Memory & Cognition, 10*(4), 324–332. doi:10.3758/BF03202424

Thompson, C. P., Skowronski, J. J., Larsen, S. F., & Betz, A. (1996). *Autobiographical memory: Remembering what and remembering when.* Hillsdale, NJ: Lawrence Erlbaum Associates.

Wagenaar, W. A. (1986). My memory: A study of autobiographical memory over six years. *Cognitive Psychology, 18*(2), 225–252. doi:10.1016/0010-0285(86)90013-7

Walker, W., Vogl, R. J., & Thompson, C. P. (1997). Autobiographical memory: Unpleasantness fades faster than pleasantness over time. *Applied Cognitive Psychology, 11*(5), 399–413. doi:10.1002/(SICI)1099-0720(199710)11:5<399::AID-ACP462>3.0.CO;2-E

Wildschut, T., Sedikides, C., Arndt, J., & Routledge, C. (2006). Nostalgia: Content, triggers, functions. *Journal of Personality and Social Psychology, 91*(5), 975–993. doi:10.1037/0022-3514.91.5.975

Zauberman, G., Levav, J., Diehl, K., & Bhargave, R. (2010). 1995 feels so close yet so far: The effect of event markers on subjective feelings of elapsed time. *Psychological Science, 21*(1), 133–139. doi:10.1177/0956797609356420

Frozen in Time: Traumatic Memories

raumatic—terrifying or life-threatening—experiences are often thought to have a special status in memory. A real example of a memory for a traumatic experience may give you a sense of some of the qualities of trauma memories. This memory was reported by a man in his 20s who recalled the outcome of a serious argument his parents had when he was 8. His father emerged from the fight wearing socks on his arms that were "crimson red and dripping like a leaky faucet." The reason for this became apparent when the father ordered the son to remove the socks from his arms. All the skin had been cut off with a razor. The father exclaimed, "'[L]ook what your mother did to me.' . . . [M]y dad was asking for drug money. Every time she wouldn't give him any he would slice his wrist. This is a terrible memory and I fear I'll never be able to forget how I felt when that happened" (peacefulbeing, 2012). Over a decade and a half later, the man is still tormented by this memory, with all of its vivid details and intense emotion. In this chapter we explore how memories for such traumatic experiences differ from memories for more mundane experiences, and what role the memories play in the development and maintenance of posttraumatic stress disorder (PTSD).

Most people don't expect to go through a traumatic experience. As we mentioned in Chapter 6, people's cultural life scripts lead them to expect their life stories to be filled with positive milestones such as marriage, career, and birth of children. Unfortunately, a person is far more likely to have a traumatic experience than not. In reality, 70% to 90% of Americans will be exposed to at least one traumatic event at some point in their lives (Breslau & Kessler, 2001; Breslau et al., 1998), such as violent crime, rape, natural disaster, domestic abuse, military combat, or motor vehicle accidents causing severe injury. The physical pain of trauma may heal, but the psychological effects may linger for many years as the memory associated with that experience comes to mind again and again.

When the memory refuses to fade and continues to intrude into daily experiences months or years later, PTSD may result. According to the fifth edition of the *Diagnostic and Statistical Manual of Mental Disorders* (*DSM-5*), PTSD is a psychiatric disorder with four clusters of symptoms: intrusions, avoidance, negative thoughts and mood, and hyperarousal (American Psychiatric Association, 2013). The first cluster of symptoms relates to memory most directly. Those who have PTSD suffer through flashbacks, in which the memory for the event occurs without intention and feels like a reliving of the experience, and recurrent nightmares about the traumatic experience. The second and third clusters also refer to memory, as the second includes avoidance of reminders of the event and the third includes amnesia for some aspects of the event. The fourth cluster is more physiological, including symptoms of being jittery, irritable, and easily startled.

A firsthand account is probably the best way to convey what re-experiencing feels like, and how it relates to memory: "It's like you're living it just as it happened but you're not. It's only a memory but it's a memory that becomes a part of you. It hooks itself onto you. You can feel the pressure of someone's hand or hear the voice of someone shatter through your ear-drum" (FarrahSpada, 2012). Even those fortunate enough to never experience severe traumas such as rape or combat exposure still experience highly stressful events that may linger in memory. For example, people may be devastated by the unexpected death of a close loved one, a painful relationship breakup, or witnessing from afar a tragedy such as the 9/11 terrorist attacks in the United States. In this way none of us is immune to the effects of stress and trauma.

Before we delve into the research about trauma and memory, take a minute to consider this question: What does trauma do to us, and how is it remembered? Your answer to that question reveals your own theory of how trauma affects people. We'll refer to this as *lay traumatology*. Our experience as researchers and teachers of memory, as well as the results of national surveys, points out ways in which lay traumatology is generally correct and several major misconceptions. We will address three separate but related beliefs prevalent in lay traumatology.

Lay Traumatology Belief #1: Trauma Memories Are "Burned" Into the Brain. According to a 2006 survey, 70% of people believe that memory for traumatic events is better than memory for mundane events (Magnussen et al., 2006). This belief is often expressed in the notion that memories for traumas are fixed, unchanging, unforgettable, and highly accurate. We will examine the evidence for the notion that memories for traumatic experiences are "flashbulb" memories and that flashbacks or unintended memories for traumatic experiences are repetitive replays of the same memory over and over.

Lay Traumatology Belief #2: Long-Term Psychological Harm Is Inevitable After a Severe Trauma. Lay traumatology says that bad events cause bad psychological outcomes. One commonly sees evidence of the belief that negative psychological effects of trauma are inevitable. For example, in the aftermath of large-scale tragedies such as shootings or terrorist attacks, mental health practitioners often attempt to intervene immediately to mitigate the negative effects (which is a bad strategy; Watson, Brymer, & Bonanno, 2011). Yet as we shall demonstrate, the eminently logical conclusion that bad things necessarily lead to bad outcomes is not well supported by extensive research on the long-term psychological effects of trauma exposure. We will show that this lay belief that bad outcomes necessarily result from bad experiences has its origins in quite recent historical events.

Lay Traumatology Belief #3: Traumatic Experiences Are Often Initially Repressed Yet Later Recoverable From Memory. In the same 2004 survey mentioned earlier, 40% of people agreed that memory for traumatic events is frequently repressed or blocked. In a different survey, 13% of people claimed that they personally had recovered a repressed memory (Golding, Sanchez, & Sego, 1996). This belief in repressed memory seems to oppose belief #1, that memory for traumatic events is actually better than other memory, but both are widely held. We will discuss this highly controversial issue regarding memory for trauma in detail, and weigh the evidence for and against it.

LAY TRAUMATOLOGY BELIEF #1: TRAUMA MEMORIES ARE "BURNED" INTO THE BRAIN

Most people are convinced by their own experience that dramatic and traumatic events are better remembered than mundane or neutral ones. In fact, there is extensive evidence supporting this phenomenon of emotional enhancement of memory. People remember words on a list referring to emotional concepts better than neutral words (Schmidt & Saari, 2007), emotion-laden pictures better than neutral ones (Hamman, Ely, Grafton, & Kilts, 1999), emotionally arousing scenes in films better than neutral ones (Guy & Cahill, 1999), and emotionally charged events from their own lives better than neutral ones (Thompson, Skowronski,

Larsen, & Betz, 1996). There is also evidence that negative emotions enhance memory more than positive (e.g., Ochsner, 2000). Theoretically, it is essential for organisms to remember situations that represent danger so they can be avoided in the future. Situations that represent opportunities for positive outcomes (food, mating, dominance) are also important, but adaptively it is more important to stay alive than to thrive.

Theorists have proposed that during a frightening event, the brain narrows its focus to the perceptual aspects of the event (images, feelings) in an effort for survival, and cannot devote resources to processing the event at a conceptual level (What is happening? What does it mean for me?; Ehlers & Clark, 2000). The perceptual aspects are burned into memory and then replay themselves randomly as the brain struggles to integrate the frightening event with conceptual views of the world and the self. The results are the familiar symptoms of PTSD: intrusive re-experiencing in the form of flashbacks and nightmares, with poor memory for some aspects of the traumatic event and fixed, exact memory of others, particularly the disturbing images and intense emotions experienced. It's difficult to test this theory with real-life traumas. But in laboratory studies, preventing people from focusing on the perceptual aspects of a mildly traumatic film reduces the number of intrusive memories (mild flashbacks) of it in the days that follow (Bourne, Frasquilho, Roth, & Holmes, 2010).

Under times of stress, then, we may focus on what we see, hear, smell, or taste, resulting in a particularly vivid memory. Most people report at least one memory in their own lives that is highly perceptual and detailed, vivid and fixed over time as if burned into the brain. These have been termed flashbulb memories. Much of the research on flashbulb memories has concerned surprising and highly negative public events, like the assassination of U.S. President John F. Kennedy, the explosion of the space shuttle Challenger, and the 9/11 terrorist attacks in New York and Washington, DC, in 2001.

Here is one woman's memory of the latter event, recorded 10 years later as a comment on a *Scientific American* story about

9/11 memories. She reported that her brother left her a voice message saying: "'Uh . . . Cara, I think we're at war. They've attacked the World Trade Center in New York City.'" She went to tell her roommate, who told her he had already received a call from a friend. The two wanted to watch the televised coverage on it, but the satellite dish had yet to be installed, so the roommate went outside to install it, which she reported took about 15 minutes. Her reaction to the live television coverage was "Shock, immediate empathy for the victims, and outrage. . . . I was too shocked to cry. Those tears came late that evening, actually around 2:00 a.m., MST, on Sept. 12, when I finally went to bed" (Carapella55, 2011).

Note the detail provided in the memory—it covers who first told her about the event, where she was, when it happened, who else was there, how she felt, exact quotations of what was said, and even time estimates for installing the satellite dish and going to bed. These are typical characteristics of a *flashbulb memory*. Brown and Kulik (1977) proposed that memories of shocking incidents are embedded in the brain at the time of occurrence by a special mechanism that makes the memory vivid, fixed, and accurate. However, further research on flashbulb memories shows that although they may be vivid, they are neither unchanging nor accurate. Like all memories, so-called flashbulb memories decay over time. One study found that memories for 9/11 were as equally detailed after 7 months as after 7 days, but the details had started to shift in content over time: "Heard it sitting in class" might become "My mom told me on the phone," for example. Memories for comparable everyday events showed exactly the same rate of decay. What remained high over time for flashbulb memories were ratings of confidence in their accuracy and of their vividness (Talarico & Rubin, 2003). Traumatic events are therefore no more likely than other events to produce fixed, highly accurate photographic representations in memory.

Although not fixed, memories for traumatic events may change somewhat less than memories for pleasant or neutral events. For example, in one study, people who had experienced recent traumas were asked to report 12 details of the event (who was there, what one was wearing, the weather, etc.), and to select a highly positive experience and report 12 details about that event. The same people were interviewed about 4 months, 3.5 years, and 4 years later and asked to remember the same 12 details. Their memory for the details of the trauma memories was better than that of the positive memories and did not decline with time. Their better memory for traumatic events may be because the participants in this study said they thought about the traumas more often than the positive events (Porter & Peace, 2007).

Thus traumatic events are somewhat better remembered in that they change less over time. However, they are not necessarily more accurate to begin with (Laney & Loftus, 2005), and they are certainly not "burned in" to the brain. Even for trauma memories, about 20% to 25% of the details changed over time. And if your memory for a traumatic event changes over time, it's actually a good sign. People who were in or near the World Trade Center towers during the 9/11 terrorist attacks showed change in the content of their memories for the event over time, with approximately 20% of the details changing over an 11-month period. However, those whose memories changed the *most* showed the *best* adjustment (Dekel & Bonanno, 2013). So a fixed and unchanging memory for a traumatic event is a marker for, or perhaps a cause of, poor psychological adjustment to the experience rather than an innate feature of trauma memory.

As we discussed in Chapter 6, autobiographical memories are constructed in a way that meets the goals of the self in the current context. As contexts change, so ought memories to change in a flexible and well-calibrated memory system. Those whose memories do not change, therefore, are truly stuck in the past, with the self being influenced by the memory rather than vice versa. It's unhealthy when the self is influenced by a memory for an awful event. Trauma survivors who feel that trauma is central to their lives are more poorly adjusted than survivors who see it as more peripheral to their life story (Berntsen & Rubin, 2007).

In summary, lay traumatology regarding the stability of memory for trauma is partially correct in that traumas are well remembered. However, the memories aren't frozen. They change over time just as all memories do. The more change a trauma memory undergoes and the less it is seen as related to the self, the better it is for the rememberer.

LAY TRAUMATOLOGY BELIEF #2: LONG-TERM PSYCHOLOGICAL HARM IS INEVITABLE AFTER A SEVERE TRAUMA

By definition in the *DSM-5*, one must experience a trauma to be diagnosed with PTSD. It and Prolonged Grief Disorder are the *only DSM-5* diagnoses that require an instigating environmental event—and deliberately so. By the logic of the *DSM-5*, the experience of a trauma therefore *causes* PTSD (Rubin, Berntsen, & Bohni, 2008). But trauma—no matter how severe—does not itself cause PTSD or other long-term psychological problems. In fact, very few people who experience trauma develop PTSD. To be precise, only about 1 in 10 people experiencing trauma develop PTSD, making it the rare exception rather than the rule. Nor is developing any other psychological disorder inevitable (or even more likely) after experiencing a trauma (Breslau, 2002). Yet both laypeople (perhaps yourself) and mental health professionals widely believe that trauma causes disorders and, more specifically, that the more severe the trauma, the more severe the symptoms it causes. Neither of these beliefs is supported by research.

Understanding the origins of these beliefs requires a trip into fairly recent history. Veterans returning to the United States from the Vietnam War in the 1970s noticed that they were experiencing symptoms such as feeling angry and depersonalized, sleeping problems, and sometimes flashbacks and nightmares of their combat experiences. These symptoms were often labeled "post-Vietnam syndrome." They weren't the first veterans to experience such problems. World War I and II veterans were described as having "shell shock" or "combat stress reaction" (also "battle fatigue"), respectively, both convenient shorthand labels rather than a formal diagnosis. Vietnam veterans lobbied for a formal diagnosis of these problems being a result of combat exposure. They reasoned that if the U.S. government and military recognized soldiers' mental and physical health problems as a side effect of their service, then the government would logically need to pay for their treatment. Otherwise, treatment costs would be borne by the suffering individuals.

In addition, there is less shame related to a diagnosis that specifies the cause of the symptoms as the traumatic experience itself (as opposed to characteristics of the person who suffers the symptoms). Before the diagnosis of PTSD was formalized, soldiers who returned from combat were expected to recover from any negative effects. Those who did not recover were viewed as having some kind of genetic or temperamental weakness. It may be difficult to imagine medical and mental health professionals as well as soldiers' families and friends pointing to the person who suffered as the cause of his or her own problems, but that has been essentially the worldview about postcombat symptoms for most of recorded history. It is only recently, since the activism of Vietnam veterans and their advocates, that we have begun to look to the trauma rather than the person as the source (Jones & Wessely, 2007).

To make very clear that war trauma rather than the person was to blame, proponents of a posttraumatic stress diagnosis wanted to emphasize symptoms that seemed to reflect most directly the trauma itself. Thus, general symptoms such as depression, anger, and emotional numbness (the most common postwar complaints) were included in the diagnosis but were joined by specific symptoms of re-experiencing the trauma (flashbacks and nightmares). There was a corresponding shift in symptoms reported over time, according to PTSD expert Bessel van der Kolk (van der Kolk & Najavits, 2013). The specific memory-related complaints became more commonly reported and were the presenting problem, and the general complaints were reported less often. As he put it, "People's clinical presentations adapt themselves to the prevailing cultural norms" (p. 517).

Some do suffer mental health problems after trauma. But trauma does not inevitably lead to psychological problems; instead, there are different patterns of response to trauma. Looking across a large number of studies in which people's adjustment was measured before, during, and after a traumatic experience allows us to see five distinct patterns of response. Bonanno (2012) estimated from such studies that about 20% of trauma-exposed people will show a brief initial period of psychological symptoms (anxiety, sadness, flashbacks, nightmares, etc.) followed by complete recovery of normal function, and about 50% of trauma-exposed people will be completely resilient to the trauma and show no psychological symptoms whatsoever. Bonanno (2012) estimated that 7% of trauma-exposed people will actually show a pattern of improvement in mental health outcomes compared to their status before the trauma. This pattern of posttraumatic growth has been demonstrated on a number of dimensions, such as realizing the value of life and improvements in self-esteem (Tedeschi & Calhoun, 1996). Another 10% of people will continue to experience the same high level of psychological symptoms that they already exhibited before the trauma. That only leaves about 13% of people whose psychological health is negatively affected for the longer term by trauma.

Even experiencing one of the most highly traumatic events imaginable, child sexual abuse, does not by itself appear to increase the risk of psychological disorders in adulthood (Rind, Tromovitch, & Bauserman, 1998). This finding is so counterintuitive that the article reporting it in 1998 caused a firestorm in the national media, eventually leading to an unprecedented attempt by the U.S. Congress to influence the publication of scientific studies. Rind and colleagues analyzed the results of 59 published studies on the long-term effects of child sexual abuse, using well-established statistical methods. They found that those who had experienced sexual contact with an adult during childhood were somewhat more likely to have psychological problems in adulthood, including anxiety, depression, paranoia, psychosis, low self-esteem, and poor sexual and social adjustment. However, these psychological problems statistically need not be explained by the experience of sexual contact with an adult, but merely by the presence of an unhealthy family environment. That is, experiencing the traumatic event of child sexual abuse was a symptom of being brought up in a toxic home environment—which was the real problem. The authors never argued that child sexual abuse is acceptable; they explicitly stated in the article that "lack of harmfulness does not imply lack of wrongfulness" (p. 47). They simply showed that the trauma-to-disorder connection is much weaker than most people believe it to be.

When these results were reported in the media, they were widely misinterpreted as condoning the sexual abuse of children. A well-known and influential media pop psychologist, Dr. Laura Schlessinger, famously called this study "junk science" on her syndicated talk radio show. In response, several members of the U.S. House of Representatives presented a bill repudiating the results of the study and condemning the American Psychological Association (APA) for having published it in one of their journals. The resolution passed unanimously in both the House and the Senate. The APA responded by sending the article out for additional review by the American Association for the Advancement of Science, which ended the matter by stating that it would not question the peer-review process of the APA ("Rind et al. controversy," 2014). The moral of the story? It is so counterintuitive as to be *offensive* to suggest that long-term psychological harm from trauma is the exception rather than the rule.

But, you may ask, how can this possibly be true? The answer is straightforward (though not necessarily simple): People *recover* from traumatic experiences, just as they recover from physical injuries. Evidence points to the involvement of the psychological immune system (Gilbert, Pinel, Wilson, Blumberg, & Wheatley, 1998). Humans come equipped with not only a physical immune system but also a psychological immune system. For most encounters with potentially sickening agents, the physical immune system does its job just fine, protecting us from becoming ill without the need for living in a plastic bubble on a constant diet of antibiotics. In the same way, the psychological immune system enables us to resist being psychologically sickened by encounters with potentially pathology-inducing stresses and traumas.

The psychological immune system is composed of ways of thinking and acting that reduce the impact of traumatic events and daily stresses on our minds. So, for example, a person who loses her job might make herself feel better by reminding herself that she has some money in savings to fall back on or by telling herself that now she has the opportunity to search for a job she might enjoy more than her previous one. A person who is severely injured in an automobile accident might find himself newly appreciating the preciousness of life or easing his sadness by spending time with friends and loved ones. In other words, traumas don't occur in a vacuum. They happen to a living, active person whose thoughts, feelings, and relationships aid in recovery.

Like the physical immune system, the psychological immune system does its job silently, outside of our awareness. We are amazingly ignorant that we will cope with and make sense of stressful events, so we tend to predict that our reactions to events will be more intense and lasting than they actually turn out to be. For example, assistant professors were asked to estimate their happiness with life in the 5 years after their tenure decision if they were to be denied tenure (fired). They expected to experience a happiness level of only 3.4 on a scale of 1 to 7. But assistant professors who really had been denied tenure actually experienced a happiness level of 4.7 in the 5 years after this negative outcome, no different from those who had received tenure (happiness level 5.2; Gilbert et al., 1998). The psychological immune system brought people back to a sunny outlook to an unforeseen extent.

Like its physical counterpart, the psychological immune system actually seems to be *stimulated* by the experience of stress or trauma: It takes exposure to bad experiences to get it going. Several studies have found that the more stress or distress people experience, the more active coping efforts they engage in, and consequently the better off they are down the line (Joseph,

2012). Some studies find that there is a limit to this stimulating effect. With extreme, repeated trauma or for people whose psychological health is fragile, the immune system is not engaged as all mental efforts must be directed toward simple day-to-day living tasks (Kunst, 2010).

The psychological immune system cannot be photographed in action, but its effects have been documented in research studies. In one study, participants were asked to predict their emotional state on Valentine's Day and then reported their actual emotional state on the day itself. They also described what they did that day so researchers could code these descriptions for mentions of effective coping strategies. Those who were in a dating relationship expected to feel happier than they actually did, and those who were not in a dating relationship expected to feel sadder than they actually did. More importantly, those who mentioned using good coping strategies had not previously predicted being better off, but were in fact much better off than those who did not mention using good coping strategies. Their psychological immune system was both effective and invisible to them (Hoerger, 2012). This cloak of invisibility gives the psychological immune system its power. After all, if we were aware that we could cope efficiently with most of what life throws at us, we would not take proper precautions to avoid danger or to protect ourselves and our loved ones from trauma.

Knowing about the psychological immune system and its stealthy manner of operation may help us to explain why such wrath was aroused by the Rind and colleagues' (1998) article about childhood sexual abuse. Because we are often ignorant of the psychological immune system, when we imagine going through a traumatic experience, we imagine it having a devastating and long-lasting impact. To assert that someone may experience trauma and turn out okay seems illogical as well as insensitive.

As we shall see, the topic of child sexual abuse is always controversial and emotional, so any research that addresses this topic is likely to cause heated argument. But another reason might be that talking about recovery as normative seems insensitive to those who have experienced trauma, as if we're waving it off and saying, "Whatever, you'll be fine." The wrath of the media and lawmakers toward Rind and colleagues (1998) begins to make sense if their article was seen as dismissive of those who have had to suffer abuse. However, showing evidence for the psychological immune system in no way minimizes the experience of those exposed to trauma.

Logically, it is not just long-term damage that we want to prevent, but also the short-term pain of experiencing a trauma. Our legal system awards compensation for pain and suffering even if that pain was temporary. As a society, we are so concerned about pain that we have laws to limit the pain not just of humans but of nonhuman animals in research and in food production. We are not only concerned with the long-term effects of pain; we also care about the mere experience of pain at all. No one wants another being to suffer unnecessarily. Therefore, instead of asserting that trauma inevitably leads to long-term psychological problems such as PTSD, we will learn the most by (a) trying to prevent traumas from occurring so that both short- and long-term psychological symptoms are reduced, and (b) trying to ascertain *which* people are more vulnerable to such problems so that we may intervene appropriately.

In short, the lay traumatology belief that bad things lead to bad mental health, in proportion to their badness, is not upheld by the results of research. First, people cope with bad things much better than they (or we) expect. Second, there is no objective scale of badness. People experience traumatic and stressful events in different ways because of their life experiences, age, coping skills, social support, belief system, and so on, making only some people at particularly high risk for experiencing long-term aftereffects of trauma. Third, this belief that bad things lead inevitably to bad mental health seems to be historically and culturally bound— meaning, the belief came about in latter 20th-century United States. Humans are usually resilient in the face of adversity. This resilience is truly inspiring and ought not to make us minimize our efforts to help those who are not resilient to trauma. Rather, we should be working to prevent traumatic experiences and to identify people at risk of long-term psychological harm from trauma and to treat them most humanely and effectively.

LAY TRAUMATOLOGY BELIEF #3: TRAUMATIC EXPERIENCES ARE OFTEN INITIALLY REPRESSED YET LATER RECOVERABLE FROM MEMORY

This belief is by far the most controversial of the three we address in this chapter. Debate about this issue was widespread in the 1990s and came to be referred to as the Memory Wars (Ost, 2003). The idea arose that traumatic experiences can be stored yet buried. It was based on the anecdotal reports of combat veterans who reported that they could not remember the actual traumatic incident of being on the battlefield but nonetheless were distressed by the experience, and on clinical reports of adults' suddenly remembering sexual abuse from their early childhood.

Case Studies

For example, take the case of Claudia (Bower, 1993). As an adult, she began to experience flashbacks of being sexually abused by her brother. During group therapy sessions, she reported full memories of the abuse coming back to her for the first time since the abuse occurred at age 4. Perhaps seeking some form of closure, or perhaps doubting the veracity of her memories, Claudia returned to her parents' house to search the bedroom of her now-dead brother. Her parents had kept the room intact since he had left to serve—and died—in Vietnam. Claudia found a diary in which her brother had kept records of the abuse she remembered experiencing, validating details of her newfound memories such as handcuffing her and burning her with cigarettes. She even found

215

a pair of handcuffs among his belongings. Claudia's case contains the essential elements of repression and recovery: childhood sexual abuse, a long period of amnesia for the abuse, and a return of the memories in adulthood, often in the context of therapy. It has been estimated that almost half of adult clients who seek psychotherapy for child sexual abuse report having an extended period of amnesia for the abuse itself (Brewin & Andrews, 1998).

Given what we've learned about memories for trauma so far, this amnesia followed by full remembering is a decidedly unusual pattern. Normally memories for a trauma such as childhood sexual abuse would be better and longer-lasting than other memories (although of course not perfectly accurate; Laney & Loftus, 2005). Moreover, the notion that amnesia can be motivated by the sheer horror surrounding an event was grounds for skepticism among many memory researchers. Nevertheless, the increasing incidence of reports of recovery led to increased interest, motivated in part by Freud's theory that distressing memories would be prevented from entering the conscious mind by an unconscious process of pushing the memories away (Breuer & Freud, 1895/1974). Meanwhile mainstream memory researchers continued to assert that nothing like repression and recovery had ever been demonstrated in the laboratory or carefully documented in a case study (e.g., Holmes, 1995).

The usually professional back-and-forth of the scientific process exploded in the late 1990s with the reporting of an allegedly airtight documented case study of abuse, repression, and recovery (Corwin & Olafson, 1997). A woman pseudonymously referred to as Jane Doe, who was allegedly abused by her mother, described the incident to her court-appointed psychiatrist on videotape at age 6. Then, 11 years later, the psychiatrist contacted Jane to ask whether she would be willing to discuss her memory of the abuse. Jane was interested in being interviewed and especially in watching the videotape made when she was a child, as she reported not being able to remember the abuse any longer. She seemed to remember more and more details during the interview, including new details she had not reported at age 6. Upon being shown the original recording of herself as a child reporting the event, she experienced shock as the memories flooded back to her. Jane Doe's case was seen by many as a textbook case of repression and recovery.

Reactions to this case study show how complicated the issue of repression and recovery is. Several psychologists expressed enthusiasm about the content of the memory and the nature of Jane's emotional reactions and the strong support these provided for repression and recovery (e.g., Armstrong, 1997; Ekman, 1997). Others expressed mild doubts about whether the abuse was truly never remembered between age 6 and 17, and whether the age 17 memory was truly the same as the age 6 memory (Neisser, 1997; Schooler, 1997). Loftus and Guyer (2002) investigated the Jane Doe case thoroughly and expressed doubt that the abuse incident even happened at all. Instead, they argued, Jane Doe was a case study of a false memory suggested to Jane as a child by her father and stepmother in order to gain custody, as opposed to a case study of repression and recovery.

In other words, even this, one of the best-documented alleged cases of abuse, repression, and recovery, does not reliably demonstrate all of the hallmarks of the process. Rather than critiquing this single case study further, some memory researchers turned their attention to attempts to demonstrate a repression-like pattern of memory for neutral or mildly unpleasant stimuli in the lab. Several types of findings seemed to corroborate the buried-then-recovered pattern. Bear with us, it's about to get a little technical. It's critical to understand exactly what has been demonstrated in the lab and the extent to which these findings map onto the real-world issue of repressed memories for childhood trauma.

Laboratory Evidence of Repression-Like Phenomena

First consider the phenomenon of *hypermnesia*, meaning better memory over time. Usually memory becomes worse over time, with fewer and fewer items or details being recalled over successive days, weeks, or months (e.g., Squire, 1989; Wickelgren, 1972). But occasionally memory becomes better over time, with more items or details being recalled (Erdelyi, 2010). Hypermnesia is particularly likely for meaningful materials and when participants are given a series of blanks and encouraged to guess rather than given a list of items for yes/no judgments (Erdelyi, 2010). In the real world, a traumatic life event is unarguably meaningful, and there may be occasions upon which people allow their minds to roam free, to "guess" what might have happened to them during childhood. Hypermnesia therefore *may* occur for real-world events, although 40 years of research has produced very few successful laboratory demonstrations of hypermnesia for real events (Bluck, Levine, & Laulhere, 1999; Campbell, Nadel, Duke, & Ryan, 2011).

Other clues from the laboratory suggest an additional mechanism by which repression might work. There is a subset of people categorized as *repressors*, who report low anxiety but are high in defensiveness (meaning that they tend to "fake good" on self-report measures; Weinberger, Schwartz, & Davidson, 1979). These people cope with unpleasant information by avoiding it, as is theoretically the case with repression of a traumatic experience, by pushing it out of conscious memory. In fact, repressors do report fewer negative autobiographical memories and do a better job of forgetting negative information they have been instructed to forget, especially when their memory is tested privately (Myers & Derakshan, 2004). Moreover, repressors have intact implicit memory for negative self-relevant information even though they successfully push away explicit memory of it (Fujiwara, Levine, & Anderson, 2008). Thus it may be possible for a person motivated to avoid thinking of a trauma to forget (explicitly) and yet preserve a record of the event (implicitly) that might be called up again years later.

Still other findings in the laboratory have been offered as evidence of normal memory mechanisms that happen in all people and that could lead to unwanted memories being forgotten. For example, there is the memory suppression (inhibitory control) effect demonstrated by Anderson and Green (2001). In their studies participants learn a list of word pairs. Then one word of a pair was presented on the screen and participants were instructed to either respond out loud with the associated word, or to suppress and not think about the associated word. Afterward, participants were given different cues that ought to bring to mind the suppressed items. The more times the word had been suppressed, the less likely participants were to remember it later.

Thus, people can simply choose to keep information that they do not wish to recall out of memory by inhibiting recall of it. Anderson and Levy (2002) argued that such a process, if repeated frequently enough, could lead to complete forgetting, even of negatively emotionally charged experiences. Presumably, the horror of childhood abuse would be so often and so fully inhibited over and over that forgetting could result. Compelling though such an argument is, there are two missing pieces in this laboratory demonstration that prevent it from providing direct evidence of repression and recovery. First, the amount of forgetting in these studies is not terribly impressive; the majority of information presented was still remembered with the alternative cue (about 70%). Second, there was no evidence that the forgotten information could be readily recovered later.

More direct evidence of both repression and recovery in the laboratory was provided by Smith and Moynan (2008). In their studies, participants learned lists of words that fit into a category (e.g., death). Then half of participants performed a variety of unrelated distractor tasks, and the other half were re-exposed to some but not all of the word lists. Then all participants were asked to recall the names of the word list categories. Those who had been re-exposed to some of the lists recalled the names of those lists better than the ones to which they had not been re-exposed; no surprises there. But these participants actually *forgot* more of the names of the lists to which they had *not* been re-exposed (remembering only 25%) than those in the distractor condition who had only seen each list once (remembering 60%). That is, by turning their attention to competing information, participants actually forgot information they had previously learned. Crucially, some of these forgotten word lists contained highly emotional and unpleasant information (death, diseases, expletive words).

What's special about this kind of forgetting is that the forgotten information can be recovered later. After the recall test for the names of the word lists, Smith and Moynan (2008) re-presented all the list names to all participants and asked them to try to recall words that had been on each of the lists. The results are compelling: Participants in both conditions performed equally well. Put differently, people who had previously forgotten that an experience (list) happened at all were able to remember as much about it as someone with continuous memory for the experience, once provided with the right cue (name of the list). All the ducks are in a row to establish the reality of repression and recovery: Unpleasant information is encountered, an ordinary memory mechanism (interference) produces forgetting of that information, and a cue encountered later restores the memory for that unpleasant information.

Even more impressive is laboratory evidence for a similar sequence of remember/forget/recover for unpleasant experiences rather than mundane word lists. One group of researchers (Barnier, Conway, Mayoh, Speyer, Avizmil, & Harris, 2007) used a slightly different forgetting method than the inhibition of recall or rehearsal of other information to produce forgetting. In this study, participants were given a list of word cues (such as "hurt," "fulfilled," and "punctual") and asked to write down a memory for a life experience that the cue brought to mind. Afterward, they were presented with half these cues one at a time and asked to report the memory they had written down for that cue previously. Then half of participants were told that the memories they had just recalled for these cues (List 1) were "just for practice" and that they should forget those memories; they wouldn't need to recall them again in the experiment. (This *directed forgetting* instruction usually leads to true forgetting [MacLeod, 1999].) The other half were told that they should continue to remember the memories they had just recalled as they would be asked about them later. The remaining cue words were then presented and participants were asked to recall the memories they had originally written down for those cues (List 2).

Then participants were given a recall test in which they were asked to recall all of the memories they had originally written down, whether they had been told to forget or remember them earlier (i.e., List 1 and List 2 memories). Half of participants simply tried to remember all of the memories on their own. For them, a directed forgetting effect was obtained, such that those who had previously been told to forget the memories in List 1 recalled fewer of them than those told to remember them. The other half of participants were given the cue words for List 1 and List 2 and asked to remember all of the memories they had originally written down. For them, no directed forgetting effect was obtained. Instead, those who had been told to forget the List 1 memories did as well at remembering as those who had been told to remember them. The pattern was the same for unpleasant memories and pleasant and neutral memories. Barnier and colleagues (2007) therefore successfully demonstrated that unpleasant life events can be recalled, then forgotten, then recalled again given the right cue. To some memory researchers, the preponderance of evidence points to a number of ordinary memory mechanisms by which memories can be repressed and then later recovered.

Caveats Regarding Repression-Like Patterns in Memory

Despite these demonstrations of forgetting followed by remembering, other research casts doubt on the validity of the remember/forget/recover pattern. One group of memory researchers argued that child sexual abuse is not a new phenomenon, but recovery of memories from childhood appears to be. If, indeed, traumas often lead to repressed and then recovered memories, then surely there would be mentions of it in writings throughout history. For example, history is replete with descriptions of both real and fictional people who hear voices that others do not hear (i.e., schizophrenia), or who are suicidal and eschew food and sleep (i.e., major depressive disorder), or who have irrational fears of specific objects (i.e., specific phobia). These descriptions occur in the literature of many cultures as well, so we do not doubt the validity of the disorders they represent. Pope, Poliakoff, Parker, Boynes, and Hudson (2007) proposed that unlike those disorders, repression and recovery is a culture-bound modern syndrome, gaining popularity in Western cultures in about 1800 along with a growing fascination with the unconscious mind. Pope and colleagues challenged anyone to find an example of a character in literature prior to 1800 who was described as experiencing a traumatic event, forgetting about it, and then remembering it later. Although over a hundred submissions were received, none fit the repression-and-recovery criteria. They concluded that there is no real neurological condition of repression and recovery.[1]

Note also that, despite the suggestive evidence reviewed in the previous section, there is no controlled research showing all steps of the process. The research would need to demonstrate that (a) a traumatic experience can be remembered immediately, then (b) completely unremembered soon after, and (c) once again remembered years later. Traumatic experiences cannot ethically be doled out to research participants in the laboratory, but researchers can scientifically study memory among real-world trauma survivors immediately after the traumatic event. The possibility of repression can then be investigated prospectively rather than retrospectively. We know of no study that has shown prospectively that a traumatic event was immediately forgotten, without traumatic brain injury having occurred (e.g., Gil, Caspi, Ben-Ari, Koren, & Klein, 2005; Kleim & Ehlers, 2008). Certainly people do forget traumatic events, but forgetting occurs over time intervals of months or years, not immediately as would be the case for repression, and at a similar rate as for ordinary memory decay (Engelhard, van den Hout, & McNally, 2008; Lalande &

Bonanno, 2011). Moreover, traumatic events are *less* likely to be forgotten than other types of mildly stressful events (e.g., financial difficulties, moves; Lalande & Bonanno, 2011).

Instead of remember/forget/recover, prospective studies have shown some evidence of the formation of (probably) false memories over time that were (likely) misperceived as being recovered. In one study, participants were 50 patients who had suffered a traumatic brain injury during an accident and were unable to remember the accident itself immediately afterward. Then, 2 years later, 40% of these participants claimed to have "recovered" a memory for the event (Harvey & Bryant, 2001). However, without having encoded the original event, recovering it ought not to be possible. Therefore the authors suggested that most of these participants were reconstructing a (false) memory of the accident based on details told to them by others. A few may have retained "islands" of memory for the event and have filled in the details in a similar manner, and some may have had intact implicit memory for the event that was then used to create a plausible explicit memory. In any case, the details in all likelihood came from a place external to the person's own memory for the event.

Indeed, people can be fairly readily induced to remember events that never happened to them. As mentioned in Chapter 3, a large literature now demonstrates that false memories can be implanted into unsuspecting participants. In this research, an event is selected that has demonstrably *not* happened to the group of participants in question, which we will term a false event. There are several ways to identify a false event, including giving a preliminary survey to the participants or their parents asking them to check off which of a list of childhood experiences happened to the participant. Another method is to select an event that is impossible, such as meeting Bugs Bunny at Disneyland (Bugs Bunny is a Warner Brothers character, not a Disney character). Next, a combination of suggestion and imagination is imposed upon participants. They are told that their parents said the false event in question happened, or in some cases shown a doctored photograph. Participants are then told that they should be able to recover the memory of the event if they spend time imagining how it could have happened and trying to fill in as many sensory details as they can. Finally, participants are asked to indicate their confidence that the false event did in fact happen to them. On average, 31% of participants fall prey to false-memory implantation using these techniques (Lindsay, Hagen, Read, Wade, & Garry, 2004). The kinds of memories that have been implanted by these techniques vary widely, as does the rate of susceptibility to the false memory. Table 7.1 shows some examples.

The pseudomemories created by false-memory implantation techniques feel quite real and are in many ways indistinguishable from real memories. First, true and false memories are equally emotional in content (Laney & Takarangi, 2013; Laney & Loftus, 2008). Second, true and false beliefs that an event happened both influence behavior via the directive function we discussed in Chapter 6. Participants convinced that a costumed Pluto at Disneyland licked their ear in a creepy way were willing to pay less for a Pluto stuffed animal afterward (Berkowitz, Laney, Morris, Garry, & Loftus, 2008). Participants convinced they once got sick eating egg-salad sandwiches ate fewer egg-salad sandwiches 4 months later (Geraerts et al., 2008). A false memory affects our decisions in the present moment in the same way as a true memory.

Because so many reports of memory recovery come from those who have recently undergone psychotherapy, the motivation behind false-memory implantation studies is to simulate how inappropriate and suggestive psychotherapy techniques may lead to false memories. Psychotherapists may directly suggest repressed child abuse as a cause of current symptoms, and people seeking psychotherapy often believe they have repressed memories of abuse (Rubin & Berntsen, 2009). Moreover, procedures to "recover" memories, much like that used in laboratory studies of false-memory implantation, were reported to be used by 71% of psychotherapists in 1995 (Poole, Lindsay, Memon, & Bull, 1995). The confluence of suggestive therapists, willing patients, and false-memory–producing techniques is likely responsible for

TABLE 7.1 **A SAMPLING OF PSEUDOMEMORIES INVESTIGATED IN LABORATORY RESEARCH**

False Event	% of Participants "Remembering"	Reference
Received a medical rectal enema	0%	Pezdek et al. (1997)
Met Bugs Bunny at Disneyland	16%	Braun, Ellis, & Loftus (2002)
Caught parents having sex	20%	Laney & Loftus (2008)
Spilled punch bowl on bride's parents	25%	Hyman & Pentland (1996)
Got lost in a shopping mall	25%	Loftus (1993)
Ear licked by Pluto at Disneyland	35%*	Berkowitz et al. (2008)
Got sick after eating egg salad	35%*	Geraerts et al. (2008)
Attacked by an animal	37%	Porter et al. (1999)
Gave someone a black eye	41%	Carey & Takarangi (2013)
Rode in a hot-air balloon	50%	Wade et al. (2002)
Visited a burns unit	55%	Otgaar, Smeets, & Peters (2012)
Saw [nonexistent] attack ad on Obama	68%	Frenda et al. (2013)
Put "Slime" toy in teacher's desk	70%	Lindsay et al. (2004)

*Includes both those with a clear memory and those who expressed a belief that the event happened without a clear memory.

many cases of claimed repression and recovery. In 2004, about 1,300 people who later realized that they falsely accused others of sexual abuse based upon a pseudomemory were identified (McHugh, Lief, Freyd, & Fetkewicz, 2004). Therefore, false memories of childhood trauma have been demonstrated in both the laboratory and the real world. To some memory researchers, then, the preponderance of evidence points to claims of recovered memory being errorful.

Middle Ground

What shall we make of this inconsistent mess of case studies, anecdotal reports, laboratory studies, and prospective studies? Whom shall we believe—those who argue that child sexual abuse can be forgotten and then remembered again, or those who argue that such experiences would be well remembered and are therefore likely to be false memories if recalled in adulthood? Neither wholesale acceptance nor utter rejection is necessary. There is plenty of room in the middle, although the middle ground receives less attention in the media. We'll discuss two ways one can be a fence-sitter in the debate about recovered memories and yet still account for the evidence on all sides.

One middle ground is to conceptualize cases of valid memory recovery as instances of *forgetting of previous remembering*. Virtually all evidence of repression and recovery relies upon the rememberer's self-report of forgetting. People are actually not very good at remembering when and whether they have remembered or forgotten information. Laboratory studies show that people may remember something but when asked later whether they remembered it, fail to report that they did so (Arnold & Lindsay, 2002). Thus, a 35-year-old who says he is remembering something he has not remembered since he was a 5-year-old child may simply be mistaken about his memory.

A study with participants who did or did not identify as survivors of child sexual abuse categorized the participants as having a continuous memory of the abuse (they said they always remembered it), a discontinuous memory of the abuse (they said they repressed and then recovered it), or no abuse (they said they were never abused). All participants were given word lists to remember at two different times, then were asked later to think back and judge which words they had remembered and which they had forgotten. All three groups had difficulty with this task, but the discontinuous memory group (repressed and recovered) was especially likely to claim that they failed to remember words that they actually had remembered (Geraerts et al., 2006). In other words, people who claim to experience repression and recovery also tend to forget that they did remember information. This study suggests a specific memory deficit in people who claim repression and recovery. These people may well have remembered being abused all along but have simply forgotten that they remembered, giving them the impression of repression and recovery. Seen in this light, people's "recovered" memories are accurate in content. It's only people's subjective experience of having repressed and recovered the memory—a form of metamemory—that is inaccurate.

Another middle ground is to see memory recovery due to repression as a *viable, but rare, phenomenon*. Two lines of research demonstrate different mechanisms that would support such a view. In one line of research, survey respondents who reported having been physically or sexually abused as children were then asked whether they had ever failed to remember the abuse for some time. Then they were asked why or in what way they forgot it: like any other memory; because they avoided thinking about it; or because it became buried and inaccessible and then popped back up. Very few people self-reported the third (repression and recovery) option. Instead, people tended to report the other two, which are based on ordinary memory mechanisms (Epstein & Bottoms, 2002). Thus, we can conceptualize most cases of claimed memory recovery as a semantic issue, a failure to understand that there is nothing special about the way this memory acted. Only (in the researchers' estimates) about 1% of the time would repression and recovery occur, even if we took as fact the reports of everyone who claims it, after we interview them to see which pattern their memory really followed.

Viable but rare is also the conclusion from another line of research. People who said they remembered being abused were asked whether they had always remembered it ("continuous" memory), or had repressed and recovered it ("discontinuous" memory). Those in the recovered memory group were then asked whether they had recovered the memory in the course of psycho-therapy, or in some other everyday context. Then the researchers set about trying to find objective corroborating evidence that the claimed abuse truly occurred, using criteria similar to that that a court of law would allow. The researchers found that none of the memories recovered in therapy could be corroborated in any way. But 37% of the memories recovered outside of therapy could be corroborated. Approximately the same percentage, 45%, of the continuous memories could be corroborated (Geraerts et al., 2007). Therefore, the authors concluded, memories recovered in therapy are likely false and implanted, whereas memories recov-ered outside of therapy are likely true—or as likely to be true as any other memory (see Chapters 3 and 6).

The lessons from all of this research on repression and recov-ery: First, you and your loved ones should avoid a therapist who ignores the problem that brought you to see him or her and instead attempts to convince you that you have repressed a mem-ory that you need to recover, and you should be skeptical of the validity of any memory recovered in this way. Second, know that accurate memories are likely to be reported by those who expe-rienced the recovery of the memory in the real world (outside of therapy), but that doesn't mean that the person actually ever repressed them. He or she may simply have forgotten or avoided them or may be wrong about having forgotten the incident in between its occurrence and the recent memory of it. And when it comes down to it, metamemory is of interest primarily to mem-ory geeks such as the authors of this book. The accurate content of the memory (not the metamemory) is of the utmost importance.

In summary, the lay belief that traumas are often repressed then potentially recovered is difficult to judge as right or wrong. It depends on how one defines repression, and whether one trusts people's reports of their own memory. The evidence suggests that most alleged cases of repression and recovery are the result of either mistaken metamemory or harmful and discredited psychotherapy techniques. Only a very few may be genuine.

WHAT CAN WE DO?

We began this chapter by noting that traumatic experiences will happen to most people (70% to 90%) in their lifetime. Despite all of the controversy and the complicated research results, there are a few solid pieces of information you can use to guide you should you or a loved one experience a trauma.

1. Define yourself in ways that are irrelevant to the trauma. Don't make the trauma central to who you are. Research shows that people who think of a traumatic experience as central to their definition of the self experience more psychological symptoms of anxiety and depression as well (Berntsen & Rubin, 2006). You aren't the person to whom trauma happened; you are *you*.
2. Understand the normalcy of intrusive thoughts, including that they will very likely decline over time on their own. Within a month of the 9/11 terrorist attacks, people in New York City and those who watched the media coverage reported a large number of unwanted intrusive thoughts about the attacks. But the number of these thoughts reduced in frequency soon afterward (Silver, Holman, McIntosh, Poulin, & Gil-Rivas, 2002). Research shows that people who become concerned with intrusive thoughts continue to experience them at a high rate. People who accept them

as normal see a reduction in intrusive thoughts and other PTSD symptoms (Halligan, Michael, Clark, & Ehlers, 2003).

3. Wait and see before you go to a psychotherapist's office. Remember that many (most) people have only short-term rather than long-term pain as a result of a traumatic experience, and that you have a psychological immune system that will fight for you. Research shows that immediate clinical psychological intervention after traumatic experiences does not help, and may even worsen, posttraumatic symptoms (McNally, Bryant, & Ehlers, 2003). Let your mind work through it in its own way, understanding that it will take time. You also don't need to try to "make sense" of the trauma (Park, 2010). It may never make sense to you, and that's all right. Coming to terms with it and accepting it seem to be the most important aspects of healthy coping with a trauma. If you continue to experience a high rate of upsetting and uncontrollable memories, sleep problems, and anxiety after a period of months, then find a skilled psychotherapist to work with you to reduce these symptoms.

4. Don't feel that it is necessary to "recover" from memory any aspects of the trauma that you do not fully remember in order to heal from it. Remember that forgetting of both pleasant and unpleasant experiences is natural, normal, and *healthy*. No matter what you have experienced, you have the rest of your life to live and many memories ahead of you.

NOTE

1. Later, the authors were pointed to a single example that did fit—a character in a 1786 opera—but this single counterexample they deemed insufficiently convincing to overturn their prior conclusion (news.brown.edu/pressreleases/2009/07/memory).

REFERENCES

American Psychiatric Association. (2013). *Diagnostic and statistical manual of mental disorders* (5th ed.). Washington, DC: Author.

Anderson, M. C., & Green, C. (2001). Suppressing unwanted memories by executive control. *Nature, 410*(6826), 366–369. doi:10.1038/35066572

Anderson, M. C., & Levy, B. (2002). Repression can (and should) be studied empirically. *Trends in Cognitive Sciences, 6*, 502–503.

Armstrong, J. (1997). Exploring the lines of Jane Doe's picture of pain. *Child Maltreatment, 2*(2), 121–122. doi:10.1177/1077559597002002004

Arnold, M. M., & Lindsay, D. (2002). Remembering remembering. *Journal of Experimental Psychology: Learning, Memory, and Cognition, 28*(3), 521–529. doi:10.1037/0278-7393.28.3.521

Barnier, A. J., Conway, M. A., Mayoh, L., Speyer, J., Avizmil, O., & Harris, C. B. (2007). Directed forgetting of recently recalled autobiographical memories. *Journal of Experimental Psychology: General, 136*, 301–322. doi:10.1037/0096-3445.136.2.301

Berkowitz, S. R., Laney, C., Morris, E. K., Garry, M., & Loftus, E. F. (2008). Pluto behaving badly: False beliefs and their consequences. *The American Journal of Psychology, 121*(4), 643–660. doi:10.2307/20445490

Berntsen, D., & Rubin, D. (2006). The centrality of event scale: A measure of integrating a trauma into one's identity and its relation to post-traumatic stress disorder symptoms. *Behaviour Research and Therapy* [Serial online], *44*(2), 219–231. Available from PsycINFO, Ipswich, MA.

Berntsen, D., & Rubin, D. C. (2007). When a trauma becomes a key to identity: Enhanced integration of trauma memories predicts post-traumatic stress disorder symptoms. *Applied Cognitive Psychology, 21*, 417–431. doi:10.1002/acp.1290

Bluck, S., Levine, L. J., & Laulhere, T. M. (1999). Autobiographical remembering and hypermnesia: A comparison of older and younger adults. *Psychology and Aging, 14*, 671–682.

Bonanno, G. A. (2012). Resilience and variability following oil spill disasters. *Psychiatry: Interpersonal and Biological Processes, 75*(3), 236–242. doi:10.1521/psyc.2012.75.3.236

Bourne, C., Frasquilho, F., Roth, A. D., & Holmes, E. A. (2010). Is it mere distraction? Peri-traumatic verbal tasks can increase analogue flashbacks but reduce voluntary memory performance. *Journal of Behavior Therapy and Experimental Psychiatry, 41*(3), 316–324. doi:10.1016/j.jbtep.2010.03.001

Bower, B. (1993). Sudden recall: Adult memories of child abuse spark a heated debate. *Science News.* Retrieved from www.thefreelibrary.com/Science+News/1993/September/18-p510

Breslau, N. (2002). Epidemiologic studies of trauma, posttraumatic stress disorder, and other psychiatric disorders. *The Canadian Journal of Psychiatry/La Revue Canadienne de Psychiatrie, 47*(10), 923–929.

Breslau, N., & Kessler, R. C. (2001). The stressor criterion in *DSM-IV* posttraumatic stress disorder: An empirical investigation. *Biological Psychiatry, 50*(9), 699–704. doi:10.1016/S0006-3223(01)01167-2

Breslau, N., Kessler, R. C., Chilcoat, H. D., Schultz, L. R., Davis, G. C., & Andreski, P. (1998). Trauma and posttraumatic stress disorder in the community: The 1996 Detroit Area Survey of Trauma. *Archives of General Psychiatry, 55*(7), 626–632. doi:10.1001/archpsyc.55.7.626

Breuer, J., & Freud, S. (1974). Studies on hysteria (J. Strachey & A. Strachey, Trans.). In *The Pelican Freud library* (Vol. 3). Harmondsworth, UK: Penguin. (Original work published 1895)

Brewin, C. R., & Andrews, B. (1998). Recovered memories of trauma: Phenomenology and cognitive mechanisms. *Clinical Psychology Review, 18,* 949–970. doi:10.1016/S0272-7358(98)00040-3

Brown, R., & Kulik, J. (1977). Flashbulb memories. *Cognition, 5*(1), 73–99. doi:10.1016/0010-0277(77)90018-X

Campbell, J., Nadel, L., Duke, D., & Ryan, L. (2011). Remembering all that and then some: Recollection of autobiographical memories after a 1-year delay. *Memory, 19*(4), 406–415. doi:10.1080/09658211.2011.578073

Carapella55. (2011, September 12). *My brother called me . . .* [Online forum comment]. Retrieved from www.scientificamerican.com/article.cfm?id=911-memory-accuracy

Corwin, D. L., & Olafson, E. (1997). Videotaped discovery of a reportedly unrecallable memory of child sexual abuse: Comparison with a childhood interview videotaped 11 years before. *Child Maltreatment, 2,* 91–112. doi:10.1177/1077559597002002001

Dekel, S., & Bonanno, G. A. (2013). Changes in trauma memory and patterns of posttraumatic stress. *Psychological Trauma: Theory, Research, Practice, and Policy, 5*, 26–34. doi:10.1037/a0022750

Ehlers, A., & Clark, D. M. (2000). A cognitive model of posttraumatic stress disorder. *Behaviour Research and Therapy, 38*, 319–345.

Ekman, P. (1997). Expressive behavior and the recovery of a traumatic memory: Comments on the videotapes of Jane Doe. *Child Maltreatment, 2*(2), 113–116. doi:10.1177/107755959700 2002002

Engelhard, I. M., van den Hout, M. A., & McNally, R. J. (2008). Memory consistency for traumatic events in Dutch soldiers deployed to Iraq. *Memory, 16*, 3–9. doi:10.1080/09658210701334022

Epstein, M. A., & Bottoms, B. L. (2002). Explaining the forgetting and recovery of abuse and trauma memories: Possible mechanisms. *Child Maltreatment, 7*, 210–225. doi:10.1177/ 1077559502007003004

Erdelyi, M. (2010). The ups and downs of memory. *American Psychologist, 65*, 623–633. doi:10.1037/a0020440

FarrahSpada. (2012, August 1). *I have PTSD* [Online forum comment]. Retrieved from www.experienceproject.com/stories/Have-Ptsd/ 2462547

Fujiwara, E., Levine, B., & Anderson, A. K. (2008). Intact implicit and reduced explicit memory for negative self-related information in repressive coping. *Cognitive, Affective and Behavioral Neuroscience, 8*(3), 254–263. doi:10.3758/CABN.8.3.254

Geraerts, E., Arnold, M. M., Lindsay, D., Merckelbach, H., Jelicic, M., & Hauer, B. (2006). Forgetting of prior remembering in persons reporting recovered memories of childhood sexual abuse. *Psychological Science, 17*(11), 1002–1008. doi:10.1111/j.1467-9280 .2006.01819.x

Geraerts, E., Bernstein, D. M., Merckelbach, H., Linders, C., Raymaekers, L., & Loftus, E. F. (2008). Lasting false beliefs and their behavioral consequences. *Psychological Science, 19*(8), 749–753. doi:10.1111/j.1467-9280.2008.02151.x

Geraerts, E., Schooler, J. W., Merckelbach, H., Jelicic, M., Hauer, B. A., & Ambadar, Z. (2007). The reality of recovered memories: Corroborating continuous and discontinuous memories of childhood sexual abuse. *Psychological Science, 18*, 564–568. doi:10.1111/j.1467-9280.2007.01940.x

Gil, S., Caspi, Y., Ben-Ari, I. Z., Koren, D., & Klein, E. (2005). Does memory of a traumatic event increase the risk for posttraumatic stress disorder in patients with traumatic brain injury? A prospective study. *The American Journal of Psychiatry, 162*, 963–969. doi:10.1176/appi.ajp.162.5.963

Gilbert, D. T., Pinel, E. C., Wilson, T. D., Blumberg, S. J., & Wheatley, T. P. (1998). Immune neglect: A source of durability bias in affective forecasting. *Journal of Personality and Social Psychology, 75*(3), 617–638. doi:10.1037/0022-3514.75.3.617

Golding, J. M., Sanchez, R., & Sego, S. A. (1996). Do you believe in repressed memories? *Professional Psychology: Research and Practice, 27*(5), 429–437. doi:10.1037/0735-7028.27.5.429

Guy, S., & Cahill, L. (1999). The role of overt rehearsal in enhanced conscious memory for emotional events. *Consciousness and Cognition: An International Journal, 8*(1), 114–122. doi:10.1006/ccog.1998.0379

Halligan, S. L., Michael, T., Clark, D. M., & Ehlers, A. (2003). Posttraumatic stress disorder following assault: The role of cognitive processing, trauma memory, and appraisals. *Journal of Consulting and Clinical Psychology, 71*, 419–431. doi:10.1037/0022-006X.71.3.419

Hamann, S. B., Ely, T. D., Grafton, S. T., & Kilts, C. D. (1999). Amygdala activity related to enhanced memory for pleasant and aversive stimuli. *Nature Neuroscience, 2*(3), 289–293. doi:10.1038/6404

Harvey, A. G., & Bryant, R. A. (2001). Reconstructing trauma memories: A prospective study of "amnesic" trauma survivors. *Journal of Traumatic Stress, 14*, 277–282. doi:10.1023/A:1011108816888

Hoerger, M. (2012). Coping strategies and immune neglect in affective forecasting: Direct evidence and key moderators. *Judgment and Decision Making, 7*, 86–96.

Holmes, D. S. (1995). The evidence for repression: An examination of sixty years of research. In J. L. Singer (Ed.), *Repression and dissociation: Implications for personality theory, psychopathology, and health* (pp. 85–102). Chicago, IL: University of Chicago Press.

Jones, E., & Wessely, S. (2007). A paradigm shift in the conceptualization of psychological trauma in the 20th century. *Journal of Anxiety Disorders, 21*, 164–175. doi:10.1016/j.janxdis.2006.09.009

Joseph, S. (2012). What doesn't kill us . . . . *The Psychologist, 25*, 816–819.

Kleim, B., & Ehlers, A. (2008). Reduced autobiographical memory specificity predicts depression and posttraumatic stress disorder after recent trauma. *Journal of Consulting and Clinical Psychology, 76*, 231–242. doi:10.1037/0022-006X.76.2.231

Kunst, M. J. (2010). Peritraumatic distress, posttraumatic stress disorder symptoms, and posttraumatic growth in victims of violence. *Journal of Traumatic Stress, 23*(4), 514–518. doi:10.1002/jts.20556

Lalande, K. M., & Bonanno, G. A. (2011). Retrospective memory bias for the frequency of potentially traumatic events: A prospective study. *Psychological Trauma: Theory, Research, Practice, and Policy, 3*, 165–170. doi:10.1037/a0020847

Laney, C., & Loftus, E. F. (2005). Traumatic memories are not necessarily accurate memories. *The Canadian Journal of Psychiatry/La Revue Canadienne de Psychiatrie, 50*(13), 823–828.

Laney, C., & Loftus, E. F. (2008). Emotional content of true and false memories. *Memory, 16*, 500–516.

Laney, C., & Takarangi, M. T. (2013). False memories for aggressive acts. *Acta Psychologica, 143*(2), 227–234. doi:10.1016/j.actpsy.2013.04.001

Lindsay, D., Hagen, L., Read, J., Wade, K. A., & Garry, M. (2004). True photographs and false memories. *Psychological Science, 15*(3), 149–154. doi:10.1111/j.0956-7976.2004.01503002.x

Loftus, E. F., & Guyer, M. J. (2002, May/June). Who abused Jane Doe? The hazards of the single case history, part 1. *Skeptical Inquirer, 26*(3). Retrieved from www.csicop.org/si/show/who_abused_jane_doe_the_hazards_of_the_single_case_history_part_1

MacLeod, C. M. (1999). The item and list methods of directed forgetting: Test differences and the role of demand characteristics. *Psychonomic Bulletin and Review, 6*(1), 123–129. doi:10.3758/BF03210819

Magnussen, S., Andersson, J., Cornoldi, C., De Beni, R., Endestad, T., Goodman, G. S., . . . Zimmer, H. (2006). What people believe about memory. *Memory, 14*(5), 595–613. doi:10.1080/09658210600646716

McHugh, P. R., Lief, H. I., Freyd, P. P., & Fetkewicz, J. M. (2004). From refusal to reconciliation: Family relationships after an accusation based on recovered memories. *Journal of Nervous and Mental Disease, 192*, 525–531. doi:10.1097/01.nmd.0000136301.18598.52

McNally, R. J., Bryant, R. A., & Ehlers, A. (2003). Does early psychological intervention promote recovery from posttraumatic stress? *Psychological Science in the Public Interest, 4*(2), 45–79. doi:10.1111/1529-1006.01421

Myers, L. B., & Derakshan, N. (2004). To forget or not to forget: What do repressors forget and when do they forget? *Cognition and Emotion, 18*, 495–511. doi:10.1080/02699930341000419

Neisser, U. (1997). Jane Doe's memories: Changing the past to serve the present. *Child Maltreatment, 2*(2), 123–125. doi:10.1177/1077559597002002005

Ochsner, K. N. (2000). Are affective events richly recollected or simply familiar? The experience and process of recognizing feelings past. *Journal of Experimental Psychology: General, 129*(2), 242–261. doi:10.1037/0096-3445.129.2.242

Ost, J. (2003). Seeking the middle ground in the "memory wars." *British Journal of Psychology, 94*, 125–139. doi:10.1348/000712603762842156

Park, C. L. (2010). Making sense of the meaning literature: An integrative review of meaning making and its effects on adjustment to stressful life events. *Psychological Bulletin, 136*, 257–301. doi:10.1037/a0018301

peacefulbeing. (2012, October 15). *I have complex PTSD* [Online forum comment]. Retrieved from www.experienceproject.com/stories/Have-Complex-Ptsd/2647199

Poole, D. A., Lindsay, D., Memon, A., & Bull, R. (1995). Psychotherapy and the recovery of memories of childhood sexual abuse: U.S. and British practitioners' opinions, practices, and experiences. *Journal of Consulting and Clinical Psychology, 63*(3), 426–437. doi:10.1037/0022-006X.63.3.426

Pope, H. G., Poliakoff, M. B., Parker, M. P., Boynes, M., & Hudson, J. I. (2007). Is dissociative amnesia a culture-bound syndrome? Findings from a survey of historical literature. *Psychological Medicine, 37*, 225–233.

Porter, S., & Peace, K. A. (2007). The scars of memory: A prospective, longitudinal investigation of the consistency of traumatic and positive emotional memories in adulthood. *Psychological Science, 18*, 435–441. doi:10.1111/j.1467-9280.2007.01918.x

Rind et al. controversy. (2014, May 28). In *Wikipedia*. Retrieved from http://en.wikipedia.org/wiki/Rind_et_al._controversy

Rind, B., Tromovitch, P., & Bauserman, R. (1998). A meta-analytic examination of assumed properties of child sexual abuse using college samples. *Psychological Bulletin, 124,* 22–53. doi:10.1037/0033-2909.124.1.22

Rubin, D. C., & Berntsen, D. (2009). Most people who think that they are likely to enter psychotherapy also think it is plausible that they could have forgotten their own memories of childhood sexual abuse. *Applied Cognitive Psychology, 23*(2), 170–173. doi:10.1002/acp.1462

Rubin, D. C., Berntsen, D., & Bohni, M. (2008). A memory-based model of posttraumatic stress disorder: Evaluating basic assumptions underlying the PTSD diagnosis. *Psychological Review, 115,* 985–1011. doi:10.1037/a0013397

Schmidt, S. R., & Saari, B. (2007). The emotional memory effect: Differential processing or item distinctiveness? *Memory and Cognition, 35*(8), 1905–1916. doi:10.3758/BF03192924

Schooler, J. W. (1997). Reflections on a memory discovery. *Child Maltreatment, 2*(2), 126–133. doi:10.1177/1077559597002002006

Silver, R., Holman, E., McIntosh, D. N., Poulin, M., & Gil-Rivas, V. (2002). Nationwide longitudinal study of psychological responses to September 11. *JAMA: Journal of the American Medical Association, 288*(10), 1235–1244. doi:10.1001/jama.288.10.1235

Smith, S. M., & Moynan, S. C. (2008). Forgetting and recovering the unforgettable. *Psychological Science, 19,* 462–468. doi:10.1111/j.1467-9280.2008.02110.x

Squire, L. R. (1989). On the course of forgetting in very long-term memory. *Journal of Experimental Psychology: Learning, Memory, and Cognition, 15*(2), 241–245. doi:10.1037/0278-7393.15.2.241

Talarico, J. M., & Rubin, D. C. (2003). Confidence, not consistency, characterizes flashbulb memories. *Psychological Science, 14,* 455–461. doi:10.1111/1467-9280.02453

Tedeschi, R. G., & Calhoun, L. G. (1996). The Posttraumatic Growth Inventory: Measuring the positive legacy of trauma. *Journal of Traumatic Stress, 9*(3), 455–472. doi:10.1002/jts.2490090305

Thompson, C. P., Skowronski, J. J., Larsen, S. F., & Betz, A. (1996). *Autobiographical memory: Remembering what and remembering when.* Hillsdale, NJ: Lawrence Erlbaum Associates.

van der Kolk, B., & Najavits, L. M. (2013). Interview: What is PTSD really? Surprises, twists of history, and the politics of diagnosis and treatment. *Journal of Clinical Psychology, 69*, 516–522. doi:10.1002/jclp.21992

Watson, P. J., Brymer, M. J., & Bonanno, G. A. (2011). Postdisaster psychological intervention since 9/11. *American Psychologist, 66*(6), 482–494. doi:10.1037/a0024806

Weinberger, D. A., Schwartz, G. E., & Davidson, R. J. (1979). Low-anxious, high-anxious, and repressive coping styles: Psychometric patterns and behavioral and physiological responses to stress. *Journal of Abnormal Psychology, 88*(4), 369–380. doi:10.1037/0021-843X.88.4.369

Wickelgren, W. A. (1972). Trace resistance and the decay of long-term memory. *Journal of Mathematical Psychology, 9*(4), 418–455. doi:10.1016/0022-2496(72)90015-6

Memory Loss:
Amnesia and Other
Memory Disorders

o truly understand how important and central memory is to us, it is important to understand what life is like for people who experience memory loss, or *amnesia*. In general, amnesia refers to a decline in memory ability without a corresponding decline in other cognitive abilities, such as reading, reasoning, and perception. Amnesia comes in a variety of forms that depend upon which portion of the brain has been damaged or is not functioning properly. We will focus on four types of amnesia. First, we will examine the amnestic syndrome, which has been widely studied and the knowledge of which has significantly influenced theories of memory. The abilities and nonabilities of those with amnestic syndrome demonstrate that there are multiple independent systems of memory.

Second and third are two controversial diagnoses, the main feature of which is memory loss—dissociative identity disorder (DID) and psychogenic or dissociative amnesia. DID was formerly called multiple personality disorder. It involves different states, called *alters*, that recurrently take possession of a person's mind, with a reported lack of memory by one alter of what happens while another alter is in charge. Psychogenic amnesia usually occurs after a traumatic experience and involves loss of memory for not only past events but also one's own identity and often the identity of others. Controversial though these two diagnoses may be, case studies show the complexity of what it means to remember and to forget, and demonstrate that sometimes forgetting is fully reversible. Fourth, we will discuss a form of memory loss that does not fit the technical definition of amnesia because it eventually affects not just memory but all cognition: Alzheimer's disease (AD). Sadly, AD is common among older adults and demonstrates how a worsening loss of memory and cognition can lead to a complete disruption of everyday life. (For further discussion of the differences between and the etiology of these different amnesias, see Markowitsch & Staniloiu, 2012.)

THE AMNESTIC SYNDROME

The best known and most studied type of amnesia is called medial temporal lobe (MTL) amnesia, or the amnestic syndrome. It results from an injury or illness that destroys a part of the temporal lobe of the brain called the hippocampus. This unassuming little fingerlike piece of tissue extends into each of the two sides of the brain. Its name arises from its shape: It translates to *seahorse*, which the hippocampus rather resembles. Damage to the hippocampus and surrounding tissue results in a dense amnesia. The defining properties of this amnesia are that it occurs for information coming in through any of the senses, and that immediate memory, perception, and intelligence remain intact despite it (Squire, Stark, & Clark, 2004). We will introduce you to some individuals who suffered from temporal lobe amnesia to help you understand the nature of this form of amnesia.

The most famous MTL amnesiac was Henry Molaison, for many years known to memory researchers from case study reports that identified him as H. M. Henry, who was born in 1926 and as a teenager began to suffer severe daily epileptic seizures. In 1953 his doctor William Scoville performed a frankly experimental brain surgery, removing the hippocampus on both sides of the brain. It was known that seizures often started deep in the brain, and surgeries removing only one of the hippocampi had been performed and resulted in a reduction in seizures with few notable side effects. In light of the severity of Henry's epilepsy, Dr. Scoville removed both of the hippocampi and some of the surrounding tissue. Scoville went in through Henry's eye socket, inserted a spatula-shaped device to lift the frontal lobes, and then inserted a surgical straw that was used to suck out the seahorse-shaped structures in each of the temporal lobes (Scoville & Milner, 1957).

Henry's seizures did improve, but he was left with a memory impairment so profound that he was unable to live unassisted. Henry was unable to form any new memories for his experiences, at least none that lasted longer than a minute before fading. He was unable to remember the names or faces of any of his doctors or what happened between the time of the surgery and the present moment. He also lost access to almost all of his autobiographical memories for specific experiences in his life. He retained the facts about his life prior to 1953, but in all the years of testing, he produced only two solid autobiographical memories of his former life. One was a memory of flying a plane as a copilot when he was 13 years old. The other was of the time he smoked his first cigarette and coughed afterward. That was it for Henry's autobiographical world—flying and coughing, all he had to ground him in the rooms full of strange faces, equipment, furniture, and conversations that he seemed to always be entering midstream (Corkin, 2013).

In contrast to his profound memory deficit, his intelligence, vocabulary, and personality remained intact, as did his knowledge of the world prior to 1953. And his ability to perform fairly complex intellectual tasks was unimpaired—he had been an avid crossword puzzler prior to the surgery and continued to work crosswords until his death in 2008. He was also able to remember a normal quantity of information for about 30 seconds at a time. He even retained some circumscribed learning and memory abilities. He was able to learn new tasks involving motor skill, such as mirror tracing, and he learned a number of new facts about the world and himself, such as that Jonas Salk invented the polio vaccine and that he himself was of interest to science due to his memory impairment (Corkin, 2013).

That first set of abilities, learning new tasks, relies on a form of memory that is referred to as *nondeclarative* or *implicit* memory. It is memory being used to accomplish some other goal rather than as an end in itself. From the earliest testing, Henry demonstrated that he could improve at motor tasks with practice. His ability to draw a shape while looking at it reflected in a mirror, to adjust a stylus to track a single spot on a rotating disk, to tap different places on two circles with his left and right hand simultaneously, and to track targets onscreen by moving a mechanical arm all improved over time and were learned at about the same rate as people without amnesia (Corkin, 1968). These are forms of procedural memory—like learning to ride a bicycle. The medial temporal structures removed from Henry are not necessary for this form of learning.

In addition, Henry showed normal priming effects, evidence that information already in memory has recently been activated. For example, if he was presented with a list of words containing the word "DRUMS," Henry would be unable to recall which words he had seen within 30 seconds of them being taken away from him. However, if presented with a list of words with blank spaces to be filled in to form any words he chose, Henry would be very likely to complete the item DR_ _ _ as DRUMS rather than DRAKE or DRYER or any other word—just as people without amnesia would do. His performance showed evidence, for a few minutes or hours at least, of having previously been presented with information—that is, *memory* (Gabrieli et al., 1994).

Finally Henry showed some intriguing clues that he was learning about the world—new semantic memory. With any new experimental task, at first Henry would be awkward and require many repetitions of the instructions and sometimes would seem to forget that he was involved in a task in the middle of it. But eventually, after multiple days at a task, he would sit at the apparatus more quickly, ask fewer questions, and pay attention to the task with greater ease. On some level, he remembered doing the task and remembered the "rules" (Corkin, 2013). Moreover, he seemed to be more comfortable in familiar settings and with familiar people, even seeming to recognize on some level Dr. Suzanne Corkin, who worked with him over several decades. This kind of memory isn't exactly a motor skill, and it's not quite the same as classical conditioning. Instead it is a nondeclarative form of semantic memory that shows up when one is in a familiar environment.

A similar pattern of deficit and ability was found in another profoundly amnesic person. Clive Wearing was a world-renowned conductor born in 1938 who acquired encephalitis in 1985. The infection destroyed his hippocampi on both sides, as well as some of his frontal lobes. Clive has been unable to retain any new information about his experiences and has been unable to produce memories from before his illness as well (Wilson, Kopelman, & Kapur, 2008).

He still knows who he is, recognizes his children and his wife, and knows some of the facts about his life before his illness. And he knows the layout of his apartment in the care facility in which he lives, moving about it efficiently. He knows where coffee cups are kept, going immediately to the correct cabinet if someone asks him to make a cup of coffee. He also recognizes the facility from the outside, removing his seat belt once he sees it while in a car (Wearing, 2005). Clive also seems to know that his wife does not live with him and has a long drive to reach him.

When she arrived fairly early in the day, he looked at his watch and noted that she must have been "up at the crack of dawn" to get there at that time (Colorado State University, 1999). None of these pieces of information could he verbalize if asked; his behavior shows that he remembers implicitly rather than explicitly. It's important not to overstate the case for new learning in people with MTL amnesia like Henry and Clive. Their implicit memory is usually intact, and they can sometimes acquire nuggets of new information about the world. But the latter ability is still quite impoverished and may require that some of the posterior portions of the MTL be intact (Bayley, O'Reilly, Curran, & Squire, 2008).

Similar symptoms to the amnestic syndrome are experienced reversibly in a type of amnesia called *transient global amnesia*. Caused by blood flow changes to the brain arising from exertion or intense physical activity, transient global amnesia causes symptoms just like Henry's or Clive's but disappears on its own within a matter of hours or days. A particularly interesting example is that of 59-year-old Alice, who in 2009 experienced sudden confusion and loss of memory one morning after having sex with her husband. She was unsure of the month, day, or year and, after being rushed to the hospital, started asking the same series of questions of her family and doctors over and over without remembering the answers. She remembered who she was and who her husband was, as well as other details about her life, but ongoing events made no impression on her. She even kept making the same joke to her husband upon hearing that she was in the hospital due to complications from sex: "You owe me a 30 carat diamond!" Finally after several hours in the hospital, her confusion subsided and her memory returned—all except the memory of that morning with her husband (Park, 2009). Worried readers might be comforted by the knowledge that the condition is quite rare, generally occurs only in those age 50 and older, and is more likely to occur among people who experience frequent headaches or migraines. Indeed, Alice reported having had a headache the night before her frightening amnesia experience.

If for some reason you want to experience firsthand and temporarily what the amnestic syndrome is like, it is reproduced with brief-acting amnestic drugs used during surgeries that do not require full anesthesia and that yet would be unpleasant to witness. Patients are medicated before the procedure so that they are aware of what is happening as the procedure unfolds but immediately forget what has happened. On second thought, there wouldn't be much point in experiencing temporary amnesia as you wouldn't remember what it was like later . . . right?

PSYCHOGENIC AMNESIA

Another type of amnesia is called *psychogenic* (or functional or dissociative) amnesia. It is a usually temporary amnesic state that occurs without any clear organic or physical explanation, and it often occurs after times of trauma or stress, or mild head trauma that leaves no visible damage. The person suffering from psychogenic amnesia experiences severe retrograde amnesia, forgetting not just episodic life events, but also semantic information about the self. That is, the person loses not only his or her memory, but also his or her identity. The person may or may not remember public (nonself) events, such as political or sporting events (Markowitsch & Staniloiu, 2012).

Thus, a person with psychogenic amnesia may recognize a picture of the current U.S. president or be able to name the president when asked, but be unable to remember any incidents of his or her life or even general self-knowledge such as his or her name, address, whether he or she is married or has children, where he or she works, and so forth. He or she is not in a completely confused and eternally forgetting state like Henry or Clive; rather, he or she is able to learn new information at the usual rate. Psychogenic amnesia therefore differs from repression in that the person forgets not just the precipitating traumatic event, but also everything else that came before it. Psychogenic amnesia differs from the amnestic syndrome in that the person forgets only what came before (retrograde amnesia) but is able to store new memories of what comes after the precipitating event (no anterograde amnesia; Markowitsch & Staniloiu, 2012).

As an example, a 19-year-old woman had a minor fall from her motorcycle and was found wandering around in front of her school (which she did not recognize). School staff recognized her and had her taken to the hospital, where she was alert and tested negative for drug and alcohol intoxication. She did not know who she was or how she had gotten in front of the school, nor did she recognize her parents when they came to the hospital to see her. She started to memorize some information about herself, but none of it felt familiar, and she could not remember any events before the day she was taken to the hospital. Her memory of famous people and events, however, was normal. Her amnesia was limited to her own life. Starting 3 days later, her memories began to return, with full memory returning by the end of 3 weeks except for a tiny 1-hour window around the moment the amnesia had set in (Stracciari, Mattarozzi, Fonti, & Guarino, 2005).

Interestingly, when psychogenic amnesia begins to lift, it seems to progress from first remembering general, abstract self-knowledge to next remembering specific event memories (Stracciari et al., 2005). Functional brain imaging tests performed while the amnesia state is in effect show reduced activity in the frontal lobes (which would be involved in memory search) and increased activity in the posterior parietal cortex (Arzy et al., 2011; Glisky et al., 2004). Psychogenic amnesia, therefore, differs from temporal lobe amnestic syndrome in that it affects both semantic and episodic memory about the self, and does not prevent the amnesic person from remembering new information and experiences. Psychogenic amnesia is rare and poorly understood and remains controversial as a diagnosis.

DISSOCIATIVE IDENTITY DISORDER

A third type of amnesia is one of the defining features of the psychiatric disorder known as *dissociative identity disorder*, or DID. Formerly called multiple personality disorder, DID is present when a person has different states or personalities, often called *alters*, that take control of the person's identity and functioning at different times. Amnesia is also part of the diagnosis, specifically "recurrent gaps in the recall of everyday events, important personal information, and/or traumatic events." This amnesia usually manifests as lack of memory for events experienced by different alters. Many people refer to this state as a "split personality" (Markowitsch & Staniloiu, 2012).

(Spoiler alert!) Movies such as *Psycho* and *Fight Club* revolve around the main character's lack of knowledge of the activities (and indeed the existence of) a troublesome alter. For example, the narrator of *Fight Club* has sex with the character Marla and plots explosive demolitions of buildings while he (as the narrator alter) is asleep and Tyler Durden (the other alter) is in charge. The narrator is amnesic for Tyler's activities, but Tyler appears to know about the narrator's activities (Bell & Fincher, 1999). This one-way amnesia is relatively common in DID, where one alter is in charge and the other(s) is/are subordinate and therefore amnesic (Dorahy, 2001). If one alter is unable to remember what happens to the other, this is called inter-identity amnesia.

Former professional American football player Herschel Walker is a well-known person who was diagnosed with DID. He experienced extreme mood swings, blackouts, and acts that endangered himself and others as his mind jumped from alter to alter. He claims to have had over a dozen alters, which he named by their roles, such as the Warrior, the Hero, and the Daredevil. Walker's ex-wife became familiar with the different alters surfacing; when one of the violent alters took control, his voice would change and his eyes would take on a gleam that she described as "evil." Walker has no memory of having once threatened to kill her with a knife, as it occurred under the direction of one of his dangerous alters. Other alters were benevolent and caring. Once Walker retired from playing football, his various alters could no longer organize themselves toward a common goal, and his life began to fall apart. Fortunately, Walker is responding well to psychotherapy and is now an outspoken advocate for mental health (Falco, 2008).

We cannot talk about DID without mentioning the controversy surrounding it. More than half of psychiatrists surveyed in 1999 thought that there were serious problems with the diagnostic category of DID, and more than two thirds thought that there was insufficient evidence for it (Pope, Oliva, Hudson, Bodkin, & Gruber, 1999). Many psychiatrists think it is faked by patients or coaxed out of them by overzealous therapists (see Chapter 7 for a similar argument regarding recovered memories). Some people misdiagnosed with DID may indeed have something to gain by faking: If they act as if they have separate personalities, they may evade responsibility for their misdeeds.

A well-known case of faking DID is that of Kenneth Bianchi, also known as the Hillside Strangler. He was arrested for serial rape and murder in 1979 on the basis of a great deal of damning evidence. During his trial, Bianchi claimed that one of his alters, "Steve Walker," committed the crimes, and pled not guilty by reason of insanity. He managed to convince two psychiatrists he had the disorder, but a third saw through Bianchi's ruse and testified for the prosecution. Bianchi later changed his plea to guilty and is currently serving a life prison sentence (Boardman & Barnes, 1984). Others misdiagnosed with DID may have been convinced by their therapists that they have other personalities just waiting to come out. If they try to humor the therapist by role-playing how they imagine these alters would act, the therapist rewards them with attention and approval (Piper & Merskey, 2004).

Perhaps more mental health professionals would be convinced of the validity of DID if there were hard scientific evidence of the types of memory problems that would occur if one really had separate personalities ignorant of one another's experiences. Imagine we gave a list of words to Tyler Durden to memorize, then waited until the narrator alter ("Jack") returned (*Fight Club*, 2014). Would Jack be able to remember the words? If not, would we be able to tell whether he merely claimed not to remember (faking) or if he truly did not remember?

Such research has in fact been conducted on real people with a diagnosis of DID. Because of the controversy surrounding DID as a real versus imagined or faked condition, this research has the unusual feature of comparing DID patients to control participants, the latter of whom are instructed to try to *fake* what they think someone would do if they were merely claiming to have inter-identity amnesia. When the results of those diagnosed with DID and so-called *simulators* are identical, we must infer that DID memory symptoms can be faked (and therefore that there is not anything demonstrably unusual about the memory of the DID patients). Remember, we do not know for sure whether someone whose responses are identical to those of fakers is (a) intentionally faking the symptoms of DID, (b) unintentionally displaying the symptoms of DID, or (c) truly experiencing memory symptoms that simply happen to be guessable by simulators. The best evidence for alters with different memories comes from studies that show inter-identity amnesia that looks different from the pattern faked by simulators.

There are several studies that show such evidence. In one, people diagnosed with DID had different physiological and neurological responses to hearing a description of memories for their traumatic experiences when in two different identity states. People attempting to simulate nonresponsiveness did not show the same pattern (Reinders, Willemsen, Vos, den Boer, & Nijenhuis, 2012)—partly because neural and low-level physiological responses would be very difficult to control enough to fake. This finding suggests that the DID patients truly do not remember the traumatic incident when in a different identity state.

Unfortunately, such results are relatively rare. More often, DID patients show intact knowledge of information learned in one alter state when tested in another alter state. For example, DID patients also seem to have intact implicit memory in a second alter state for stimuli encountered in another alter state. They respond more quickly and accurately in implicit memory tests such as making decisions about line drawings, some of which they had previously seen, and completing word stems, some of which could be completed with words they had previously encountered (Huntjens et al., 2002). Maybe the DID patients were just faking, you might wonder? Simulator participants show different patterns, mainly of failure to transfer both implicit *and* explicit memory across feigned alter states (Eich, Macauley, Loewenstein, & Dihle, 1997).

There are several possible explanations for the "leakage" of some types of information and not others across alter states. One is that it depends on how deeply and conceptually the information has been processed. Information processed at a low, perceptual level will transfer, whereas information processed at a higher, conceptual level will not (Dorahy, 2001).

A second possible explanation is poor metamemory. DID patients sometimes actively deny having memory that they nonetheless demonstrate behaviorally. In one study, DID patients and control participants were presented with words in one alter state, then given a recognition test later to either the same or a different alter ("yes," I've seen this word earlier, versus "no," I have not). DID patients were slow to respond "no" to words they had learned as a different alter, suggesting a state of conflict between saying "yes" because they really did remember the word, and saying "no" because they knew they *shouldn't* remember the word as this alter. Even more compellingly, a psychophysiological measurement was used to determine whether participants truly forgot the words (versus merely claiming to forget them). When a person learns information and then is presented with that same information again, the brain produces a characteristic "That's familiar!" response. Measured with electrodes placed on the scalp, evoked response potentials show that words learned by one alter produced a familiarity response when presented to a different alter, even though DID patients denied recognizing these words (Allen & Movius, 2000).

Denial of memory for information learned by a different alter, along with behavioral demonstration of intact memory for that information, has been found in other studies as well (Huntjens et al., 2006; Kong, Allen, & Glisky, 2008). In other words, people diagnosed with DID *claim* that they don't remember what happens to them in the different identity states, whereas in reality they *do* remember. They may be trying to convince themselves of their inter-identity amnesia (Huntjens et al., 2006), or they may have extremely poor metamemory skills. What feels like poor memory to them is actually perfectly good memory (Huntjens et al., 2002). The explanation is at this point elusive, and this diagnosis too remains controversial (Gillig, 2009).

ALZHEIMER'S DISEASE

A fourth syndrome with amnesia as one of its major defining symptoms is AD, a progressive disease in the brain. For reasons that are still unknown, normal processes in the brain begin to go awry. Beta amyloid plaques and neurofibrillary tangles begin to form. The former are caused by proteins in the neuron's cell membrane being snipped off in an abnormal process that allows them to collect together into masses that obstruct the communication between neurons. The latter is caused by abnormal proteins being produced, which then fail to hold portions of the neuron together and cause it to die. This leads to failed communication between neurons as well. These plaques and tangles begin to form up to 10 years before symptoms of AD are evident. But the process is unceasing, and eventually cell death is significant enough to cause shrinkage of the brain. Problems in everyday memory appear in the early stages of the disease, followed by greater and greater loss of memory, failures of judgment, and eventually even difficulties with basic self-care. There is no known cure for AD, nor are its causes well understood. Research continues into this fatal disease that currently affects about 5 million Americans and 50% of those who reach the age of 85 (National Institute on Aging, 2011, 2014; National Institutes of Health, 2010).

The phenomenological experience of losing one's memory abilities to AD is well described in the poignant words of Ted, who reports that he frequently loses his train of thought while typing and must rely on his wife to help him reconstruct what he must have been thinking. "I have few new memories to speak of, as recent events just do not stay in my mind on a consistent basis. As a result, I feel that I am robbed of any future, because while I will live in it, I will be unlikely to remember it" (Alzheimer's Organization, 2014).

AD is different from normal aging. People's memory performance does tend to decline with age, and occasional incidents of misplacing one's keys, forgetting to pay a bill, or briefly forgetting what day of the week it is will occur with increasing frequency as you get older. But these so-called senior moments are merely embarrassing and don't interfere with job performance or relationships in normal aging (National Institute on Aging, 2011). You can still remember—it's just harder—and you lose a few items from memory now and again.

In contrast, AD patients show the same severe autobiographical and episodic memory deficits exhibited by Henry Molaison, Clive Wearing, and others with MTL amnesia. In the early stages, only episodic autobiographical memory is impaired—the ability to remember what happened on a particular day, just like Henry's inability to remember any incident that happened to him after his surgery. In the middle stages of AD, however, semantic self-knowledge is also impaired—the ability to remember general facts about one's past (Seidl, Lueken, Thomann, Geider, & Schröder, 2011). And unlike other amnesias, AD has a broad effect on memory and cognition even in its early stages. For example, AD affects semantic memory and language in the early stages, particularly the speed and fluency of naming items or coming up with words (Verma & Howard, 2012). Working memory is also affected; holding information in one's head and operating on it is impaired in early stage AD (Huntley & Howard, 2010). Implicit memory is affected in early stage AD in a more nuanced way. Implicit memory that relies on low-level perceptual processing remains intact, whereas implicit memory that requires high-level perceptual processing is damaged. For example, reading a word aloud once will facilitate reading it again later in both AD and healthy participants, whereas producing an example of a category once will facilitate producing it again later only in healthy participants (Fleischman et al., 2005).

Eventually all cognitive abilities are affected by the disease; it's just a matter of time. With our aging population and the high risk for AD with increasing age, research into AD prevention and treatment is critical. There are a number of promising treatments on the horizon, some pharmacological, some behavioral. You will probably have a family member diagnosed with AD in your lifetime, and you may even develop it yourself. We encourage you to learn more about AD and to get involved in research on this deadly disease.

EFFECTS OF AMNESIA ON THE INTEGRITY OF THE SELF

Considering how integral memory is to our lives, it is inevitable that each of these forms of amnesia affects the amnesic person and his or her loved ones. As we discussed in Chapter 6, some of the functions of memory include forming a foundation for the self-concept and for social bonds with other people. Therefore we will explore how amnesia influences one's sense of identity as well as the ability to form and maintain relationships with others. As we will see, some aspects of identity and relationships are severely damaged, whereas others remain undamaged, when memory is removed from the picture. Thus we can determine the aspects of identity and relationships that rely on an intact memory system.

Anecdotal and laboratory evidence show some disruptions in the sense of self and identity of those suffering from amnesia. First of all, two of the amnesias we have discussed have a disrupted self-concept as part of the very definition. In psychogenic amnesia, there is a hole where the self should be, as the disorder is characterized by the inability to remember not just life events, but also personal semantic knowledge of who the self is. In fact, psychogenic amnesia even leads to changes in behaviors that seem to be deeply ingrained into the self, such as eating and smoking (Staniloiu, Markowitsch, & Brand, 2010). In DID, there is a fragmented identity composed of alters with more or less coawareness (Markowitsch & Staniloiu, 2012). Thus both of these amnesic disorders clearly compromise the self.

The matter is more complicated for MTL amnesia and AD. Some individuals diagnosed with MTL amnestic syndrome have so little sense of self that they actually construct a momentary self from their current surroundings. Amnesic patient A. D., who was unaware of his memory deficits, would take on roles suggested by cues in his present environment and would confabulate self-knowledge consistent with that role. For instance, when being interviewed by a physician in a white coat, he would claim to be a doctor himself. On one occasion he claimed to be specifically a cardiologist, and began to discuss his salary, fees, and experience in the field without prompting (Conchiglia, Della Rocca, & Grossi, 2007). Thus, patient A. D. seemed to be the self whose particulars he could generate on the spot, with that self changing as the context changed, a series of selves infinitely replacing the one just abandoned. Patient A. D's case is unusual, however, because he had not only amnesia due to hippocampal damage, but also damage to the frontal lobes that prevented him from inhibiting the tendency to incorporate aspects of the present environment into his identity.

One study found that people with AD had not only poorer autobiographical memory skills than age-matched participants without AD, but also a less certain sense of self. Specifically, AD participants generated fewer and more vague responses to the prompt: "I am . . ." In addition, the researchers found that the greater the degree of autobiographical memory impairment in people with AD, the weaker their sense of self was. That is, the more of their personal past people with AD had forgotten, the less certain they were in their sense of self. This relationship did not hold for age-matched participants without AD (Addis & Tippett, 2004). Therefore, it appears that the loss of autobiographical memory for one's own life experiences, rather than general cognitive decline, interferes with a sense of identity. The reports of caregivers of people with AD frequently stress the AD patient's diminishing sense of self as the disease progresses (MacRae, 2010). People with advanced AD often cannot recognize recent pictures of themselves (although they recognize the self in old pictures; Hehman, German, & Klein, 2005).

On the other hand, the picture is not necessarily as bleak as the preceding information would suggest. When those with AD are asked about their sense of self, they rarely if ever cite having AD as a central aspect of the self—even though almost all remember the fact that they have an AD diagnosis. They also express a continuous sense of being the same person they have always been (MacRae, 2010). It is only in the late stages of AD that identity begins to show a serious breakdown (Caddell & Clare, 2010).

Similarly, with MTL amnesia, Henry Molaison did recognize himself in the mirror and in old photos (Corkin, 2013). He seemed to have a sense of self, albeit an impoverished one due to the inability to engage in mental time travel or to recall detailed narratives of discrete experiences (Corkin, 2013). Even the profoundly amnesic Clive Wearing seems to present a continuous and coherent sense of identity. He was once a world-class conductor, and describes himself as such, so his identity is particularly notable when he performs or enjoys music. Clive's wife Deborah refers to the self that emerges when he plays or sings as his "musical self." After conducting old friends in a choir at the

hospital chapel, he had a wonderful time returning to this familiar activity. Afterward, he even chatted up the singers. Deborah
described him at that moment as "charming, engaging, debonair
and completely himself" (Wearing, 2005, p. 201). She goes on to
say, "His memory loss had no effect on his sense of identity . . .
Clive's 'soul' . . . was intact" (Wearing, 2005, p. 206).

The distinction is between so-called *episodic* and *semantic*
self-knowledge. Episodic self-knowledge is memory for individual days and specific behaviors in one's life. Semantic self-
knowledge is more abstract and general information about
one's personality traits, likes and dislikes, and physical appearance. Neurological and behavioral evidence shows that episodic
and semantic self-knowledge are independent—that is, you can
damage one without it affecting the other. They seem to require
different parts of the brain that don't regularly interact with each
other (Klein & Lax, 2010). People who are amnesic and cannot remember new (or old) instances of what they have done
can nonetheless remember what they are like, even when this
information changes. People without amnesia answer questions
about what they are like without accessing information about
the specific times they have exhibited these qualities. So, for
example, a person with amnesia can describe himself as outgoing, even if he can't remember a single time he has been outgoing in the past. He can even accurately tell you that he is not
outgoing if he has changed on that dimension since the onset
of his amnesia. And a person without amnesia can tell you that
she is outgoing without activating memories of times that she
has been outgoing in the past (Klein, Rozendal, & Cosmides,
2002). Our conclusions about the self in general are independent of the memories of specific experiences that inform those
conclusions.

Angie is a particularly compelling case of a person with damaged episodic but intact semantic self-knowledge (Duff, Wszalek, Tranel, & Cohen, 2008). Angie developed amnesia after a car
accident damaged her hippocampus. She is unable to retain any
memories of specific experiences she has had since the accident.

She nonetheless holds a job as a successful project manager for an educational testing company. She knows that she works as a project manager, but she has no memory of any individual project. She must refresh her memory from her notes before every meeting or work task that needs to be done. She knows about her memory impairment, remembers that she has a husband and stepdaughter, and describes her general organizational system accurately but without any memory of the specific strategies she uses ("I keep lists"). Angie is decidedly unusual, but other amnesiacs have been shown to have an intact sense of self, because they learn to rely on their undamaged repertoire of semantic information about the self as the basis of self-definition (Rathbone, Moulin, & Conway, 2009).

People with amnesia continue to create a life story after the onset of the amnesia, even though that story may be impoverished. They still know the structure stories are supposed to have, so they work with the information available in memory to create such stories. One strategy amnesiacs use is to import memories from before their accident to substantiate the conclusions they have drawn from semantic self-knowledge. For example, an amnesic woman mistakenly claimed she was dissatisfied with her job and had an upcoming job interview when in fact that interview had been scheduled years ago before her brain injury. Another strategy is to borrow memories told to them by other people. A different amnesic woman mentioned a car accident in which she had driven into a ditch, admitting when questioned that she did not remember it but that her sister had told her that she had done this (Medved, 2007). In other words, amnesiacs who have some limited memories continue to populate their life stories with specific memories even though it takes some maneuvering to do so. They may still have a sense of a self to whom things are happening.

To summarize, memory loss has a somewhat limited effect on a person's sense of identity. If the impairment is acquired in adulthood, does not involve a division of the self (multiple alters), and is localized to episodic autobiographical memory (rather than the progressive deterioration present in AD), many people can maintain a continuous and meaningful sense of self. The semantic knowledge of one's own life seems to inform identity directly, with specific memories of one's life experiences acting as fodder for that semantic knowledge.

EFFECTS OF AMNESIA ON INTERPERSONAL RELATIONSHIPS

In Chapter 6, we discussed the social function of autobiographical memories—that sharing memories facilitates relationship development and maintenance. If you don't have memories to share, relationships will surely suffer. The effects of psychogenic amnesia on relationships is poorly documented, and conclusions cannot be drawn at this point in time. DID seems to disrupt relationships inasmuch as there is a claimed tendency for people with DID to be in poor-quality relationships (Putnam, 1989; Williams, 1991). But the literature on DID is too sporadic to let us determine whether the amnesia between alters, the abrupt switching of affective style between alters, the traumatic experiences the person with DID may have had, or some other variable is the cause of these poor relationships (Covalt, 2000).

A richer database is available on the effects of AD and the MTL amnestic syndrome on relationships. The requisite skills involved in relationships begin to suffer in AD. For example, AD impairs the ability to recognize the emotion expressions on other people's faces. It is harder for a person with AD to determine whether her caregiver is sad, angry, or just concentrating really hard. This emotion decoding inability then leads to problems in behavior around other people, likely arising from misinterpretations of others' intentions (Shimokawa et al., 2001). As the disease progresses, the inability to visually recognize significant others will have a chilling effect on relationships (Hayes, Boylstein, & Zimmerman, 2009).

Yet the effects of the cognitive decline in AD on relationships are not entirely negative. For example, AD is about as likely to have no effect on the sex life of the patient and spouse as it is to lead to decreased or increased sexual activity (Kuppuswamy, Davies, Spira, Zeiss, & Tinklenberg, 2007). Some couples report that AD improves their emotional and physical intimacy by causing them to value their time together more. Others, particularly wives of husbands with AD, report decreased comfort with physical intimacy as the disease progresses (Hayes et al., 2009). The conflict between being a caregiver (mother) and wife (lover) is difficult to negotiate. But for those who are able to maintain a fulfilling relationship, there are emotional and physical benefits. Over time, closer relationships with primary caregivers predict slower cognitive decline among AD patients (Norton et al., 2009). The lesson of this research: It's essential to keep caregivers healthy and to maintain the quality of the relationship between the caregiver and the AD patient. Otherwise AD symptoms interfere with relationship functioning, relationship quality suffers, and AD symptoms progress as a result.

The evidence regarding temporal lobe amnestic syndrome and relationship formation and maintenance is similarly mixed. Studies show a lack of empathy in people with MTL amnesia. They score lower on trait measures of empathic concern for others, and they have a hard time taking another person's perspective (you would have to remember not only your view but also another's to see how they differ). They also fail to experience normal emotional reactions to news of another's suffering (Beadle, Tranel, Cohen, & Duff, 2013). Relatedly, amnesiacs have difficulty communicating with others linguistically, particularly when they need to lay out what needs to be done in a series of steps. It's hard for them to keep track of what other people know and don't know (Duff, Hengst, et al., 2008). Moreover, amnesiacs are (not surprisingly) highly repetitive in their conversations. Clive Wearing likely wears on his caregivers' patience with his repeated monologues about the same half-dozen topics (music, architecture, telephones, space travel, Queen Victoria, and the subway, among them; Wearing, 2005).

But anecdotal evidence suggests some relationships can be maintained, and even new ones formed despite the inability to form new memories. Although Angie was abandoned by close friends and a fiancé after the accident that led to her memory loss, she met a new man whom she married, and she successfully took on a new role as stepmother to her husband's daughter (Duff, Wszalek, et al., 2008). Henry Molaison formed what appeared to be a mutually rewarding friendship with a janitor at the rehabilitation center where he was placed in the 1970s. The janitor took Henry under his wing and found tasks at which he could succeed despite his memory impairment. When he was transferred, the janitor became emotional and expressed his love for Henry and his intention to continue to care for him (Hilts, 1995). Henry was described as pleasantly social, readily engaged in conversation with anyone who approached him. Those who cared for and worked with Henry over the years became very fond of him even though he couldn't remember a single interaction they had ever had with him (Corkin, 2013). It is not clear the extent to which these emotional attachments were reciprocated by Henry, who was an unusually placid fellow.

Clive Wearing is able to maintain at least one highly meaningful social connection despite his amnesia. After his illness, his wife Deborah divorced him and attempted to find love again, but eventually remarried him. As she put it, "I could not modify the facts of my existence. I loved Clive, he loved me. I couldn't live with him, I couldn't live without him" (p. 239). The amnesic Angie met and married her second husband after her accident. She cannot report a single experience the two of them have shared, yet she clearly loves her husband and he her. Thus amnesiacs can continue to have significant, loving relationships with others even without the ability to retain information about events or conversations that take place with those others.

Overall the evidence points up a distinction between types of memory loss. The loss of only episodic or autobiographical memories, as in those with temporal lobe amnesia or early stages of AD, presents a significant but surmountable obstacle in relationships. Conversations are awkward and repetitive, and important moments spent together cannot be shared and retold. Yet the relationship itself may nonetheless thrive as long as the amnesiac retains a sense of self at the semantic level, a sense of "me" and "you" and "us." The loss of personal semantic memories—as in the late stages of AD and in DID patients, some of whose alters have no knowledge of the others—appears nearly insurmountable. Relationships become one-sided caregiving rather than partnerships. Overall, semantic memory of the self seems a prerequisite to identity and to relations with other people, with episodic autobiographical memory making identity and relationships richer and more satisfying.

AMNESIA VERSUS FORGETTING

Before we close this chapter on amnesia, we must take a moment to distinguish these severe forms of memory loss from everyday memory errors and forgetting. As we discussed in Chapters 2 and 3, forgetting is natural, and everyone does it. So just because you can't remember what you ate for lunch a year ago today, or have to make a written list if your grocery needs exceed seven items, or have gradually forgotten all the Spanish you learned in high school, or just now realized you didn't take your multivitamin this morning, or forgot where this very long sentence started, does not mean that you are suffering from amnesia. And it is perfectly natural for your memory skills to decline somewhat as you get older, just as your muscle mass and your hearing may decline somewhat. You need not monitor your every instance of forgetting to check for the sudden onset of amnesic-type symptoms.

You might try instead to adopt an attitude of appreciation for forgetting. Everyday forgetting is necessary and even healthy! After you learn information about a topic, you tend to remember portions of that information that you practice and forget portions of that information you don't practice. For example, imagine that you learn that American pygmy shrews have a diet consisting of insects and spiders, and that their gestation period is 18 days. If you keep rehearsing the fact that pygmy shrews eat insects and spiders, and do not rehearse the fact that their gestation period is 18 days, then later, when you are asked what you know about pygmy shrews' diet you will be quite good at recalling that it consists of insects and spiders. If you are later asked what you know about pygmy shrews' gestation period, you will be quite bad at recalling that it is 18 days. What is surprising is that your memory for the 18 days fact may be *worse* than that of someone who had not rehearsed either fact at all. This phenomenon is known as *retrieval-induced forgetting*. Practicing the retrieval of one fact inhibits the memory for the other when the same cue is used for both. Retrieval-induced forgetting can be a good thing—you will want to remember information that is important enough to be used and forget information that is never used.

Just how good a thing is retrieval-induced forgetting? As it turns out, the ability to forget unwanted information also predicts the ability to set aside useless and distracting information in other types of thinking. Participants who were good at retrieval-induced forgetting were also good at solving creative problems after having been given a distracting piece of information. They were able to overcome mental fixation on the distracting piece of information and allow their creative faculties to function more fully (Storm, 2011). Moreover, participants who were good at retrieval-induced forgetting were also better at recalling positive autobiographical memories and worse at recalling negative autobiographical memories (Storm & Jobe, 2012). If more forgetting yields more creativity and helps us maintain a positive view of our lives, we then say bring on the forgetting! We'd rather be creative and happy than remember every detail of every experience—a phenomenon we will discuss in Chapter 9.

REFERENCES

Addis, D., & Tippett, L. J. (2004). Memory of myself: Autobiographical memory and identity in Alzheimer's disease. *Memory, 12*(1), 56–74. doi:10.1080/09658210244000423

Allen, J. B., & Movius, H. (2000). The objective assessment of amnesia in dissociative identity disorder using event-related potentials. *International Journal of Psychophysiology, 38,* 21–41. doi:10.1016/S0167-8760(00)00128-8

Alzheimer's Organization. (2014). *Ted's story.* Retrieved from www.alz.org/living_with_alzheimers_8929.asp

Arzy, S. S., Collette, S. S., Wissmeyer, M. M., Lazeyras, F. F., Kaplan, P. W., & Blanke, O. O. (2011). Psychogenic amnesia and self-identity: A multimodal functional investigation. *European Journal of Neurology, 18,* 1422–1425. doi:10.1111/j.1468-1331.2011.03423.x

Bayley, P. J., O'Reilly, R. C., Curran, T. T., & Squire, L. R. (2008). New semantic learning in patients with large medial temporal lobe lesions. *Hippocampus, 18*(6), 575–583. doi:10.1002/hipo.20417

Beadle, J. N., Tranel, D. D., Cohen, N. J., & Duff, M. C. (2013). Empathy in hippocampal amnesia. *Frontiers in Psychology, 4,* 69. doi:10.3389/fpsyg.2013.00069

Bell, R. G. (Producer), & Fincher, D. (Director). (1999). *Fight club* [Motion picture]. USA: 20th Century Fox.

Boardman, A. (Writer), & Barnes, M. (Director). (1984). The mind of a murderer. In M. Barnes (Producer), *Frontline.* New York, NY: Public Broadcasting Service. Retrieved from www.pbs.org/wgbh/pages/frontline/criminal-justice

Caddell, L. S., & Clare, L. (2010). The impact of dementia on self and identity: A systematic review. *Clinical Psychology Review, 30*(1), 113–126. doi:10.1016/j.cpr.2009.10.003

Colorado State University (Producer). (1999). Clive Wearing, part 2: Living without memory. In *The Mind,* 2nd ed. Retrieved from www.learner.org/resources/series150.html

Conchiglia, G., Della Rocca, G., & Grossi, D. (2007). On a peculiar environmental dependency syndrome in a case with frontal-temporal damage: Zelig-like syndrome. *Neurocase, 13*(1), 1–5. doi:10.1080/13554790601160558

Corkin, S. (1968). Acquisition of motor skill after bilateral medial temporal-lobe excision. *Neuropsychologia, 6*(3), 255–265. doi:10.1016/0028-3932(68)90024-9

Corkin, S. (2013). *Permanent present tense: The unforgettable life of the amnesic patient, H. M.* New York, NY: Basic Books.

Covalt, P. M. (2000, February). A phenomenological study of committed relationships in which one member is diagnosed with dissociative identity disorder. *Dissertation Abstracts International, 60,* 4211.

Dorahy, M. J. (2001). Dissociative identity disorder and memory dysfunction: The current state of experimental research and its future directions. *Clinical Psychology Review, 21,* 771–795.

Duff, M. C., Hengst, J. A., Tengshe, C., Krema, A., Tranel, D., & Cohen, N. J. (2008). Hippocampal amnesia disrupts the flexible use of procedural discourse in social interaction. *Aphasiology, 22*(7–8), 866–880. doi:10.1080/02687030701844196

Duff, M. C., Wszalek, T., Tranel, D., & Cohen, N. J. (2008). Successful life outcome and management of real-world memory demands despite profound anterograde amnesia. *Journal of Clinical and Experimental Neuropsychology, 30*(8), 931–945. doi:10.1080/13803390801894681

Eich, E., Macaulay, D., Loewenstein, R. J., & Dihle, P. H. (1997). Memory, amnesia, and dissociative identity disorder. *Psychological Science, 8*(6), 417–422. doi:10.1111/j.1467-9280.1997.tb00454.x

Falco, M. (2008, April 15). *Herschel Walker reveals many sides of himself.* Retrieved from http://edition.cnn.com/2008/HEALTH/conditions/04/15/herschel.walker.did

Fight Club. (2014). Retrieved from http://en.wikipedia.org/wiki/Fight_Club

Fleischman, D. A., Wilson, R. S., Gabrieli, J. E., Schneider, J. A., Bienias, J. L., & Bennett, D. A. (2005). Implicit memory and Alzheimer's disease neuropathology. *Brain: A Journal of Neurology, 128*(9), 2006–2015. doi:10.1093/brain/awh559

Gabrieli, J. E., Keane, M. M., Stanger, B. Z., & Kjelgaard, M. M. (1994). Dissociations among structural-perceptual, lexical-semantic, and event-fact memory systems in Alzheimer, amnesic, and normal subjects. *Cortex: A Journal Devoted to the Study of the Nervous System and Behavior, 30*(1), 75–103.

Gillig, P. (2009). Dissociative identity disorder: A controversial diagnosis. *Psychiatry, 6*(3), 24–29.

Glisky, E. L., Ryan, L., Reminger, S., Hardt, O., Hayes, S. M., & Hupbach, A. (2004). A case of psychogenic fugue: I understand, *aber ich verstehe nichts. Neuropsychologia, 42,* 1132–1147. doi:10.1016/j. neuropsychologia.2003.08.016

Hayes, J., Boylstein, C., & Zimmerman, M. K. (2009). Living and loving with dementia: Negotiating spousal and caregiver identity through narrative. *Journal of Aging Studies, 23*(1), 48–59. doi:10.1016/j.jaging.2007.09.002

Hehman, J. A., German, T. P., & Klein, S. B. (2005). Impaired self-recognition from recent photographs in a case of late-stage Alzheimer's disease. *Social Cognition, 23*(1), 118–123.

Hilts, P. J. (1995). *Memory's ghost: The nature of memory and the strange tale of Mr. M.* New York, NY: Simon & Schuster.

Huntjens, R. C., Peters, M. L., Woertman, L., Bovenschen, L. M., Martin, R. C., & Postma, A. (2006). Inter-identity amnesia in dissociative identity disorder: A simulated memory impairment? *Psychological Medicine, 36,* 857–863. doi:10.1017/S0033291706007100

Huntjens, R. C., Postma, A., Hamaker, E. L., Woertman, L., Van Der Hart, O., & Peters, M. (2002). Perceptual and conceptual priming in patients with dissociative identity disorder. *Memory and Cognition, 30,* 1033–1043. doi:10.3758/BF03194321

Huntley, J. D., & Howard, R. J. (2010). Working memory in early Alzheimer's disease: A neuropsychological review. *International Journal of Geriatric Psychiatry, 25,* 121–132. doi:10.1002/ gps.2314

Klein, S. B., & Lax, M. L. (2010). The unanticipated resilience of trait self-knowledge in the face of neural damage. *Memory, 18*(8), 918–948. doi:10.1080/09658211.2010.524651

Klein, S. B., Rozendal, K., & Cosmides, L. (2002). A social-cognitive neuroscience analysis of the self. *Social Cognition, 20*(2), 105–135. doi:10.1521/soco.20.2.105.20991

Kong, L. L., Allen, J. B., & Glisky, E. L. (2008). Interidentity memory transfer in dissociative identity disorder. *Journal of Abnormal Psychology, 117,* 686–692. doi:10.1037/0021-843X.117.3.686

Kuppuswamy, M., Davies, H. D., Spira, A. P., Zeiss, A. M., & Tinklenberg, J. R. (2007). Sexuality and intimacy between individuals with

Alzheimer's disease and their partners: Caregivers describe their experiences. *Clinical Gerontologist: The Journal of Aging and Mental Health, 30*(3), 75–81. doi:10.1300/J018v30n03_06

MacRae, H. (2010). Managing identity while living with Alzheimer's disease. *Qualitative Health Research, 20*(3), 293–305. doi:10.1177/1049732309354280

Markowitsch, H. J., & Staniloiu, A. (2012). Amnesic disorders. *The Lancet, 380*, 1429–1440. doi:10.1016/S0140-6736(11)61304-4

Medved, M. I. (2007). Remembering without a past: Individuals with anterograde memory impairment talk about their lives. *Psychology, Health and Medicine, 12*(5), 603–616. doi:10.1080/13548500601164404

National Institute on Aging. (2011). *Understanding Alzheimer's disease* (NIH Publication No. 11-5441). Retrieved from www.nia.nih.gov/sites/default/files/understanding_alzheimers_disease.pdf

National Institute on Aging. (2014). *Inside the brain: Unraveling the mystery of Alzheimer's disease* [Video file]. Retrieved from www.nia.nih.gov/alzheimers/alzheimers-disease-video

National Institutes of Health. (2010). Preventing Alzheimer's disease and cognitive decline. *NIH Consensus and State-of-the-Science Statements, 27*(4). Retrieved from http://consensus.nih.gov/2010/docs/alz/ALZ_Final_Statement.pdf

Norton, M. C., Piercy, K. W., Rabins, P. V., Green, R. C., Breitner, J. S., Østbye, T., . . . Tschanz, J. T. (2009). Caregiver-recipient closeness and symptom progression in Alzheimer disease. The Cache County Dementia Progression Study. *The Journals of Gerontology: Series B: Psychological Sciences and Social Sciences, 64B*(5), 560–568. doi:10.1093/geronb/gbp052

Park, M. (2009, November 5). *Sex, then amnesia . . . and it's no soap opera.* Retrieved from www.cnn.com/2009/HEALTH/11/04/transient.global.amnesia/index.html

Piper, A., & Merskey, H. (2004). The persistence of folly: A critical examination of dissociative identity disorder. Part I. The excesses of an improbable concept. *The Canadian Journal of Psychiatry/La Revue Canadienne De Psychiatrie, 49*, 592–600.

Pope, H. R., Oliva, P. S., Hudson, J. I., Bodkin, J., & Gruber, A. J. (1999). Attitudes toward *DSM-IV* dissociative disorders diagnoses among board-certified American psychiatrists. *The American Journal of Psychiatry, 156*, 321–323.

Putnam, F. W. (1989). *Diagnosis and treatment of multiple personality disorder*. New York, NY: Guilford Press.

Rathbone, C. J., Moulin, C. A., & Conway, M. A. (2009). Autobiographical memory and amnesia: Using conceptual knowledge to ground the self. *Neurocase, 15*(5), 405–418. doi:10.1080/13554790902849164

Reinders, A., Willemsen, A. M., Vos, H. J., den Boer, J. A., & Nijenhuis, E. S. (2012). Fact or factitious? A psychobiological study of authentic and simulated dissociative identity states. *PLoS ONE, 7*(6), e39279. doi:10.1371/journal.pone.0039279

Scoville, W., & Milner, B. (1957). Loss of recent memory after bilateral hippocampal lesions. *Journal of Neurology, Neurosurgery and Psychiatry, 20*, 11–21. doi:10.1136/jnnp.20.1.11

Seidl, U., Lueken, U., Thomann, P. A., Geider, J., & Schröder, J. (2011). Autobiographical memory deficits in Alzheimer's disease. *Journal of Alzheimer's Disease, 27*, 567–574.

Shimokawa, A., Yatomi, N., Anamizu, S., Torii, S., Isono, H., Sugai, Y., & Kohno, M. (2001). Influence of deteriorating ability of emotional comprehension on interpersonal behavior in Alzheimer-type dementia. *Brain and Cognition, 47*(3), 423–433. doi:10.1006/brcg.2001.1318

Squire, L. R., Stark, C. L., & Clark, R. E. (2004). The medial temporal lobe. *Annual Review of Neuroscience, 27*, 279–306.

Staniloiu, A., Markowitsch, H. J., & Brand, M. (2010). Psychogenic amnesia—A malady of the constricted self. *Consciousness and Cognition: An International Journal, 19*, 778–801. doi:10.1016/j.concog.2010.06.024

Storm, B. C. (2011). The benefit of forgetting in thinking and remembering. *Current Directions in Psychological Science, 20*(5), 291–295. doi:10.1177/0963721411418469

Storm, B. C., & Jobe, T. A. (2012). Retrieval-induced forgetting predicts failure to recall negative autobiographical memories. *Psychological Science, 23*(11), 1356–1363. doi:10.1177/0956797612443837

Stracciari, A., Mattarozzi, K., Fonti, C., & Guarino, M. (2005). Functional focal retrograde amnesia: Lost access to abstract autobiographical knowledge? *Memory, 13*, 690–699. doi:10.1080/09658210444000331

Verma, M. M., & Howard, R. J. (2012). Semantic memory and language dysfunction in early Alzheimer's disease: A review. *International*

Journal of Geriatric Psychiatry, 27(12), 1209–1217. doi:10.1002/gps.3766

Wearing, D. (2005). *Forever today: A memoir of love and amnesia.* London, UK: Doubleday.

Williams, M. B. (1991). Clinical work with families of MPD patients: Assessment and issues for practice. *Dissociation: Progress in the Dissociative Disorders, 4*(2), 92–98.

Wilson, B. A., Kopelman, M., & Kapur, N. (2008). Prominent and persistent loss of past awareness in amnesia: Delusion, impaired consciousness or coping strategy? *Neuropsychological Rehabilitation, 18*(5/6), 527–540. doi:10.1080/09602010802141889

Memory Is Everything: Having Superior Memory

W e're nearing the end of our whirlwind journey through the wonderful world of memory. Along the way, we hope you've learned interesting and valuable lessons, including the following: Memory is *complicated*. It's not any one thing, but rather is a system of coordinated processes. Memory is *reconstructed*. Even if it feels like a literal replaying of the past, it's not. Instead, little bits and pieces from all over the brain are bound together temporarily to give rise to the experience of recollection. Memory is *fallible*. We like to believe that our own memories are accurate, maybe even perfect, but they're subject to all kinds of errors and biases—and some of them are of events that never even happened at all. Memory is *important*. It not only allows us to get all of our daily tasks done without a written list, but it also provides a sense of identity, motivates action, facilitates communication with others, and gives us something to reflect upon to provide life with meaning. Memory is critical to the *legal system*, a system that is only just learning these facts about memory and therefore may unwittingly be leading to unjust verdicts. Memory can be *haunting*. It can either help us to transcend or make us stuck in the traumatic experiences of our lives.

As we discussed in Chapter 1, memory intersects with every area of psychology and is relevant to every moment in everyday life. Memory is also a major contributor to intelligence. The influential Cattell-Horn-Carroll theory includes short-term and long-term memory as two of the defining components of intelligence (McGrew, 1997). All major intelligence tests (such as the widely used Wechsler Adult Intelligence Scale—Fourth Edition) include tests of memory (Benson, Hulac, & Kranzler, 2010). Working memory (discussed in Chapter 2) in particular is closely related to intelligence (Nisbett et al., 2012). If memory makes you smarter, perhaps we should all be doing everything we can to improve our memory abilities. The idea of enhanced memory appeals to millions of people. Memory improvement books, supplements, and seminars comprise a $450 million per year industry in the United States alone (Adams, 2005). A quick Internet search reveals the many products available and the promises they make. Nutritional supplements promise "a pill that enhances things like focus, memory, speech and productivity. Esentially [sic] everything you need to be smarter. If you've ever seen the movie *Limitless* then you will get an idea of what I'm talking about here" (HealthGenius, 2013), or to "accelerate[s] the rate of learning by up to 40% and increase[s] the length of time that short-term memory is retained" (Profiderall, 2014). Brain training software promises that you can "Develop a Perfect, Computer Like Memory In Just 5 Minutes A Day!" (Memory Improvement Techniques, n.d.). Memory improvement programs will allow you to "enjoy being considered a genius by friends, family and coworkers. You finally achieve the success and financial freedom you deserve. Your children start getting better grades in school and securing their future for success in life" (Farrow, n.d.). Doesn't that sound great? How does one get a genius memory like this? You've got three basic choices: easy ways, hard ways, and a mysterious way just recently discovered.

THE EASY WAYS

Many people's thoughts go immediately to a quick and easy way to enhance mental abilities, in the form of a pill or supplement. Can you achieve superior memory by taking a drug or eating a particular food? Despite the ubiquitous ads for nonprescription pills that allegedly improve memory, there isn't much evidence that supplements help. Some seem to stave off cognitive decline in older adults and may help those diagnosed with mild cognitive impairment (a sort of pre-Alzheimer's condition) to improve slightly (McDaniel, Maier, & Einstein, 2002). For example, folic acid supplements improved memory performance over a 3-year period, but the participants were older adults (Durga et al., 2007). A nutritional supplement (not yet available commercially) called Souvenaid has been shown to help the brain form synapses, the basis of new learning. In one study, Souvenaid prevented decline in the functional connectivity among neurons in people with early-stage Alzheimer's, but it didn't affect memory (de Waal et al., 2014). In another study it did improve long-term retention in people with early Alzheimer's (Scheltens et al., 2010). But for healthy young adults, there does not appear to be any supplement or food that improves memory.

What about drugs? We are quite aware of the enthusiasm many students have for prescription stimulant drugs as memory enhancers. For example, 8% to 18% of college students report using Adderall or Ritalin for other-than-prescribed uses (Moore,

Burgard, Larson, & Ferm, 2014; Teter, McCabe, LaGrange, Cranford, & Boyd, 2006). Do they work (presuming that improved memory rather than recreation is the goal)? Sort of. Some studies find small improvements in working memory in healthy young adults after taking prescription stimulants (de Jongh, Bolt, Schermer, & Olivier, 2008). However, only people with poor working memory skills before taking the stimulant show these minor improvements; those with good working memory skills show no effect or even declines in performance (Ilieva, Boland, & Farah, 2013). Interestingly, participants *thought* they did better after taking the stimulants whether they actually did or not, which may help to explain the popularity of stimulants despite their minor effectiveness (Ilieva et al., 2013). But prescription stimulants are dangerous drugs, and we recommend against them for recreational or memory-enhancement purposes.

You have a better alternative. For occasional bursts of enhanced memory, you can use over-the-counter energy drinks. They improve memory performance, particularly if you're sleep-deprived, by 5% to 9% (Wesnes, Barrett, & Udani, 2013). That may not sound like much, but it's about the same effect that prescription drugs have on cognitive performance (Husain & Mehta, 2011). And prescription drugs often impair some forms of cognition while improving memory (Husain & Mehta, 2011), which over-the-counter energy drinks do not. In the short term, chugging an energy shot from the grocery store is by far the safer option on days you feel you need optimum memory performance.

In the long term, if you want to maintain a healthy memory you need to lead a healthy lifestyle. Cigarettes and hard drugs are off limits; regular physical exercise and a good diet are your best friends (Hackley, 2011; Scarmeas et al., 2009). A Mediterranean-style diet, high in plant foods and fish, low in other meats and high-fat dairy products, and with moderate alcohol consumption is associated with reduced cognitive decline and reduced risk of Alzheimer's disease. And exercise is best if it involves not only physical activity, but also learning new skills. For example, jogging around the same track every day is good for you, but learning to tap dance or ride a unicycle is even better (Curlik & Shores 2013). Positive lifestyle choices like these will help keep your mind sharp throughout your life.

What about exercising your brain? We're referring here to so-called "brain training," and especially to the many online games that have been developed for this purpose. In the service of science (or, well, anecdotal evidence), one of the authors of this book submitted her own brain to one of these training programs for a month and kept a diary. The brain training program itself involves a series of online computer games, like the poorest-quality and most boring video games you could imagine. For example, imagine raindrops falling down the screen with numbers in them that you must add and type in before each drop reaches the bottom of the screen. Thrilling? No. But the tasks do require the exercise of a variety of cognitive abilities, such as working memory, logic, spatial reasoning, numerical operations, and hand–eye coordination.

The author dutifully completed series of such games 3 to 5 days a week for 4 weeks. Her performance on each individual game rocketed from depressingly low percentile scores in the low teens to much more encouraging scores in the upper 80th percentiles by the end. Nonetheless, her abilities to remember to go to meetings, what she talked about at such meetings later, to pick up dog food on the way home, and the names of the artists of 30-year-old songs on the radio were completely unimproved. The author's experience accords well with the results of far more systematic research. Most studies show marked effects of brain training on the particular games being played, but no particular effect of brain training on performance in everyday life (Hackley, 2011; Harrison et al., 2013). In short, you get better at anything you practice, but it doesn't generalize to other contexts, in the same way practicing typing on a computer keyboard won't help you hit the right keys on a piano.

It's a matter of so-called transfer of training. Skills gained at one task improve performance at another task only to the degree that those two tasks are similar (near transfer). If they are dissimilar (far transfer), there will be no transfer. If they are quite different, there can even be interference effects. For example, if you train for a long time in the lab to hit the right-arrow key every time you see the letter "e" you might find your typing of actual text to be slowed down afterward. Your brain (and therefore your finger) will want to type the right-arrow key rather than the "e" key when you are typing an e-mail or a homework assignment or a memo.

To demonstrate this phenomenon with memory training, Harrison et al. (2013) had participants undergo extensive training (20 days) at one of several types of working memory tasks. They had to make decisions about stimuli while adding a list of other items to their working memory. Participants all improved dramatically at their performance of the specific trained task in the course of the training. They also improved their performance of similar working memory tasks to those on which they had been trained. But their fluid intelligence as measured by tasks such as Raven's progressive matrices (a reasoning, rule-finding task) was not improved. A similar study by Redick et al. (2013) found that working memory training improved performance on the working memory task but did not transfer to measures of fluid intelligence. Interestingly, participants in the working memory training compared to the control conditions *thought* their overall memory and intelligence had been improved by the training despite no objective evidence of improvement.

Some research has examined whether memory training might be more effective for those most in need of improvement, such as those with injured or aging brains. The news is similar: Improvement, but no generalization. For example, a group of four survivors of traumatic brain injury showed improved cognitive performance after a program of brain games, but these improvements were specific to the tasks practiced and did not generalize to other tasks (Zickefoose, Hux, Brown, & Wolfe, 2013). The effects don't seem to be any more encouraging for elderly adults who are undergoing cognitive decline or for those with illnesses or disorders (Buitenweg, Murre, & Ridderinkhof, 2012; Hackley,

2011). Thus merely "working out the brain"—even by focusing on working out the memory component of the brain—does not lead to improved overall memory or reasoning performance. It might *feel* like it does, though.

There's little harm (except to your wallet) of engaging in brain training, and if you enjoy playing games and solving puzzles, you might give it a try. You might convince yourself your memory has improved, and that might be worth a few dollars a month. Anything new and active you can do with your mind helps to ward off some of the normal memory decline that comes with aging. It just won't prevent Alzheimer's disease or give you a perfect memory.

THE HARD WAYS

In short, there's no magic pill or training program that gives you superior memory. But you *can* achieve fantastical feats of mnemonic superiority—you, too, can gain the ability to almost instantly memorize dozens of cards or hundreds or thousands of digits, or even (more usefully) a roomful of new names and faces. But it's not easy, it's not quick, it's not magical, and frankly, it isn't a lot of fun. It simply takes a strategy and a lot of practice—months or years of practice. The further bad news is that undergoing such practice doesn't actually give you a better memory in general. If you get good at memorizing the order of shuffled playing cards, you will be good at remembering . . . well, the order of cards, but not necessarily names and faces—unless you spend many hours practicing that particular task, too.

To understand why this is so, let's take a look at some well-known and well-studied *mnemonists*, a term for people who demonstrate superior memory abilities. Chao Lu has memorized pi to 67,890 digits (Guinness World Records, 2014). Rajan Mahadevan can memorize a 20 × 20 array of digits in a matter of seconds

(Ericsson, Delaney, Weaver, & Mahadevan, 2004). Nelson Dellis can memorize the order of a deck of shuffled cards in 40.65 seconds—which places him only 22nd in the world (World Memory Sports Council, n.d.). Dominic O'Brien memorized the sequence of 54 decks of cards shuffled together with less than 0.3% errors ("Dominic O'Brien," 2014). T. M. could instantly learn the names of a roomful of strangers, could produce any of 15,000 hotel phone numbers on command, and could calculate square roots and products of numbers almost instantly (Wilding & Valentine, 1994a).

What is unusual about these people that might explain their memory abilities? Some early studies hinted at possible inborn or natural differences (Wilding & Valentine, 1994b). But the more research that has been done, the clearer the evidence has become that these mnemonists are simply skilled strategists. Superior memory at these sorts of tasks is learned, not innate. Most mnemonists acknowledge that they use strategies acquired through patient practice. Chao Lu practiced memorizing pi for 4 years (Guinness World Records, 2014). Rajan practiced for 1,000 hours to perfect a system for memorizing digit arrays (Ericsson et al., 2004). Nelson Dellis practices card memorization 5 hours a day (Hannah, 2012). Dominic O'Brien spent months creating his own system that links numbers with names of famous people and has practiced it for 10 years (O'Brien, 2009). T. M. had systems of linking names with people he knew, and numbers with images, which he practiced 2 to 3 hours daily (Wilding & Valentine, 1994a).

Because they rely on strategies, mnemonists are often stymied by memory tasks outside their practiced domain. For example, Rajan performed more poorly than control participants at remembering spatial locations of stimuli (Biederman, Cooper, Fox, & Mahadevan, 1992), and T. M. couldn't apply his strategy to remembering a story (he scored a dismal 3rd percentile; Wilding & Valentine, 1994b). And finally, neuroimaging reveals nothing special about the structure of the brains of world memory champions. They simply relied more on spatial areas of the brain when processing incoming information, consistent with the use of spatial encoding strategies (Maguire, Valentine, Wilding, & Kapur, 2003).

Even memory novices can perform at expert mnemonist levels if they are given appropriate strategies. Almost half of ordinary college students trained to use a mnemonic system linking numbers to letters to form words were able to perform at an extremely high level previously thought to be possible only for exceptional memorists (Higbee, 1997). These students practiced the memory system for only 6 hours. Performance becomes particularly impressive after people practice applying the strategies for hundreds of hours. They spontaneously begin to break material into larger groups, organize the material in memory, and gain speed at memorizing just like memory experts do (Ericsson, 2003). The journalist Joshua Foer became curious about how memory champions managed to do the amazing "tricks" he witnessed at the U.S. Memory Championship. He interviewed several memory champions, practiced their strategies for a year, and entered the Memory Championships. Much to his surprise, he won. He was never a good memorizer before he learned the strategies from expert mnemonists (Foer, 2011). So you too can improve your memory performance if you just learn a few strategies, which we'll reveal.

Overall, the difficulty of improving one's memory with drugs, supplements, brain training, or even strategies brings us back to one of the major themes of this book—memory isn't any one thing. It's difficult to make your memory better in a holistic sense because memory is composed of a number of different systems working together. Strategies applied to individual tasks therefore tend to be specific to those tasks and tend not to generalize to global memory functioning. Ready to learn the secrets of super memory anyway? We'll discuss some of the most commonly used strategies first, then add some new ones to the list that you might not have thought of. Some of these strategies are even counterintuitive to most people. You might want to keep this list handy for future reference.

Rehearsal

Most people think repeating things is the best way to get things into memory. One of us even heard a motivational speaker say that if you repeated a list of information every day for 90 days, the information would be forever imprinted in your memory. Unfortunately that is not true. Information needs to be frequently used to remain accessible. So if you're going to use rehearsal to retain information in memory, you need to keep at it. A more efficient way to use rehearsal is to make it more conceptual, into what is termed *elaborative rehearsal*, by adding meaning to the to-be-remembered information. Examples include creating a story that links to-be-remembered items together (such as remembering CAT, HORN, and FIRE, with a story about a cat beeping a car horn that sounds like a fire alarm), or translating meaningless into meaningful information (such as remembering the notes of the treble clef lines—EGBDF—with the sentence Every Good Boy Does Fine), or organizing the information into categories (such as with a grocery list, grouping the frozen food items together and the produce items together; Belezza, 1981).

Anything you can do to work with the information and think about it leads to deeper processing, and thereby better memory, as discussed in Chapter 2. For example, simply categorizing words as describing oneself versus not describing oneself can double the number of those words remembered later, compared to processing the words' meaning more generally (Rogers, Kuiper, & Kirker, 1977). In an actual college course, being assigned to relate course material to the self improved exam grades by 6 percentage points, more than half a letter grade (Barney, 2007). Or, like the mnemonist A. C. Aitken, you can reflect on the deeper meaning that lurks behind to-be-remembered information. He described his technique as "let[ting] the properties of the material reveal themselves" (Hunter, 1977, p. 158). For example, he would see tones and tempos in a list of digits and see stories and meanings in a list of words. Whatever deeper meaning you can find, it's certainly worth a try. Aitken's technique allowed him to remember various word lists for over 2 decades without ever having thought of them in between.

The "Memory Walk" or Method of Loci

One of the strategies most frequently used by mnemonists is the method of loci. To use this strategy, you imagine walking a familiar route, then imagine the to-be-remembered items in various locations along the route. You might need to remember the list of points you're going to make in an oral presentation, for example. Let's say you want to remember to open with a joke about lawyers, then discuss a point about saving money, follow with a discussion of buying a home, and conclude with a point about avoiding use of credit cards. You might imagine the walk from your house to a nearby park, and mentally place each point in a notable landmark along this route. You might visualize walking past your mailbox, and opening it to see a group of lawyers laughing. Next you might visualize the street sign at the corner, with a treasure chest of money under it. Then you might visualize the next landmark, a large house, with a "sold" sign in front of it. Finally you might visualize the sign at the entrance of the park as a giant credit card with a circle and a line through it. A similar method is called the peg-word technique. First you memorize a list of memory "pegs," then you "hang" the to-be-remembered items onto them. The example most often used in textbooks is this one: One is a bun, two is a shoe, three is a tree, four is a door . . . all the way up through ten. You can then picture the first to-be-remembered item in combination with a bun, the second in combination with a shoe, and so on.

For a list of random words, the method of loci improves memory by about 20%. To maximize its efficacy, it's best to use an outdoor route with locations that are distinctive from one another (Massen, Vaterrodt-Plünnecke, Krings, & Hilbig, 2009). It's a great tool because the method of loci does not suffer from repeated use as a mnemonic device (Massen & Vaterrodt-Plünnecke, 2006). The images placed on the memory walk should be bizarre, vivid, even sexually provocative, to be maximally efficient at improving memory (Foer, 2011; Marks, 1973; McDaniel & Einstein, 1986). Learning to create such images on the fly requires a good deal of creativity along with frequent practice. So start now—choose a well-worn path with distinct landmarks, preferably an outdoor path, and try to form images of the following items in order in each of the locations (obtained from a random word generator): epidemic; train; schedule; sunburn; robot; bullfight; church; salmon; strategy; young man. For example, you might visualize your driveway overrun with workers in protective suits holding syringes and looking panicky for the item "epidemic." Keep practicing for about a year, and you might be good enough to compete nationally!

Chunking

Another memory boosting technique is to combine bits of to-be-remembered information into larger units called chunks. A list of 30 items that can be "chunked" into five-item pieces transforms into only six units to be remembered. For example, participants placed in an object-filled experiment room seemed to naturally group the objects that were located close together into a single unit in memory (Sargent, Dopkins, Philbeck, & Chichka, 2010). The chunking process reduces information overload demands on memory, as the chunk is treated as an individual item (Sargent et al., 2010). Students tasked with memorizing long lists of digits spontaneously began to chunk the digits into meaningful units the longer they practiced (Ericsson, 2003).

Foer's interviews revealed that the most common mnemonic strategy among memory champions is the Person–Action–Object system. The mnemonist creates and memorizes 100 different images of a person performing an action on an object, to represent the numbers 0 through 99. So your PAO image for the number 42 might be Barack Obama making a sandwich. The PAO images are random and unique to you; you simply spend hours per day for many months memorizing the associations and practicing transforming sequences of numbers into these PAO units, and forming them into a story using the method of loci (Foer, 2011). It's strategy on top of strategy on top of strategy on top of strategy. It is highly effective once you take the time to master it.

Enactment

This one is a little easier to learn. It helps when memorizing information to engage as many modalities as possible—visual, verbal, and so forth. One modality people often don't think about but that is spectacularly effective as a memory strategy is to use physical gestures, also known as enactment, at encoding especially, but also at retrieval. Most of the laboratory research on enactment has used materials that lend themselves particularly well to enactment, phrases such as "open the book" or "put the string in the wallet." Participants enact some of these phrases and verbalize others. Enacting to-be-remembered object–action pairs when you encounter them yields 37% to 50% better memory over simply saying the pairs out loud (Hainselin et al., 2014; Mangels & Heinberg, 2006). But how can you enact something like the periodic table of the elements?

To learn to use the enactment method with a variety of different to-be-remembered materials, we turn to the literature on active experiencing, a technique developed from research on stage actors. To learn the countless lines required to perform, actors have a variety of strategies, but the overarching strategy is to understand the character's goal and to try to communicate that to the audience as fully as possible. Back to the periodic table. Imagine how you would convey the meaning of the periodic table to another person, perhaps a child sitting in the room with you. Maybe you would explain what the rows and columns represent. Maybe you would try to explain why each element is placed where it is, and as you do so you would point to the correct location and name each element. Turn it into a lecture that you imagine giving to an audience. What's most intriguing about the active experiencing strategy is that it doesn't require effortful memorization. The powerful effects come from focusing on the meaning of the information (elaboration), and using multiple channels to rehearse the information (Noice & Noice, 2006). The active experiencing technique helped a man in his 70s to remember the entire text of Milton's *Paradise Lost*, all 10,565 lines of it, virtually perfectly (Seamon, Punjabi, & Busch, 2010). This same man forgot where he left his keys and blanked on people's names as often as any other person in his 70s, so there's nothing exceptional about his memory abilities. It's the technique he used, along with the practice he put in (he estimated 3,000 hours; Seamon et al., 2010).

Distributed Versus Massed Practice

Most people think that the best way to get information in your memory is to cram it in right before you're about to be tested (Cohen, Yan, Halamish, & Bjork, 2013). But spacing out your study sessions over time rather than cramming right before a test is in fact the best way to study. In fact, optimal spaced rehearsal increases the amount remembered by 150% to 300% (Cepeda et al., 2009; Sobel, Cepeda, & Kapler, 2011). For most educational settings where you need to remember information for a period of a few days, the best amount of time between study sessions is 1 day. Put simply, all you need to do is to start studying early, review the materials briefly, then put them aside. Wait a day or two, study briefly again, then put the materials aside. Repeat about four times, and you should be able to hold onto a lot more information for tests. If you want to remember information for some duration (say, retain it 6 months later), the best amount of time between study sessions is a week or more (Cepeda et al., 2009).

Repeated Testing

You don't need to study the material over and over until you feel it must be thoroughly engraved in your brain. Students will often report to us that they spent hours reading and re-reading the textbook and lecture notes the night before an exam. These are almost always students who are puzzled that they didn't do well on the exam. They are using a method known as repeated studying. It's popular because, first, it is somewhat effective at improving memory, and second, it feels reassuring to see the information and to feel that sense of familiarity increase with each round of studying.

But repeatedly studying the to-be-remembered materials isn't the most efficient way to commit it to memory. Instead, you ought to repeatedly test yourself—try to generate the material from memory either with or without prompts. It's best to test with feedback: Check your answers by restudying to be sure you're right. You'll retain about 40% more information than you would with repeated studying (Karpicke & Smith, 2012). Repeated testing is equally rapid at producing learning and is more effective at allowing you to hold onto the information for the longer term. In fact, repeated testing works better than elaborative encoding (Karpicke & Smith, 2012) and better than the active learning method of generating one's own explanations for why information is important and how it is linked to other information (Larsen, Butler, & Roediger, 2013).

One of us (Denise) uses repeated testing with feedback to learn student names at the beginning of every semester. She studies the photo and name of each student before the first day of class, then forgoes studying any further. She then repeatedly tests herself by looking at each photo and trying to generate the name. She does not check each name to see if she is right, she only checks the name if the face fails to trigger it. The key to this technique is that the process of retrieval itself solidifies memories (Karpicke & Roediger, 2008). Educators are just beginning to build distributed practice and repeated testing into courses. Frequent and cumulative tests will improve memory for course material considerably, and requires little change to the structure of a course. We hope to see these memory techniques become standard practice in all educational settings.

Write It Out

If you are like most people, when you attend a lecture or a speech that you want to remember, you'd prefer to take notes using your laptop and typing what the speaker said. You might even look askance at the old-fashioned pen-and-paper note-taker sitting next to you—how could he possibly be catching all the important details? Well, if you are like most people, you're doing it wrong! People remember material from lectures and speeches better when they take notes by hand rather than by typing. It's true that writing by hand reduces the quantity of information recorded, as handwriting is slower than typing. Nevertheless, people who were instructed to handwrite notes had 14% better performance on factual questions about the lecture material and 20% better performance on deeper conceptual questions. Inspection of the actual notes taken reveals that handwriters don't simply duplicate what the lecturer says; they process it as they write it, thus engaging in a deeper form of encoding that benefits memory (Mueller & Oppenheimer, 2014).

As college professors, we see fewer and fewer students taking notes by hand every year. In fact, we have had to change the way we give exams because many students are so unused to handwriting that they can only write for a few minutes at a time before their hand muscles fatigue. The situation is likely to get worse before it gets better. Cursive handwriting in the United States is a victim of the Common Core federal standards and is no longer on the curriculum. As of this writing, seven U.S. states are fighting to keep cursive education alive (Carr Smyth, 2013). We hope that once educators learn about the memory-boosting power of handwriting they will reinstate cursive education.

Stop Taking Pictures!

This final memory strategy is about what *not* to do, and it may be the least intuitive of all. Almost all of us use cameras (mostly in our cell phones) to record the special moments in our lives for posterity. And indeed photographs can serve as vivid recall triggers (Hodges, Berry, & Wood, 2011). But the reality is that we almost never look at the many hundreds of photos we take, so they cannot act as a memory aid. Worse, the mere act of taking a picture actually impairs memory. In an experiment in which participants were instructed to observe items at a museum, and take pictures of some of them, taking photos caused a 10% to 15% decrement to memory (Henkel, 2014).

There are several possible reasons for this photo-taking–impairment effect. First, the act of taking the picture distracts one's attention from the photographed object, and dividing attention impairs memory. Second, we trust the camera to preserve the moment, so we don't work hard to commit it to memory (i.e., we fail to apply any of the aforementioned memory strategies; Jaffe, 2013). When exciting things are happening around you, put your cell phone aside and just be present in the moment. If you cannot resist taking pictures, take some time to review the photos you take at the end of each day and try to bring back as many details of the experiences as you can. Use your photos as triggers for memories rather than letting them take the place of memories.

THE AS-YET-UNKNOWN WAY

For all our discussion of the sweat involved in becoming a superior memorizer, we must admit that there is a recently discovered group of really unusual people with extraordinary memory abilities who apparently don't use strategies or constantly practice. The first such individual was discovered in 2006 (Parker, Cahill, & McGaugh, 2006). The pseudonym assigned to her in the first published case study was A. J., but she has since come forward and identified herself as Jill Price. People like Jill have highly superior autobiographical memory (HSAM), defined as near-perfect memory for the experiences of their lives, yet ordinary or inferior memory for other information.

Give HSAM people a date in their lives, and they can tell you instantly and accurately exactly what they did that day, down to what they ate and what they were wearing, and even what song was playing in the background. Ask them what happened a year ago today, and you'll get a flood of details about specific experiences. When they talk about their lives, they (unlike the rest of us) may spontaneously throw in references to the exact day and date: "Right, that was the day we went on a picnic and I got all those mosquito bites; it was Sunday, May 23, 1982." We had to google that date to see which day of the week it fell on, but people with HSAM simply *know* it—as long as the date occurred during their own lifetime. Their amazing memory is specific to their own life experiences. Presented with a list of words or a video of a conversation, people with HSAM are no better than the rest of us at remembering (LePort et al., 2012). About 50 people with HSAM have been identified at the time of this writing, with more coming forward as media coverage of HSAM expands and people recognize their own abilities being described.

People with HSAM aren't mnemonists like Dominic O'Brien or Chao Lu. They don't use strategies. They do tend to rehearse and journal about their life events more than others, but not to a degree that would account for their near-perfect memory (LePort et al., 2012). People with HSAM are also no better at encoding than other people, they are just better at retaining that information. To quote memory researcher James McGaugh, "They are not exceptional learners. They are very poor forgetters" (Stahl, 2014). Neuroimaging reveals some differences between HSAM brains and those of others. Their brains show better linkage of frontal and medial portions via white matter in areas specific to autobiographical memory, which suggests better ability to transfer information around the brain (LePort et al., 2012). Thus some preexisting brain differences may precede the onset of HSAM, which reportedly occurs around age 8 to 10 (LePort et al., 2012; Price & Davis, 2008). On the other hand, a pair of 11-year-old identical twins have been found of whom only one has HSAM (Stahl, 2014). The existence of these twins, who share

100% of the same genes, casts doubt on any inborn differences causing HSAM. The process by which HSAM occurs therefore remains an intriguing mystery at present.

Even if we could discover how to acquire HSAM, it's not clear that you would really want it. The 11 HSAM participants studied by LePort et al. (2012) claimed their memory ability was a good thing and said that they didn't find their memories intrusive or distracting. But the evidence suggests some serious downsides to HSAM. Jill Price described her remembering as "non-stop, uncontrollable, and totally exhausting" (Price & Davis, 2008, p. 5). The perseverative nature of HSAM thoughts goes hand in hand with some other cognitive deficits. For example, Jill Price is impaired in her reasoning skills, her ability to think in an abstract way (Parker et al., 2006). With all of the details ever-present in her mind, it may be difficult to think in terms of generalities. As she put it, "I remember all of the clutter" (Price & Davis, 2008, p. 45). Also, obsessive–compulsive symptoms tend to co-occur with HSAM (LePort et al., 2012). Most common are contamination fears, hoarding, and obsessive need for organization. It's yet to be determined whether this obsessiveness causes HSAM or is a side effect of the need for rehearsal that seems to underlie HSAM.

In addition, those with HSAM have difficulties adjusting after unpleasant experiences, because their memory system doesn't strip away the unpleasant emotions like the rest of ours does (Beike & Wirth-Beaumont, 2005; Walker, Vogl, & Thompson, 1997). As Jill Price put it, negative comments from others are "seared into my brain with all of the intensity that I felt about them the moment they were spoken" (Price & Davis, 2008, p. 118). She experiences "acute, persistent regret" regarding her everyday decisions (Price & Davis, 2008, p. 122).

Similarly, a 10-year-old with HSAM woke up sad on the anniversary of a day his father had scolded him, with the full vivid memory of how he had felt that day. In his own words, "The worst thing is that I can remember every bad thing that happened to me. . . . I remember this from *The Lion King*: (sings) 'Leave the past behind.' But I can't do that" (Stahl, 2014). He will likely continue to suffer after every letdown much longer than the rest of us do.

People with HSAM not only have trouble coping, but also may have trouble relating to others. They recognize when their friends' memories are in error and often cannot resist pointing out the errors. For example, Jill Price confessed that her HSAM interfered with the process of family therapy, as she compulsively corrected others' memories rather than listening to their points of view (Price & Davis, 2008). In her interview with HSAM people, journalist Leslie Stahl pointed out that an unusually large percentage of them were unmarried. Poignantly, one responded that he thought it was a "coincidence" (Stahl, 2014). But imagine how difficult it might be to live with someone who cannot forget any hurtful word you utter in anger. And it might be hard to tolerate someone who constantly corrects your memory like some form of memory police. We suspect that those with HSAM face relationship difficulties unique to their situation.

MEMORY IS ALL RIGHT JUST THE WAY IT IS

After considering the difficulty of attaining a superior memory, as well as the possible downsides to it, we have a radical suggestion: Maybe you shouldn't bother trying to improve your memory at all! We began this book by discussing how everything we do involves memory, then showed you a cavalcade of its errors, biases, and complications. We'd like to end on an optimistic note. Memory is fallible and has its foibles, but for reasons that are basically healthy and functional. Let's look collectively at memory's many foibles, which memory researcher Dan Schacter (1999) refers to as the Seven Sins of Memory. Briefly, they are

1. *Transience* (memories fade over time; see Chapter 2)
2. *Absent-mindedness* (we forget information we don't pay attention to; see Chapter 2)

3. *Blocking* (the wrong memory comes to mind; see Chapter 3)
4. *Misattribution* (we misremember the source of information; see Chapter 3)
5. *Suggestibility* (we "remember" something just because someone else said it happened; see Chapter 3)
6. *Bias* (the present unduly influences our memory of the past; see Chapter 7)
7. *Persistence* (we wish we could forget extremely unpleasant things but cannot; see Chapter 8)

We add to this list an eighth sin—that of *self-enhancement*. The self-enhancement bias is the tendency to process information in a way allowing the most positive view of the self. As we discussed in Chapter 6, we tend to forget negative feedback about ourselves, and to distort information so that it is more positive. In short, we don't quite know the truth about ourselves and our lives, because memory keeps slipping a pair of rose-colored glasses on us.

Looking over these many sins tempts us to conclude that memory is somewhat of a jackass, an old friend you keep relying on even though he or she has repeatedly made you look foolish. But that's only true when you focus on the occasional slip-ups. When you look at the big picture, you see a system that operates with efficiency and focus. The sins of memory occur in the service of protecting us from worrying about a million nagging, upsetting, and pointless details. Thanks to the basic principles of memory, we tend to forget information that is old, obsolete, boring, unimportant, temporarily unnecessary, unconfirmed by others, inconsistent with our beliefs, or unflattering to ourselves. If you can't remember everything (and no system can), what better types of things to forget than these sorts of information? As we mentioned in Chapter 8, the ability to forget is a gift that allows creative thought.

We rather like memory just the way it is. Memory is the repository of all our life experiences and study sessions. Memory comes to mind automatically, presenting us (usually) with just the word we want to say, or (usually) just the fact we need at our disposal, or (usually) just the recollection we seek. Memory updates itself as things change; it's dynamic and interactive and makes itself into what we need. Memory gives us something to talk about with loved ones and even strangers. Memory provides a sense of identity, an anchoring "me-ness" in the seas of time. Memory helps us plan and motivates our actions. Memory warns us of danger (sometimes too loudly) and blunts the emotional effects of our failures and faults (sometimes too much). It enables us to bring the past into the present so we can anticipate the future.

In short, *memory is everything*. Yes, this is a sweeping statement. Think for a moment, though, about what you cherish most. Everything you truly value is related somehow to memory. With regard to purchases, people are happier when they spend their money on experiences (memories) instead of material objects. The same $500 will lead to more happiness if you spend it on a vacation rather than on jewelry (Van Boven & Gilovich, 2003). The difference is partly that experiences are seen as one of a kind. You might be able to replace your vintage automobile (or get another one sort of like it), but you could never replace the feeling of walking across the stage at your college graduation (Rosenzweig & Gilovich, 2012). Experiences are also more valuable because people think about and savor them in memory in such a way that the experience becomes increasingly satisfying over time. The opposite pattern occurs for material goods, which quickly become less satisfying over time (Mitchell, Thompson, Peterson, & Cronk, 1997; Van Boven, 2005).

Interestingly, material possessions *can* make people happy *if* those possessions involve memory. People value objects that evoke memories more than objects that are useful or beautiful (Jones & Martin, 2006). Especially as you get older, you may start to value objects in your life because of the memories they evoke (Price, Arnould, & Curasi, 2000). In the eloquent words of 89-year-old Jane, "It's not what they're worth, it's just memories that make them valuable to me . . . reminders of the past.

I get happy feelings out of some things because of the memories with those things and sadness out of other things because it is the reminder of what was" (Price et al., 2008, p. 188). Ultimately, people value their experiences and treasure their possessions for the same reason: because they produce positive, special memories.

In fact, people are surprisingly unwilling to have new experiences similar to prior special experiences because they (correctly) fear the two will compete in memory (Zauberman, Ratner, & Kim, 2009). The first time you travel to Bora Bora for your honeymoon is so amazing that you don't want to travel to Bora Bora again for fear it will diminish the memory of that first time. So we come to our final pieces of advice for living a happy memory-filled life. Save your pennies for a variety of distinct trips, concerts, and dinners. Spend as little as possible on televisions, cars, and the latest fashions. Maybe pick up a few objects along the way that remind you of your distinctive life experiences. Use your brain rather than technology such as laptops and smartphone cameras to record these experiences. You can use any or all of the strategies in this chapter to help you. Now get out there and make some memories!

REFERENCES

Adams, M. (2005, April 4). *Memory improvement a $450 million industry, but doctors say most people have nothing to worry about.* Retrieved from www.naturalnews.com/006360.html

Barney, S. T. (2007). Capitalizing on the self-reference effect in general psychology: A preliminary study. *Journal of Constructivist Psychology, 20*(1), 87–97. doi:10.1080/10720530600992915

Beike, D. R., & Wirth-Beaumont, E. T. (2005). Psychological closure as a memory phenomenon. *Memory, 13*(6), 574–593. doi:10.1080/09658210444000241

Bellezza, F. S. (1981). Mnemonic devices: Classification, characteristics, and criteria. *Review of Educational Research, 51*(2), 247–275. doi:10.3102/00346543051002247

Benson, N., Hulac, D. M., & Kranzler, J. H. (2010). Independent examination of the Wechsler Adult Intelligence Scale—Fourth Edition (WAIS-IV): What does the WAIS-IV measure? *Psychological Assessment, 22*(1), 121–130. doi:10.1037/a0017767

Biederman, I., Cooper, E. E., Fox, P. W., & Mahadevan, R. S. (1992). Unexceptional spatial memory in an exceptional memorist. *Journal of Experimental Psychology: Learning, Memory, and Cognition, 18*(3), 654–657. doi:10.1037/0278-7393.18.3.654

Buitenweg, J. V., Murre, J. J., & Ridderinkhof, K. (2012). Brain training in progress: A review of trainability in healthy seniors. *Frontiers in Human Neuroscience, 6*, 183. doi:10.3389/fnhum.2012.00183

Carr Smyth, J. (2013, November 14). *Cursive handwriting: Seven states fight for cursive writing in school* (plus video). Retrieved from http://www.csmonitor.com/USA/Latest-News-Wires/2013/1114/Cursive-handwriting-Seven-states-fight-for-cursive-writing-in-school-video

Cepeda, N. J., Coburn, N., Rohrer, D., Wixted, J. T., Mozer, M. C., & Pashler, H. (2009). Optimizing distributed practice: Theoretical analysis and practical implications. *Experimental Psychology, 56*(4), 236–246. doi:10.1027/1618-3169.56.4.236

Cohen, M. S., Yan, V. X., Halamish, V., & Bjork, R. A. (2013). Do students think that difficult or valuable materials should be restudied sooner rather than later? *Journal of Experimental Psychology: Learning, Memory, and Cognition, 39*(6), 1682–1696. doi:10.1037/a0032425

Curlik, D., & Shors, T. J. (2013). Training your brain: Do mental and physical (MAP) training enhance cognition through the process of neurogenesis in the hippocampus? *Neuropharmacology, 64*, 506–514. doi:10.1016/j.neuropharm.2012.07.027

de Jongh, R., Bolt, I., Schermer, M., & Olivier, B. (2008). Botox for the brain: Enhancement of cognition, mood and pro-social behavior and blunting of unwanted memories. *Neuroscience and Biobehavioral Reviews, 32*(4), 760–776. doi:10.1016/j.neubiorev.2007.12.001

de Waal, H., Stam, C. J., Lansbergen, M. M., Wieggers, R. L., Kamphuis, P. H., Scheltens, P., . . . van Straaten, E. W. (2014). The effect of Souvenaid on functional brain network organisation in patients with mild Alzheimer's disease: A randomised controlled study. *PLoS ONE, 9*(1), e86558.

Dominic O'Brien. (2014). Retrieved from http://en.wikipedia.org/wiki/Dominic_O%27Brien

Durga, J., van Boxtel, M. J., Schouten, E. G., Kok, F. J., Jolles, J., Katan, M. B., & Verhoef, P. (2007). Effect of 3-year folic acid supplementation on cognitive function in older adults in the FACIT trial: A randomised, double blind, controlled trial. *The Lancet, 369*(9557), 208–216. doi:10.1016/S0140-6736(07)60109-3

Ericsson, K. (2003). Exceptional memorizers: Made, not born. *Trends in Cognitive Sciences, 7*(6), 233–235. doi:10.1016/S1364-6613(03)00103-7

Ericsson, K., Delaney, P. F., Weaver, G., & Mahadevan, R. (2004). Uncovering the structure of a memorist's superior "basic" memory capacity. *Cognitive Psychology, 49*(3), 191–237. doi:10.1016/j.cogpsych.2004.02.001

Farrow, D. (n.d.). *World's greatest memory—Dave Farrow.* Retrieved from www.worldsgreatestmemory.com

Foer, J. (2011). *Moonwalking with Einstein: The art and science of remembering everything.* New York, NY: Penguin Press.

Guinness World Records. (2014). *Most pi places memorized.* Retrieved from www.guinnessworldrecords.com/world-records/1/most-pi-places-memorised

Hackley, D. (2011). Coach your cortex: Is "brain training" a sales con or evidence-based exercise? *The Psychologist, 24*(8), 586–589.

Hainselin, M., Quinette, P., Juskenaite, A., Desgranges, B., Martinaud, O., de La Sayette, V., . . . Eustache, F. (2014). Just do it! How performing an action enhances remembering in transient global amnesia. *Cortex: A Journal Devoted to the Study of the Nervous System and Behavior, 50*, 192–199. doi:10.1016/j.cortex.2013.10.007

Hannah, J. (2012, March 23). *Spurred by love and fear, memory champ aims to inspire.* Retrieved from www.cnn.com/2012/03/23/us/nelson-dellis-memory/index.html

Harrison, T. L., Shipstead, Z., Hicks, K. L., Hambrick, D. Z., Redick, T. S., & Engle, R. W. (2013). Working memory training may increase working memory capacity but not fluid intelligence. *Psychological Science, 24*(12), 2409–2419.

HealthGenius. (2013). *Does Nootrobrain really work? (A critical review).* Retrieved from www.healthgenius.org/nootrobrain/#ixzz32 wA G4ncR

Henkel, L. A. (2014). Point-and-shoot memories: The influence of taking photos on memory for a museum tour. *Psychological Science,* *25*(2), 396–402.

Higbee, K. L. (1997). Novices, apprentices, and mnemonists: Acquiring expertise with the phonetic mnemonic. *Applied Cognitive Psychology,* *11*(2),147–161.doi:10.1002/(SICI)1099-0720(199704)11:2<147:: AID-ACP425>3.0.CO;2-Y

Hodges, S., Berry, E., & Wood, K. (2011). SenseCam: A wearable camera that stimulates and rehabilitates autobiographical memory. *Memory, 19*(7), 685–696. doi:10.1080/09658211.2011.605591

Hunter, I. M. (1977). An exceptional memory. *British Journal of Psychology, 68*(2), 155–164. doi:10.1111/j.2044-8295.1977.tb01571.x

Husain, M., & Mehta, M. A. (2011). Cognitive enhancement by drugs in health and disease. *Trends in Cognitive Sciences, 15*(1), 28–36. doi:10.1016/j.tics.2010.11.002

Ilieva, I., Boland, J., & Farah, M. J. (2013). Objective and subjective cognitive enhancing effects of mixed amphetamine salts in healthy people. *Neuropharmacology, 64,* 496–505. doi:10.1016/j. neuropharm.2012.07.021

Jaffe, E. (2013, December 12). *Digital cameras are messing with your memory.* Retrieved from www.fastcodesign.com/3023373/evidence/ digital-cameras-are-messing-with-your-memory

Jones, G. V., & Martin, M. (2006). Primacy of memory linkage in choice among valued objects. *Memory and Cognition, 34*(8), 1587–1597.

Karpicke, J. D., & Roediger, H. (2008). The critical importance of retrieval for learning. *Science, 319*(5865), 966–968. doi:10.1126/ science.1152408

Karpicke, J. D., & Smith, M. A. (2012). Separate mnemonic effects of retrieval practice and elaborative encoding. *Journal of Memory and Language, 67*(1), 17–29. doi:10.1016/j.jml.2012.02.004

Larsen, D. P., Butler, A. C., & Roediger, H. (2013). Comparative effects of test-enhanced learning and self-explanation on long-term retention. *Medical Education, 47*(7), 674–682.

LePort, A. R., Mattfeld, A. T., Dickinson-Anson, H., Fallon, J. H., Stark, C. L., Kruggel, F., . . . McGaugh, J. L. (2012). Behavioral and neuroanatomical investigation of highly superior autobiographical memory (HSAM). *Neurobiology of Learning and Memory, 98*(1), 78–92. doi:10.1016/j.nlm.2012.05.002

Maguire, E. A., Valentine, E. R., Wilding, J. M., & Kapur, N. (2003). Routes to remembering: The brains behind superior memory. *Nature Neuroscience, 6*(1), 90–95. doi:10.1038/nn988

Mangels, J. A., & Heinberg, A. (2006). Improved episodic integration through enactment: Implications for aging. *Journal of General Psychology, 133*(1), 37–65. doi:10.3200/GENP.133.1.37-65

Marks, D. F. (1973). Visual imagery differences in the recall of pictures. *British Journal of Psychology, 64*(1), 17–24. doi:10.1111/j.2044-8295.1973.tb01322.x

Massen, C., & Vaterrodt-Plünnecke, B. (2006). The role of proactive interference in mnemonic techniques. *Memory, 14*(2), 189–196. doi:10.1080/09658210544000042

Massen, C., Vaterrodt-Plünnecke, B., Krings, L., & Hilbig, B. E. (2009). Effects of instruction on learners' ability to generate an effective pathway in the method of loci. *Memory, 17*(7), 724–731. doi:10.1080/09658210903012442

McDaniel, M. A., & Einstein, G. O. (1986). Bizarre imagery as an effective memory aid: The importance of distinctiveness. *Journal of Experimental Psychology: Learning, Memory, and Cognition, 12*(1), 54–65. doi:10.1037/0278-7393.12.1.54

McDaniel, M. A., Maier, S. F., & Einstein, G. O. (2002). "Brain-specific" nutrients: A memory cure? *Psychological Science in the Public Interest, 3*(1), 12–38. doi:10.1111/1529-1006.00007

McGrew, K. S. (1997). Analysis of the major intelligence batteries according to a proposed comprehensive Gf-Gc framework. In D. P. Flanagan, J. L. Genshaft, & P. L. Harrison (Eds.), *Contemporary intellectual assessment: Theories, tests, and issues* (pp. 151–119). New York, NY: Guilford Press.

Memory Improvement Techniques (n.d.). *Learn memory improvement techniques—how to improve memory fast.* Retrieved from www.memory-improvement-techniques.com

Mitchell, T. R., Thompson, L., Peterson, E., & Cronk, R. (1997). Temporal adjustments in the evaluation of events: The "rosy view." *Journal of Experimental Social Psychology, 33*(4), 421–448. doi:10.1006/jesp.1997.1333

Moore, D. R., Burgard, D. A., Larson, R. G., & Ferm, M. (2014). Psychostimulant use among college students during periods of high and low stress: An interdisciplinary approach utilizing both self-report and unobtrusive chemical sample data. *Addictive Behaviors, 39*(5), 987–993. doi:10.1016/j.addbeh.2014.01.021

Mueller, P. A., & Oppenheimer, D. M. (2014). The pen is mightier than the keyboard: Advantages of longhand over laptop note taking. *Psychological Science, 25*, 1159–1168. doi:10.1177/0956797614524581

Nisbett, R. E., Aronson, J., Blair, C., Dickens, W., Flynn, J., Halpern, D. F., & Turkheimer, E. (2012). Intelligence: New findings and theoretical developments. *American Psychologist, 67*(2), 130–159. doi:10.1037/a0026699

Noice, H., & Noice, T. (2006). What studies of actors and acting can tell us about memory and cognitive functioning. *Current Directions in Psychological Science, 15*(1), 14–18. doi:10.1111/j.0963-7214.2006.00398.x

O'Brien, D. (2009, May 30). *How to beat forgetfulness, by eight-times world memory champion Dominic O'Brien.* Retrieved from www.dailymail.co.uk/health/article-1189706/How-beat-forgetfulness-world-memory-champion-Dominic-OBrien.html#ixzz36KCg5Ppn

Parker, E. S., Cahill, L., & McGaugh, J. L. (2006). A case of unusual autobiographical remembering. *Neurocase, 12*(1), 35–49. doi:10.1080/13554790500473680

Price, J., & Davis, B. (2008). *The woman who can't forget: The extraordinary story of living with the most remarkable memory known to science.* New York, NY: Free Press.

Price, L. L., Arnould, E. J., & Curasi, C. (2000). Older consumers' disposition of special possessions. *Journal of Consumer Research, 27*(2), 179–201. doi:10.1086/314319

Profiderall. (2014). *How it helps you think.* Retrieved from www.profiderall.com/how_it_helps_you_think

Redick, T. S., Shipstead, Z., Harrison, T. L., Hicks, K. L., Fried, D. E., Hambrick, D. Z., . . . Engle, R. W. (2013). No evidence of intelligence improvement after working memory training: A randomized, placebo-controlled study. *Journal of Experimental Psychology: General, 142*(2), 359–379. doi:10.1037/a0029082

Rogers, T. B., Kuiper, N. A., & Kirker, W. S. (1977). Self-reference and the encoding of personal information. *Journal of Personality and Social Psychology, 35*(9), 677–688. doi:10.1037/0022-3514.35.9.677

Rosenzweig, E., & Gilovich, T. (2012). Buyer's remorse or missed opportunity? Differential regrets for material and experiential purchases. *Journal of Personality and Social Psychology, 102*(2), 215–223. doi:10.1037/a0024999

Sargent, J., Dopkins, S., Philbeck, J., & Chichka, D. (2010). Chunking in spatial memory. *Journal of Experimental Psychology: Learning, Memory, and Cognition, 36*(3), 576–589. doi:10.1037/a0017528

Scarmeas, N., Luchsinger, J. A., Schupf, N., Brickman, A. M., Cosentino, S., Tang, M. X., & Stern, Y. (2009). Physical activity, diet, and risk of Alzheimer disease. *JAMA: Journal of the American Medical Association, 302*(6), 627–637. doi:10.1001/jama.2009.1144

Schacter, D. L. (1999). The seven sins of memory: Insights from psychology and cognitive neuroscience. *American Psychologist, 54*(3), 182–203. doi:10.1037/0003-066X.54.3.182

Scheltens, P., Kamphuis, P. H., Verhey, F. J., Olde Rikkert, M. M., Wurtman, R. J., Wilkinson, D., . . . Kurz, A. (2010). Efficacy of a medical food in mild Alzheimer's disease: A randomized, controlled trial. *Alzheimer's and Dementia, 6*(1), 1–11. doi:10.1016/j.jalz.2009.10.003

Seamon, J. G., Punjabi, P. V., & Busch, E. A. (2010). Memorising Milton's *Paradise Lost*: A study of a septuagenarian exceptional memoriser. *Memory, 18*(5), 498–503. doi:10.1080/09658211003781522

Sobel, H. S., Cepeda, N. J., & Kapler, I. V. (2011). Spacing effects in real-world classroom vocabulary learning. *Applied Cognitive Psychology, 25*(5), 763–767. doi:10.1002/acp.1747

Stahl, L. (Correspondent). (2014). Memory wizards. In S. Finkelstein (Producer), *60 Minutes*. New York, NY: CBS News. Retrieved from www.cbsnews.com/news/memory-wizards

Teter, C. J., McCabe, S. E., LaGrange, K., Cranford, J. A., & Boyd, C. J. (2006). Illicit use of specific prescription stimulants among college students: Prevalence, motives, and routes of administration. *Pharmacotherapy, 26*(10), 1501–1510.

Van Boven, L. (2005). Experientialism, materialism, and the pursuit of happiness. *Review of General Psychology, 9*(2), 132–142. doi:10.1037/1089-2680.9.2.132

Van Boven, L., & Gilovich, T. (2003). To do or to have? That is the question. *Journal of Personality and Social Psychology, 85*(6), 1193–1202. doi:10.1037/0022-3514.85.6.1193

Walker, W., Vogl, R. J., & Thompson, C. P. (1997). Autobiographical memory: Unpleasantness fades faster than pleasantness over time. *Applied Cognitive Psychology, 11*(5), 399–413. doi:10.1002/(SICI)1099-0720(199710)11:5<399::AID-ACP462>3.0.CO;2-E

Wesnes, K. A., Barrett, M. L., & Udani, J. K. (2013). An evaluation of the cognitive and mood effects of an energy shot over a 6h period in volunteers: A randomized, double-blind, placebo controlled, cross-over study. *Appetite, 67*, 105–113. doi:10.1016/j.appet.2013.04.005

Wilding, J., & Valentine, E. (1994a). Mnemonic wizardry with the telephone directory: But stories are another story. *British Journal of Psychology, 85*(4), 501–509. doi:10.1111/j.2044-8295.1994.tb02537.x

Wilding, J., & Valentine, E. (1994b). Memory champions. *British Journal of Psychology, 85*(2), 231–244. doi:10.1111/j.2044-8295.1994.tb02520.x

World Memory Sports Council. (n.d.). *Nelson Dellis GMM*. Retrieved from www.world-memory-statistics.com/competitor.php?id=691

Zauberman, G., Ratner, R. K., & Kim, B. (2009). Memories as assets: Strategic memory protection in choice over time. *Journal of Consumer Research, 35*(5), 715–728. doi:10.1086/592943

Zickefoose, S., Hux, K., Brown, J., & Wulf, K. (2013). Let the games begin: A preliminary study using Attention Process Training-3 and Lumosity™ brain games to remediate attention deficits following traumatic brain injury. *Brain Injury, 27*(6), 707–716. doi:10.3109/02699052.2013.775484

Index

3